1980

WOMEN'S GYMNASTICS
Coach, Participant, Spectator

STG

WOMEN'S GYMNASTICS
coach, participant, spectator

MIMI MURRAY
springfield college

ALLYN AND BACON, INC.
boston   london   sydney   toronto

Library of Congress Cataloging in Publication Data

Murray, Mimi.
  Women's gymnastics.

  Includes index.
  1.   Gymnastics for women.   I.   Title.
GV464.M87   796.4'1   78-11569
ISBN 0-205-06162-1

Printed in the United States of America

CONTENTS

3 SELLING
floor exercise   **33**

4 FLYING
side horse vaulting

111

5 STICKING
balance beam

157

7 DIRECTING
Coaching

FOREWORD

The Allyn and Bacon Sports Education Series
Arthur G. Miller, Consulting Editor

Sports play a major role in the lives of almost everyone—players, coaches, officials, and spectators! Interest in sports is the result of several factors including more time for leisure because of fewer working hours per week and more vacation periods.

There is an increased emphasis in *physical fitness,* demonstrated through greater participation in jogging, tennis, golf, skiing, and other lifetime sports. Through sports participation, children and adults not only improve and maintain fitness but also develop skills, group and personal satisfactions, and enjoyment.

Another factor in the growing interest in sports is the increase in television and radio broadcasts of sporting events. Team sports, such as baseball, football, basketball, soccer, and hockey, are seasonally covered by major networks. Lifetime sports are also receiving more air time. Activities such as gymnastics, swimming, and other aquatic sports continue to receive expanded coverage. Analysis of the skills and strategies of each sport by knowledgeable commentators using instant video replay and stop-action techniques make a game or activity more interesting to the viewer.

The *Allyn and Bacon Sports Education Series* has been developed to meet the need for players, coaches, and spectators to be informed about the basic and advanced skills, techniques, tactics, and strategies of sports. Each book in the *Series* is designed to provide an in-depth treatment of a selected sport or activity. Players find the individual skills and accompanying picture sequences very valuable. Coaches gain basic and advanced knowledge of individual and team play, along with techniques of coaching. Sports fans are provided information about the activities and are thus able to become more knowledgeable about and appreciative of the basic and finer aspects of sports.

The authors of the *Sports Education Series* have been carefully selected. They include experienced teachers, coaches, and managers of college and professional teams. Some books represent the combined effort of two or more authors, each with a different background and each contributing particular strengths to the text. For other books, a single author has been selected, whose background offers a breadth of knowledge and experience in the sport being covered.

The *Sports Education Series* was initiated in 1970, and since that time, sixteen different sports have been covered with more to be added. A number of the books have now gone into their second edition, bringing them up to date with changes in tactics, strategies and new pictures.

Among the authors and titles of some of the individual sports books in the Series are: *Dynamic Track and Field* by the well-known Jim Bush of UCLA with Don Weiskopf, *Advantage Tennis* (revised) by Jack Barnaby of Harvard, and *Women's Gymnastics* by Mimi Murray of Springfield College.

In the team sports area, Mildred J. Barnes of Central Missouri State University has recently revised *Women's Basketball.* Richard Kentwell, coach of the field hockey team at Yale collaborated with Dr. Barnes in the revision of the book *Field Hockey,* and *Winning Volleyball* by Allen E. Scates of UCLA is in preparation for its third edition.

Other team sport books include *Handbook of Winning Football* by George Allen of the Los Angeles Rams with Don Weiskopf, *The Complete Baseball Handbook* by Walter Alston, formerly coach of the Dodgers, and *Basketball: Concepts and Techniques,* by Bob Cousy and Frank Power.

Psychology of Coaching by Tom Tutko and Jack Richards offers beginning and experienced coaches in either individual or team sports, many suggestions and techniques for improving their coaching.

The *Sports Series* enables readers to experience the thrills of the sport from the point of view of participants and coaches, to learn some of the reasons for success and causes of failure, and to receive basic information about teaching and coaching techniques.

Each volume in the series reflects the philosophy of the authors, but a common theme runs through all: the desire to instill in the reader a knowledge and appreciation of sports and physical activity which will carry over throughout his or her life as a participant or a spectator. Pictures, drawings, and diagrams are used throughout each book to clarify and illustrate the discussion.

The reader, whether a beginner or one experienced in sports, will gain much from each book in the Allyn and Bacon Sports Education Series.

Arthur G. Miller
Chairman, Department of
    Movement, Health & Leisure
Boston University

PREFACE

The impact of the social-cultural phenomenon of the female athlete is evidenced by the fantastic increases in the opportunities, the number of participants, and the quality of programs for the woman in sport. One of the sports for women that is riding the crest of this wave is gymnastics. Women's gymnastics is currently one of the fastest-growing sports. It is a sport in which a female can be extremely aggressive, totally commit herself, develop great amounts of strength and flexibility, and still have the confidence that her performance will be aesthetically pleasing both for herself and for her spectators. The raison d'être for this book is to provide not only the gymnast and her teacher/coach, but also the spectators of gymnastics, with an understanding of this extremely popular sport. The materials in this book have been designed and organized in a progression from beginning to advanced skill level to help fill the void of information about women's gymnastics.

The philosophy of this author is that the acquisition of sound basics and fundamentals performed with proper execution and amplitude makes success inevitable.

The first chapter serves as an introduction and explanation of women's gymnastics. The second chapter deals with basic concepts and the preparation necessary to become an outstanding gymnast. Chapters 3–6 explain the various skills by giving a description of the skill, progressions and teaching techniques, corrections and suggestions for avoiding common errors, and suggested combinations with other skills. These chapters conclude with a section on coaching, routine construction and composition, psychology, and conditioning for the specific event. Each skill is presented so that the reader can refer to that given skill without having to read the whole chapter and/or book for understanding. Therefore, in a few places the corrections and suggestions are repeated from one related skill to another.

The last chapter presents coaching tips on the development of a philosophy, the coaching role, safety, mechanical analysis, spotting, and demonstrations.

Throughout the book, the author has attempted to present a positive, light-hearted approach to the teaching of gymnastics. If a gymnast can relate and associate necessary learning with a "one-liner," even if it seems a bit silly, she may learn more easily. As an example, the most important concept for a female gymnast and something that a large percentage of female gymnasts don't do is to maintain a total body tightness while performing any skill. This book reminds gymnasts of this important technique by admonishing them to "STG" (squeeze those glutes). The large muscle group in the back between the waist and the top of the legs are the gluteals, or "glutes." If the gymnast squeezes this muscle group, a whole body tightness will result. Rather than the teacher/coach constantly telling the gymnast to tighten up, straighten her legs, point her toes, keep her hips and shoulders in line, and so on, she can simply remind her to "STG." STG might even become the team's cheer or goal.

The suggestions and recommendations herein have proved effective in the author's highly successful teaching and coaching experience with all age groups and levels of gymnastics including three national championship teams; a United States team; clinics, workshops, and camps for gymnasts and their coaches throughout the country; a gymnastics summer sports school; college level physical education courses; and high school level gymnastics. This book should be an excellent source for the learner (gymnast, teacher/coach, or spectator) as well as for practicing teachers and coaches.

It is the author's desire that the reader will gain as much as she has gained both professionally and personally from an association with this new, challenging, and dynamic mode of expression for the female athlete, women's gymnastics. The rewards and joys are well worth the investment of time, energy, and enthusiasm necessary for success.

ACKNOWLEDGMENTS

The publication of this book owes much to the help, support, and patience of many. I am especially fortunate to have had several outstanding professional role models, namely, Diane Babbit, Genie Dozier, Ruth Evans, Grace Jones, Katherine Ley, Nancy Mueller, Emogene Nelson, Margaret Thorsen, and Betty Weisner. I am equally grateful to colleagues who have supported my professional endeavors, including Edie Colbane, Reuben Frost, Judith Holland, Carole Oglesby, Jesse Parks, and Thomas Sheehan.

Two special friends, Nancy Meyer and Jane Rosenkrans, made easier the difficult times during the acquisition of the knowledge and understanding that have gone into this book. I thank them for their loyalty and patience.

The photographs in the book were made available through the generosity of the Springfield College Public Relations Office and through the outstanding talent of photographers Paul Kennedy and Phil Saunders and their models, primarily the Springfield College Women's Gymnastic Team. The sketches from which the published drawings were prepared were done by gymnastic expert and friend Inie Rovegno. Thanks also to typists B. J., the Darsch, and Nance.

Special appreciation and thanks to those Springfield College Team gymnasts who were "all they could be" throughout six undefeated dual meet seasons, five Eastern Championships, and three National Championships. The champions who were able to humor, con, and do it when it counted are: Kim Andres, Barbara Block, Linda Beyer, Sue Brewer, Patti Corrigan, the Dunkleys—Deb and Ruth—Gail Goodspeed, Steph Jones, Katherine Kolemainen, Judi Markell, Debbie Mezger, Lucy Miller, Bonnie Remo, Nancy Shultz, and Karen Stewart.

To my Motherbird, Gerda Murray; my sister, Barbara Rathbun; my brother, Gordan Murray II; as well as to the McLeans—my love and thanks (What a family!), for they have encouraged and supported my endeavors in sport.

HERALDING
the questions and answers about women's gymnastics

The renaissance of interest in the female athlete in the last decade has been incredible. Many factors have influenced this change, a major one being the "whole women's movement." New understanding has made it seem okay for a girl or a woman to participate in sport or, for that matter, anything else. The negative social sanctions that were once imposed on the female who desired to be an athlete have largely disappeared and this trend is likely to continue. Stellar athletic performances by females have contributed further to the change in attitude toward the woman athlete.

The sport that has led the way in terms of public acceptance is women's gymnastics. The primary reason is that gymnasts use an aesthetic and artistic approach to demonstrate athletic prowess in a sport that requires a combination of strength, agility, coordination, flexibility, and poise (Fig. 1.1).* Women's gymnastics is an exciting and visually artistic sport. A gymnast can be an extremely aggressive athlete and yet this demonstration of aggression does not offend some who continue to have a narrower concept of the female role. Certainly all of us have been amazed and hypnotized by the performances of Korbut and Comenici. These athletes have made a considerable impact on our times. If one was to ask spectators of past Olympics which athletes and performances they remembered, undoubtedly Comenici and/or Korbut would be mentioned. Their performances have further stimulated interest in the sport of women's gymnastics in the United States and thus helped to make it the fastest-growing sport for girls and women.

*Figure 1.1 is on the preceding page.

THE 10.00 PERFORMANCE In Communist countries gymnastics is the most popular national sport, very much like football and baseball are in the United States. The ultimate goal of many individuals in Communist countries is to be successful athletes, for athletic achievement affords them the opportunity to rise socially, to receive cash awards. Consequently, they and their families live more comfortably than other citizens. Thus the motivation in Communist countries to be the best gymnast is complete because it is one of the few avenues by which the average citizen can experience social mobility and economic improvement. Is it any wonder, then, that gymnasts from Czechoslovakia, Romania, Hungary, East Germany, and the USSR have historically dominated the sport of women's gymnastics at the international level? Korbut and Comenici are products of these countries' highly sophisticated systems, which are designed to turn out the perfect gymnast for the express purpose of political propaganda. A country's performance in sports, whether good or bad, affects the national image. Many countries anxious to show their political superiority actively promote and encourage excellence in sport. The Soviet and American governments both have been known to use athletics as an instrument of foreign policy, which, of course, also affects policy at home.

The preparation, concern, and intensity with which athletes train for competition often reflects the political structure of their homeland. Having observed the Soviet system and having visited the Physical Culture Institute in Moscow, one U.S. delegation felt that the Russians are achieving much of their success in athletics because of an intense program to somatotype and muscle-test their youth. They program four- and five-year-olds into sports for which they are best suited, according to the Russian scientists' concept of the ideal body shape, muscle strength, and physical characteristics for a given sport. It appears that athletes there have little choice of sport. Soviet athletic achievements have been heralded the world over as the finest in human history and their athletes receive recognition in proportion to their excellence. To be a superior athlete in Russia is the ultimate achievement for the state and for the self. Russian press releases during international competition emphasize that the dominance of their athletes is due to their superior political system; thus the reason for the 10.00 performance.

It has often and wisely been said that sport is the great leveler. Even though the political, economic and religious system in the USSR is the antithesis of ours, we can quickly come to admire and appreciate the excellence of the Russian athlete, for in the beauty of sport political, religious, racial, and other differences disappear. Consider Cuba, for example: a relatively new entry in international competition, this young country is attempting to persuade the rest of the world of the success of their policies and also to build self-confidence through their athletes' performance in all sports. The pride and intensity with which the Cubans perform in all sports is amazing.

The emphasis different nations place on winning and athletic achievement may give cause to wonder about the validity of the old cliché, "the battles of England were won on the playing fields of Eton." Maybe the word order should be changed to "the playing fields of Eton fostered the battles of England."

The worth of the individual is of prime importance in a democracy. As Americans, we prize our freedoms—freedom of choice, self-direction, discipline, and self-realization. These freedoms do not exist for the Communist citizen. Communist athletes don't have the freedom of choice. Is there any wonder, then, that the 10.00 gymnastics performance is a habit?

GYMNASTICS PROGRAMS IN THE UNITED STATES

As previously mentioned, women's gymnastics in the United States is growing almost too rapidly to be accommodated by our present numbers and kinds of facilities, teachers, and coaches. The growth of gymnastics is evident from the increasing number of aspiring gymnasts. The purpose of this book is to provide for the interested spectator, gymnast, and coach of women's gymnastics a resource through which to acquire greater understanding and appreciations of this fast-growing sport.

THE WHAT OF GYMNASTICS

What women's gymnastics is may best be described initially by telling what it is *not*. Although women's gymnastics shares its origin, name, and several basic skills with men's gymnastics, it is neither comparable to nor synonymous with men's gymnastics.

Men's gymnastics consists of the following events: floor exercise, horizontal bar, parallel bars, long horse vaulting, pommel horse, and still rings. Men's gymnastics is further notable because of its extended history. The pommel horse, long horse, parallel bars, and horizontal bar events are rich in antiquity and contributions to physical education. The history of the pommel horse goes back to ancient Greek civilization. Apparatus similar to the present pommel horse was used during this time in training equestrians to mount and dismount a horse. The name of the handles, "pommels," comes from a part of a horse saddle. Skills performed today on the pommel horse are sophisticated and highly technical adaptations of the original skills. Another activity in which the ancient Greeks participated was bull leaping in which the athlete would run toward a bull, grasp his horns, and jump the length of the animal. Long horse vaulting descends from this rather treacherous sport. The horizontal bar and the parallel bars were the creation of Freidrich Jahn in the early 1800s, during an era of nationalism in Germany, as physical education activities. He proposed that these events would make young men stronger and thus better citizens. Jahn's gymnastic activities became so popular with the German youth that Germany's Austrian rulers grew concerned that Jahn was becoming too powerful. Jahn's motives were quite innocent and altruistic: he desired only to develop strong, healthy German citizens. Nevertheless the government had false charges brought against Jahn as a traitor. After a sojourn in jail, he was released but not permitted to teach physical education again.

Men's gymnastics as a sport is primarily designed to demonstrate male power and strength with total control. Women's gymnastic events, on the other hand, are quite different in design and purpose from the men's gymnastic events although they have grown out of the men's events. Rather than six events, which make up men's gymnastics, women's gymnastics consists of four events: side horse vaulting, uneven parallel bars, balance beam, and floor exercise. Each one of these events is a distinct and unique sport, for each requires different physical and psychological strengths and flexibilities. The women's events as they are now practiced did not become uniformly accepted until the time of the 1952 Olympics; thus, by comparison to the men's events they have a short history. Prior to 1952 the women's Olympic program consisted of the swinging rings, even parallel bars, free calisthenics, team drill with hand apparatus, side horse vaulting with pommels, and balance beam (three inches wide, compared to the current four-inch-wide beam). The reasons for the changes in these events were to eliminate the demonstration by the gymnast of the static strength required in the men's events and to make women's gymnastics a display of grace, flexibility, and moving strength, which better challenge and accommodate the female physique.

Certainly women's gymnastics is a totally new sport as compared to men's gymnastics. Because of its youth teachers and coaches need continual updating. It will keep changing and growing as we find the female is capable of performing

Figure 1.2 · The all-around gymnast

more difficult feats. The differences and improvement in routines performed by gymnasts from Olympics to Olympics and locally from one meet to the next are evidence of the sport's evolution.

The all-around gymnast (see Fig. 1.2), an athlete who participates in all four women's events is unique. The skilled all-around gymnast is one of the finest female athletes because the all-around event in women's gymnastics taxes the individual totally. The physical, mental, and emotional requirements for a good all-around gymnast are demanding. The balance beam, the uneven parallel bars, side horse vaulting, and floor exercise are the four events in which an all-around gymnast must perform.

The all-around gymnast must be extremely flexible to perform on the balance beam (Fig. 1.3). To move through a handstand, an event requirement, she must be stronger through the upper arms, shoulder girdle, upper and lower back, and abdomen than the average female athlete. An acutely accurate kinesthetic sense is necessary for successful balance beam work, as are grace, agility, and, of course, balance. The mental and emotional qualities needed for the balance beam are probably even more important than the physical qualities. The beam is the greatest psychological event in women's gymnastics. The gymnast must prepare herself mentally to exhibit complete self-control, self-confidence, and creativity. She must approach the beam with the utmost respect and work as if "caressing" it.

The uneven parallel bars require the following physical attributes: strong

Figure 1.3 · (left) Beam
Figure 1.4 · (right) Bars

abdominal muscles, upper arm and shoulder girdle strength, and coordination to make movements rhythmical and flowing. Timing is essential to a good performance on the uneven bars. This event requires a little more daring, or "gutsiness," than the other three events. In contrast to the beam, the bars must be forcefully attacked as the performer mentally seeks to completely dominate the event with her strength, coordination, and mental attitude (Fig. 1.4).

The third event, side horse vaulting, requires many other qualities. The key to effective vaulting is a perfect run, or approach. The legs of the vaulter should be as strong and as powerful as those of a fine sprinter. The body should be well tuned because the vault itself occurs within a second or two and many varied body positions and changes must be effected in this short period of time. Therefore, timing, coordination, and agility are essential. To end the vault properly, the gymnast must exhibit outstanding balance, body control, and body alignment. Mentally, the gymnast prepares herself for total commitment to coming as close to flying as possible. Once the run has begun, it should not be interrupted, nor should it or can it be stopped. This commitment is similar to that of the kamikaze pilots of World War II, those Japanese suicide flyers who were taught only to take off in airplanes and not to land them.

Floor exercise, considered by many to be the most artistic of the four women's gymnastic events, is limited only by the performer's strength, flexibility, and creativeness. In this event, the body is the primary medium. The three main components of this event are tumbling, dance, and acrobatics. Physically, tumbling requires explosive leg strength and flexibility. Dance requires coordination, efficient movements that will appear to be graceful, flexibility, complete body control, and balance. Cardiovascular endurance is also important. Acrobatics requires extreme flexibility of the upper and lower back, the hamstrings, the shoulder girdle, and the adductors of the legs. Mentally, the gymnast performing on the floor should attempt to say something through her exercise. It should be obvious that she takes great pride in her skill and that she is doing something that brings her the "joy of effort" (Fig. 1.5).

No other sport seems to be as demanding physically, mentally, and/or emotionally as the all-around category in women's gymnastics. Most other sports generally concentrate on the physical development of one or two body areas. Field hockey and lacrosse, for example, emphasize agility, cardiovascular fitness, and leg strength. Basketball requires agility and cardiovascular fitness. Volleyball demands agility, leg strength, and awareness of teammates. Swimming emphasizes arm, shoulder girdle, and leg strength. In softball the emphasis is on agility and alertness. A tennis player needs endurance and quickness. Of all the sports, track and field (if the performer were to sprint, run distances, high jump, long jump, and participate in the throwing events) most closely parallels the demands made on the all-around woman gymnast. Yet not one of these sports alone demands equal amounts of strength and flexibility in all the major muscle groups of the body, as does the all-around event in women's gymnastics.

We know that to be successful at any sport, an athlete must possess an

Figure 1.5 · Floor

aggressiveness, determination, intelligence, the ability to be coached, self-confidence, and organization. The all-around woman gymnast must have all of these qualities and great poise and she must learn to approach each event with a prescribed mental attitude, an attitude that is different for each event. Obviously the conditioning required for success in women's gymnastics is as demanding as the sport itself. The title of all-around athlete adequately describes the talents of these outstanding athletes.

Gymnastics for women is a form of nonverbal expression. Expression is an integral part of any art form and, therefore, gymnastics may be perceived as art. Individual expression is the key to modern women's gymnastics. The gymnast, using her body as the medium of expression, communicates by means of an emotional outpouring and creative insights. To interest the audience, the routines must also have meaning to the gymnast.

The degree of expression in a gymnastic exercise is greatly determined by the extent of one's movement vocabulary. Movement vocabularies may be increased by improving or adding to movement experiences; an effective method of increasing vocabulary is based on the problem-solving approach. Modern educational dance and gymnastics have made great strides in this area.

In order for true expression to occur, body control and awareness, or kinesthetic sense, must be developed. Essential to body control is the development of balance by the individual's realization of the location of the center of gravity in different body postures. The body can learn to find balance through a gesture with the free limb when it is in support position, as evidenced by the use of the arms for balance on the balance beam. The arms and hands are the natural limbs for gesture, and expression is manifested through gesture. Although these body parts can create or enhance expression, the gymnast's overall performance is ultimately affected by her facial expression and head position.

Coordinated movements and the rhythm of movement execution are essential, too, not only to efficient body movement but also to successful gymnastic performance. As a gymnast becomes more aware of her ability to move and acquires increasing confidence in herself and sureness of movement, expression increases.

Testing a gymnast's powers of expression requires an audience. The audience may be herself, her peers, her coach or teacher, a judge, or a group watching a gymnastic competition. The gymnast must learn to be articulate in her movement and, moreover, she must be herself. Being oneself effects a harmony of body movement and personality that results in true and sincere expression; therefore imposed movements and expression are to be avoided in composition construction.

Another key factor in any form of expression is the relationship of one thought to another or, in the case of gymnastics, one movement to another. Thus the connecting movements of a floor exercise, balance beam, or uneven parallel bar routine are of the utmost importance. To achieve variety in movement, the gymnast should seek changes of level, tempo, and direction. Accordingly, combinations of movements should provide contrast. In addition, a gymnast should seek total involvement in the exercise and concentrate on the total expression of the body. Spectator enjoyment will accrue when the gymnast learns to communicate and interact with the audience. This nonverbal form of expression should manifest itself in an enjoyable, moving, and inspirational performance. In performing the four events of women's gymnastics, the gymnast should surprise the audience with the unexpected and with a visually exciting performance, as well as the new, the unique, and the difficult.

THE WHO OF WOMEN'S GYMNASTICS

Any female who desires to demonstrate her skill and express herself in the new, challenging, and exciting medium of gymnastics will find opportunities available through her school team, private gymnastic clubs, sport camps, and community agencies such as the YMCA prior to and during the college years. These social institutions are becoming aware of the great interest in women's gymnastics and furthermore are realizing that sports opportunities must be provided for females. Public and private schools now include units in gymnastics as part of their physical education programs. Schools that do not have such programs should be persuaded that they are essential to the development of the well-rounded young woman. Additional instruction is available to aspiring gymnasts through private lessons in a gymnastic club or school or at a local agency. Some of the finest American gymnasts have come from such programs.

It is important to assess the strength of the program offered by a private gymnastic school or situation prior to enrollment. The educational background of the school's director, the quality of the facility, the apparatus, and particularly the safety provisions are good clues to the overall quality of a gymnastics program. Certainly observation of the school's product—their students—also will help to evaluate such programs. A further concern should be the number of pupils per teacher in the learning situation. Nevertheless, safety provisions should be of the utmost interest to those looking for additional programs in gymnastics.

A relatively new concept in gymnastics is gymnastic camp. There are both day and overnight summer camps that specialize in teaching gymnastics. Again, it is advisable to evaluate the camp and its staff before the gymnast enrolls.

The United States Gymnastics Federation has a well-established age group program designed to promote and improve the sport of gymnastics. Students from many of the private gymnastic schools participate in the USGF's age group programs, which provide beginner, intermediate, advanced, and elite competition from local to regional to national levels. Similarly, the YMCAs have age group programs. Successful participation in the elite USGF Nationals can qualify a young woman for membership on a United States team participating in international competition, the ultimate aspiration of many young female gymnasts.

High schools in the United States are adding women's gymnastic teams to their athletic programs in response to the growing demand. Under the aegis of organizations such as state secondary school principals' associations, these high school teams have the opportunity to compete with other gymnastic teams in their local leagues and to qualify for state regional meets and eventually for state championships.

The collegiate scene in gymnastics is bursting with talented performers. Since the first college-university championship for women was held in 1969 at Springfield College, programs have increased in quantity and quality. In addition, now that women are receiving athletic scholarships, a talented high school gymnast could acquire a college education because of her gymnastic expertise. The opportunities to pursue gymnastic excellence are available and will continue to be extended.

Young girls who show an interest in gymnastics can begin a program of movement (developing a movement vocabulary) dance, and tumbling as early as five years of age. Apparatus work can be included at a later age. These suggestions do not preclude the possibility of an excellent gymnast developing after beginning the sport at twelve or thirteen years of age. It is further hoped that young girls will be encouraged to participate in many different sports in addition to gymnastics. Unfortunately, in gymnastics, as in swimming, too often the brightest stars "burn out" by age sixteen due to their intensive and exclusive training as well as competitive pressure at too young an age.

THE HOW OF WOMEN'S GYMNASTICS

A girl should and can avail herself of one of the previously mentioned gymnastics opportunities and strive for perfection in all of her gymnastics efforts. To become proficient enough to enjoy gymnastics, a girl must train to achieve equal amounts of flexibility and strength and must be prepared to dedicate herself to hours of hard but well-spent work. She must find a gymnastics facility and a teacher and/or coach who will provide educationally sound learning experiences that stress the fundamental skills of gymnastics. The rewards of success in what is now one of the most popular of all sports for women are well worth the work and practice.

THE BEGINNINGS
concepts and foundations

2

Women's gymnastics is truly unique because it embraces four different sports: balance beam, uneven parallel bars, side horse vaulting, and floor exercise. Performance as well as skill is subject to judgment. So the means to the end and not just the end result itself are the keys to success in gymnastics. By contrast, in basketball getting the ball into the basket gains points; when a hockey ball or puck crosses the goal line, the offense scores; the first racer to cross the finish line is the winner, and so on. But in women's gymnastics, judges evaluate not only performance of the skill but also the way in which the gymnast performs. For this reason, performing the skills with proper technique is essential. There are a few basic concepts that apply to each event in women's gymnastics. These principles form the foundation of success in this ultimate sport.

PROPER FORM All gymnastic skills require proper form. Proper form includes pointed toes, straight knees (except during landings), good body alignment, composure, balance, and amplitude (Fig. 2.1).*

BODY POSITIONS There are three body positions in gymnastics: tuck, pike, and layout. When the back is rounded, knees to the chest, legs together, head down on chest the

*Figure 2.1 is on the preceding page.

14

Figure 2.2 • Body positions: (a) tuck, (b) pike, and (c) layout

gymnast is in *tuck* (see Fig. 2.2a). When the back and legs are straight, head down on chest, and body bent forward at the waist, the gymnast is in *pike* (sometimes referred to as jackknife), shown in Fig. 2.2b. When the body is completely stretched, back straight, head neutral, legs and arms extended and straight, the gymnast is in *layout* (Fig. 2.2c). An exercise to acquaint the novice gymnast with these body positions is to have the gymnast or whole class lie face up (supine) on a mat and assume the proper position as the teacher/coach calls it out. The teacher/coach should alter the order and tempo of the commands. A secondary but useful outcome of this exercise is that assuming the tuck or pike position from the supine position requires utilization of the abdominal muscles, and it is known that many women have notoriously weak , or "abominable," abdominals.

Figure 2.3 • Tight body, from supine position

TIGHT BODY   The preeminent concept that relates to *everything* in women's gymnastics is a tight body. A female gymnast should constantly be tightening her whole body. She may imagine she is in a complete body girdle or that she is squeezing all of her body parts to the midline. Unfortunately the majority of female gymnasts punch or initiate a skill with force and power, but once their bodies have entered space, they assume the tightness of a bowl of cooked pasta. When the body becomes loose, the initiated force dissipates and the skill is "dumped," or loses amplitude. The loose body syndrome relates directly to female gymnasts and does not appear to be a problem in men's gymnastics. If a gymnast has mastered the tight body technique a teacher/coach or another gymnast should be able to raise her whole body from a supine position to the back of her head by lifting a foot (Fig. 2.3) or from a facedown (prone) position into a handstand by lifting a leg (Fig. 2.4) or from a side-lying position onto her outstretched arm and armpit by lifting her top leg. (Fig. 2.5). The body of the gymnast must remain tight, without sags. She must *squeeze* to accomplish this skill. This is a technique that the teacher/coach must continually stress to ensure rapid progress in gymnastics. Even for some of our finest gymnasts this skill is an effective review and reinforcer. Regardless of skill level, a gymnast must continually and constantly strive for tightness of her total body. Throughout this book, the reader will note that the most commonly suggested correction is a tight body. Experience indicates that total body tightness can occur if the gymnast "squeezes her glutes." "Glutes" is a respectful contraction of the term "gluteals." The gluteals muscle group comprises muscles in the lower portion of the back or hips between the waist and the top of the thighs. Throughout this text the reader will further note the use of "STG," an abbreviation for "squeeze those glutes." It has been rumored that during training French Army Officers must keep a coin between their glutes. This is the body position that

Figure 2.4   •   Tight body, from facedown position to a handstand

Figure 2.5 • (left) Tight body, from side-lying position
Figure 2.6 • (right) Banana back

female gymnasts should affect throughout their gymnastics to tighten their whole bodies.

BODY ALIGNMENT

If you are a woman, stand up, stretch your arms over your head; and look back and down over one shoulder. What's hanging out? Unfortunately for an aspiring female gymnast the natural body posture for most women is a slight lordosis, or arched low back. This is a very weak posture and it becomes an even weaker position when a gymnast inverts into a handstand. A banana-back handstand (Fig. 2.6) is the second most common error of female gymnasts. In men's gymnastics, the so-called "hollow chest" position is the most common remedy for this weak position. To assume the hollow chest it is necessary to bring the head slightly down, stretch the arms upward in front of the ears at about the temples, and contract the pectoral, or chest, muscles. This technique is very effective with male gymnasts, but not all techniques from men's sports automatically transfer to women's sports. This position is one that is not valid for female gymnasts. The female gymnast can hollow her chest and still have a banana back. Therefore the recommended correction is to have the female tilt her pelvis forward by shortening her abominable abdominals and STG'ing. To help to learn to perform forward pelvic tilt the gymnast should assume a supine position and try to push her whole back against the floor, eliminating the space behind her waist and the mat. Eliminating this space should be easier if she bends both knees and places her heels on the mat next to the glutes. The gymnast can try to place her own hand in the space. If she can not, she should slowly extend one leg and then the other while maintaining a flat back or a forward pelvic tilt. A bonus of this exercise is that it is an excellent way to ease low back pain. An occupational hazard for most female gymnasts is a sore low back. Therefore this exercise is good for beginning, intermediate, and advanced gymnasts. The forward pelvic tilt places the gymnast in a much stronger position because of the slight contraction of the abdominal muscles.

HANDSTAND

Another characteristic that makes gymnastics different from other sports is that, more frequently than not, the sole support of the body becomes the hands rather than the feet. Therefore a gymnast can not overpractice handstands. The proper handstand is an absolutely straight one like the one shown in Fig. 2.7. A forward pelvic tilt and STG'ing make a straight handstand easier.

Teaching techniques and progressions:

1. The gymnast should perform the forward pelvic tilt and tight body drills.
2. The gymnast should kick up to a handstand on a mat with two spotters. The spotters should help by holding the gymnast's legs and assisting her to position her body in proper alignment.

Figure 2.7 • (left) Proper handstand
Figure 2.8 • (right) Wall handstand

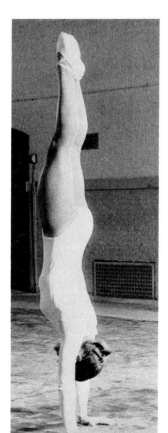

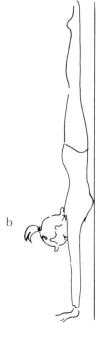

3. The gymnast lowers her body from the handstand in the direction in which she kicked up.

Corrections: The corrections that are common for the handstand relate to proper body alignment.
1. STG.
2. The head should be in neutral position and not hyperextended.
3. The hands should be shoulder width apart. If they are any wider it is very difficult to hold the position and to prevent elbow bending.
4. There should be a forward pelvic tilt eliminating a weak body position, the banana back.
5. The body should stretch toward the ceiling from the fingers to the toes.

Spotting: 1. Two spotters stand to the side, facing each other and slightly ahead of the gymnast, who places her body between the spotters. The spotter standing on the side of the gymnast catches the leg on that side with both of her hands as the gymnast kicks the handstand.

WALL HANDSTAND

This skill the gymnast can perform once she is accustomed to inverting. The purpose of this skill is to provide the kinesthesis of a straight handstand for the gymnast. The gymnast, *her back* toward the wall, places her hands on a mat and walks her feet up the wall until she is in a handstand (Fig. 2.8). Many repetitions of this drill help condition the gymnast for her sport.

For many years some teachers have instructed students to kick handstands while *facing* the wall. This practice reinforces the incorrect banana-back position. Also, an unskilled or confused student may "crash and burn" (fall out of a skill with little or no body control) into the wall and/or floor. It is amazing that this practice is such a common one and that it is often done on the floor and not on a mat.

The recommended technique does not require a spot, but it does require a mat under the gymnast.

PRESS HANDSTAND

The press handstand is a skill that the gymnast should practice daily. It is as important to gymnastics as brushing the teeth is to dental hygiene. Only when the gymnast can kick a handstand and do a controlled wall handstand should she attempt the press, but once started, she must continue to do it regularly.

The gymnast stands in a straddle position. Placing her hands on the floor in front of her, she leans forward in an attempt to bring her hips (center of gravity) over her shoulders and hands (base support). Her shoulders will overbalance or move forward of her hands. At this time, the legs release the floor and come together in the handstand (see Fig. 2.9). The gymnast slowly reverse-presses herself out of the handstand in the direction opposite the press into the handstand. As a specific conditioner, this skill is outstanding when repeated many times.

Figure 2.9 • Press handstand from straddle position

| Teaching techniques and progressions: | 1. | There should be spotters until the gymnast can perform the skill without help. |

Corrections:

1. STG, pelvic tilt, and stretch in the handstand (no banana back).
2. The head in a neutral position.
3. The hands shoulder width apart.
4. Overbalancing the shoulders as the hips are brought over them and then stretching upward at the top.
5. Straddling the legs up and then together.
6. Not jumping but lifting the hips and legs.

Spotting:

1. A spotter stands to the side and slightly forward of the gymnast. As the gymnast places her hands on the mat the spotter holds both sides from the back of the gymnast's waist. The spotter helps the gymnast overbalance her shoulders by pulling the gymnast toward her. While the gymnast is coming down from the handstand to the straddle stand, the spotter helps provide the control and balance necessary for the skill.

BALANCE

Balance in gymnastics is an indication of complete body control. The concept of balance involves showing control while moving through and holding skills (Fig. 2.10). Taking extra little steps or placing a hand down to gain balance incur

Figure 2.10 • (left) Balance
Figure 2.11 • (right) Lunge

penalties from judges. A skill that is landed without additional steps is referred to as a "stick." The coach can emphasize and assert the importance of balance. Balancing requires mental and physical discipline. The mental discipline simply involves the desire to do every skill in balance. The gymnast cannot permit herself the luxury of making up for lost balance (laziness). Rather, she should perform each skill in balance initially. The physical aspect of balance involves proper body alignment, STG, proper focus, knees bent upon landing or upon loss of balance during the performance of a skill.

The teacher/coach can aid the gymnast in understanding this concept and should insist upon the demonstration of it in the performance of a skill and during routines. She should accept nothing less than balance.

Sticking landings is extremely important because not only does it show control and balance but it is also the last thing the audience and/or judges see of the routine, so sticking or not sticking can be the lasting impression. Stick landings should be practiced while performing and alone. It is advisable for the gymnast to perform at least ten stick landings at the end of practice while jumping down from each of the following piece of apparatus: the side horse, balance beam, low bar of the unevens, and edge of the trampoline.

LUNGE

The lunge position (Fig. 2.11) prior to executing any skill requiring leg push or lift is an important one. A basic premise of this book is that the gymnast should perform the lunge and its concomitant body alignment prior to all appropriate skills, including handstands, cartwheels, front handsprings, roundoffs, and aerials. To demonstrate the importance of this skill the teacher/coach can ask gymnasts to jump as high as they can without bending their knees. Obviously, they will appreciate the need to bend the knees to get maximum push or lift. As incongruous as it may seem, many gymnasts attempt to do skills with only the power from plantar flexion in the ankles or with a straight leg push-off.

The gymnast places one leg in front of the other with the feet pointing straight ahead for maximum thrust (female gymnasts often "turn out" and consequently lose power potential). The knee of the forward leg is flexed, the rear leg is straight, the shoulders are directly over the hips. When initiating a skill, the gymnast should not pike forward at the waist but should wait until the lift of the straight (rear) leg and then the bent (forward) leg lifts and rotates the body into or through the inverted position. The emphasis is upon using the legs and not bending at the waist (pike), a movement that results in a "dumped" skill and loss of amplitude.

All tumbling skills should be learned and initially performed from a stand. A run, if added to a skill, *should not* exceed three steps.

BLOCKING

Blocking changes forward or horizontal momentum to fore-upward momentum. The lunge position is an example of blocking the hips and shoulders (preventing them from continuing forward) so that the skill can rise. Generally, the higher a skill the better. If the gymnast can thrust her body into orbit she is successful. Blocking can also be accomplished in the shoulders. Blocking in the shoulders can cause the body to rise from a hand support position, such as inverted vaulting, front handsprings, and back handsprings. In shoulder blocking, the gymnast holds her upper arms next to the temples and her hands move back so that the upper arms approximate the front of the ears, as shown in Fig. 2.12. This action must be very quick and occurs only in a small range. In reality, the gymnast in the inverted position is preventing her shoulders from continuing to move forward in the direction of the skill, and stopping this movement results in a rise of the body. This concept is not necessarily advocated in men's gymnastics; male gymnasts get the same results by slightly bending and extending their elbows. Due to a proportional (lack of) strength and body weight, it seems that most women are not strong enough to bend and extend their elbows with the necessary force in the millisecond in which it is necessary. Thus blocking is advocated and accentuated.

PRESS

The ability to ease or let the body down to a mat and lift the body up from the mat involves learning the press–reverse press concept. From a handstand position, with spotting, the gymnast should bend her elbows, easing herself down to the mat to demonstrate the reverse press. From this position, the gymnast should push herself up to the handstand with a press (Fig. 2.13). This concept is important, for occasionally the novice gymnast simply bends her arms, crashes and burns, instead of reverse pressing, or she pulls her hands away from the mat rather than pushing her body away from the mat with her hands and pressing.

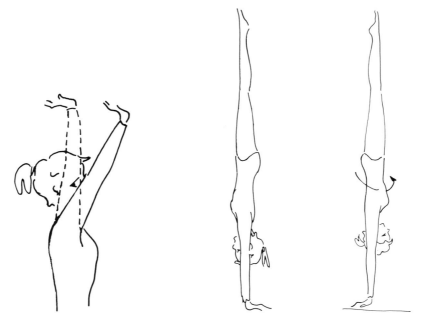

Figure 2.12 • (left) Blocking
Figure 2.13 • (center) Press
Figure 2.14 • (right) Twisting

TWISTING   Twisting (Fig. 2.14) involves a turn about the longitudinal axis of the body. Many females have difficulty twisting and it is the contention that the ones who do have never learned the fundamental gymnastics concept of a tight body and thus do not understand and cannot apply the basic principles of the mechanics of twisting. The teacher/coach should look for "spaghetti bods" when skills are performed with "banana" backs, bent knees and elbows, legs apart, heavy landings, and crashes and burns. The responsibility of the coach, then, is to encourage, expect, demand, and reward skills performed with a tight body. If the teacher/coach does not assume this responsibility, the gymnast will develop "sloppy" habits and poor technique that will haunt her later on and prevent her from progressing and performing skills of increasing difficulty.

An understanding of the basic mechanics of twisting has eluded gymnastic experts for years, leaving us with those who could twist twisting and others floundering. Currently, there are two theories regarding the twist phenomenon: the classic twist and the modern twist. In the classic twist, the gymnast initiates the turn while still in contact with the floor or the apparatus. An example of a basic skill that vividly demonstrates the classic twist is a jump pirouette turn (180° or 360°) on the floor. In order for the turn to occur, the gymnast must begin the twist as she pushes off the floor—jumping and turning with and from the same impetus. The modern twist involves a slight piking and extending in the hips. To demonstrate the modern twist, the gymnast, in a long hang from the rings, slightly pikes and extends her hip. These actions will cause her to begin to spin or twist. Most successful twisting skills in gymnastics are a combination of the classic and modern twist.

When beginning the twist, the gymnast should stretch her arms upward. She then looks over the shoulder she is twisting toward. She forcefully pulls the elbow on that side down by bending it. The other arm follows suit. While twisting, the arms are close to the body (to shorten the radius of rotation) with the hands on the chest. The body must remain tight—STG.

Usually in gymnastics the twist is added to another skill, as in the eagle pop-full twist on the unevens; full-twisting front handspring vault, front aerial full-twisting dismount from the balance beam, and back somersault full twist in floor exercise. The skill to which the twist is added must be performed with excellence prior to adding the twist; this concept must be emphasized.

SAFETY

Safety is a basic tenet and concept that warrants emphasis for the protection of the gymnast as well as the teacher/coach. Specfic safety precautions for gymnastics are:

1. Proper instruction in "how to" perform a skill is necessary.

2. Proper spotting involves an understanding of the skill to be spotted as well as the spotting techniques to be performed. Spotting is another skill to learn and practice. By moving the feet the spotter gets into position to protect the gymnast from a fall or to aid her in learning a skill.

3. Proper progressions or basics and fundamentals are the cornerstones of gymnastics. Almost all skills are built upon or relate to other skills. A gymnast should start at the beginning and work her way up to and through difficult skills and each new skill should be built upon the previous one.

4. Proper and safe equipment is basic and essential. Representatives of equipment companies can be very helpful and are most honest in response to questions regarding the safety of apparatus. Apparatus should meet the current FIG (International Gymnastics Federation) specifications, which appear in the Code of Points. The side horse and balance beam should be completely stable, and the uneven bars should be anchored to the floor so as to prevent tipping of the apparatus. After moving the apparatus or adjusting height or width, the tightness of the apparatus should be checked prior to use by the next gymnast. Local and state boards of education should approve the use of the trampoline in public schools. There should be four alert and perceptive spotters, one on each side of the trampoline.

5. Proper mat coverage is a necessity. Mats that don't "bottom out" and are placed together without spaces and without overlapping edges are critical. A double mat thickness is often advisable as is the use of dismount mats (4" thick) and crash pads (8" thick or thicker).

A teacher/coach cannot be too safety conscious.

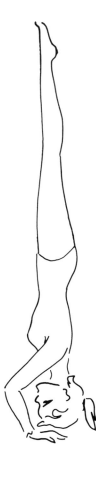

Figure 2.15 • (right) Handstand push-up

FLEXIBILITY AND STRENGTH

To be good, a gymnast should train for equal amounts of strength and flexibility. At one time a woman gymnast could get by with being very flexible, but as the difficulty of skills has increased so has the need for strength. A raging controversy within the ranks of physical educators and exercise scientists has dealt with general versus specific conditioning for sport. The generalists believe that overall strength, but particularly strength in the muscle groups used in a given sport, increases the participant's ability to perform in that sport. Advocates of specificity believe that the best way to increase ability in a given sport is to strengthen by performing the skills specific to the sport itself and that general conditioning is a waste of time. This theory is similar to Thorndike's theory of transfer of learning: only identical elements will transfer. In order not to "miss out," most coaches subscribe to both theories, although most current research supports specificity. A list of specific training and conditioning techniques, which differ for each event, follows each event chapter in this book.

Suggestions for general conditioning that may prove helpful to gymnasts involve strengthening the large muscle groups or body areas (e.g., Fig. 2.15). Table 2.1 lists several.

Any exercise in which the gymnast contracts or shortens the muscle group against resistance is also effective for general conditioning. The resistance can take the form of another gymnast, a spotter, a teacher, or a coach pushing or pulling against the desired action and making the contraction more difficult for the gymnast. Another form of resistance could be weights or a weight training

Table 2.1   General Conditioning Techniques

Muscle group or Area	Techniques	No. of Reptitions[a]
Abdominals	Bent knee sit-ups	60
	In a long hang on a bar, bring toes up to the bar	10
Hip flexors	L-Hang and hold for 20 seconds	10
Quadriceps and hamstrings (thigh muscles)	Running, jogging, and wind sprints	2 mi. 2 mi.
	Stair running	10–15 min.
	Harvard step-up	2 min., rest 30 sec. (repeat 5 times)
	Half squat jumps	40 (repeat 5 times)
Gastrocs (calf)	Straight leg jumps	40 (repeat 3 times
	Half squat jumps	40 (repeat 3 times)
Upper arm (biceps and triceps) and shoulder girdle	Push-ups	40
	Pull-ups	10–20
	Handstand push-ups	Up to 20

[a] May be decreased according to age and experience of the gymnast.

Table 2.2   Static Stretching Techniques

Muscle group	Exercise

Hamstrings (back of thigh)	Toe touching:
	  standing—straddle, legs together
	  sitting—straddle, legs together
	Stretch and contract (described above)
	Helper stretches legs in inverted split handstand, each leg forward
	Slowly going into a split with each leg forward, hips squarely facing forward
	Slowly going into a front split

Adductors (inner aspect of thigh)	Sitting in a wide straddle position on the floor, pulling forward onto feet and then into facedown position, then reverse the exercise by pushing the hips backwards Stretch and contract with side against the wall
Quadriceps (front of thighs)	Kneeling with hands on floor behind hips, keeping the shoulders and hips in line, no pike, the body is eased backwards Stretch and contract (described above)
Achilles tendon and gastrocs (heel cord and calf)	Standing with toes on the edge of an incline and stretching the heels down in back, legs kept straight Stretch and contract from supine position (described above)
Low back	Bridge position Walkovers
Upper back (should be emphasized)	From a supine position gymnast grabs the ankles of a helper who is standing with a foot on either side of the gymnast's head; with feet out or away, the gymnast pushes herself up so that arms are straight and upper back arches; helper bends over and places her hands on the gymnast's shoulder blades and pulls (gently and slowly) the gymnast toward her
Shoulder girdle	Gymnast can hold onto a broom handle or low-bar of the unevens and, without bending her elbows, evenly bring the bar behind her and then in front again
Wrist	Kneeling with hands in shoulder width position on the floor, elbows straight, the gymnast leans forward so that her shoulders are over and way past or in front of her hands
Ankle	Plantar and dorsi flexion can be increased by walking on the toes; heel, toes in, toes out, on the inside, and on the outside of the foot With one leg crossed over the other in a sitting position, the ankle of the free leg should be stretched and circled in all directions Stretch and contract (described on page 27)

machine. Contrary to popular belief, the average female will not develop bulk or bulging muscle from lifting weights. The increase in muscle bulk that occurs with males and not females from lifting weights results from higher progesterone levels in males. The weight-lifting regimen involving brief, hard exercise using heavy weights with few repetitions and short intervals is good training for power events. Endurance event training comprises prolonged moderate exercise, using light weights with many repetitions and long intervals. The teacher should be aware of the possibilities and limitations of weight training. *Caution:* An unsophisticated naive young gymnast should not be released into a weight room without a specific program of her own or supervision. A conservative suggestion is that the weight-training program for females include lifting light weights with many repetitions to increase the strength in the major muscle groups. The weights should be taken through the whole range of motion at the speed necessary in a given skill. Although many teacher/coaches endorse general conditioning, in this book the tendency is to recommend more strongly specificity in training.

Flexibility is the other basic physical attribute essential for the gymnast. Gymnasts who lack flexibility often complain, "I'm just too tight, I can't stretch." This is a convenient excuse. Flexibility, like strength, can develop over a period of time with consistent effort. At present, static stretching is considered the most effective, although we used to proclaim that one should bounce into flexibility. In the static approach, one slowly eases or stretches the large muscle groups of the body without bouncing. A totally relaxed and quiet atmosphere, in contrast to the excitement and electricity of the atmosphere when strengthening, will add to the extent of the stretch.

A popular stretching technique involves the gymnast stretching a muscle group and then contracting the same group against resistance. This combination should be repeated five times. Although this technique was designed to increase flexibility, a bonus effect is the slight strengthening that can occur as a consequence of the contraction. To demonstrate this technique, a gymnast stands with her heels and back against a wall. A helper lifts one leg (stretching the hamstrings) as high as is comfortable for the gymnast. The gymnast than pushes her leg down (contracting the hamstrings) against the resistance of the helper. Repeating this procedure five times shows the amazing degree to which flexibility increases with each repetition. The other leg is then stretched. To stretch the quadriceps, the gymnast faces the wall with her arms extended (locked) and hands on the wall. The helper lifts one of the gymnast's legs backwards as high as is comfortable. Then the gymnast attempts to push the leg down against resistance. This is a marvelous stretching technique and its principles can be applied successfully to stretch the large muscle groups of the body. Table 2.2 lists some suggested static stretching exercises for gymnasts (see also Figs. 2.16 and 2.17).

Utilization of a well-planned circuit in training and conditioning gymnasts is most effective. The exciting thing, for the coach and not the gymnast, is that a circuit design can include skills that are specific to gymnastics and accomplish strength training for explosive and endurance skills as well as flexibility skills. A

Figure 2.16 • (left) Low back stretch (bridge)
Figure 2.17 • (right) Upper back stretching

circuit should meet the needs of an individual, class, or team. It should include skills that could use improvement. The circuit is effective also because a gymnast or a group can run through a circuit in a limited amount of time and it should be possible to repeat the whole circuit as many times as necessary to accomplish the training objective. Figure 2.18 is a sample circuit for gymnastics. It is essential that the teacher/coach design the circuit to fit the needs of her gymnasts.

Since gymnasts are unique individuals, their strengths and weaknesses are very different. A coach can write out a training plan for each mature athlete and expect her to work on it above and beyond, outside of, or at the end of practice.

The most appropriate time to train is at the completion of practice. Running or a general conditioning technique can be done at any other time during the day. By conditioning at the end of practice the teacher/coach is employing the "overload principle" from exercise physiology theory. The knowledge and understanding of conditioning and even more so conditioning for female athletes is expanding daily and the conscientious, concerned teacher/coach should avail herself of the most current materials on the subject.

WEIGHT

The bane of a gymnastic coach's existence is the proverbial weight hassle. Throughout puberty females gain weight, but it may become very noticeable at about seventeen years of age. Weight is critical to one's gymnastic performance. The ratio of body weight to strength can often be the difference between accomplishing and not accomplishing a skill. Besides affecting one's ability to perform a skill, weight can also have an effect on the subjective evaluation of the performance. A natural judging thought process is, "If she is fat she obviously can't tumble as lightly or high as she should, so her amplitude isn't good and her general

28

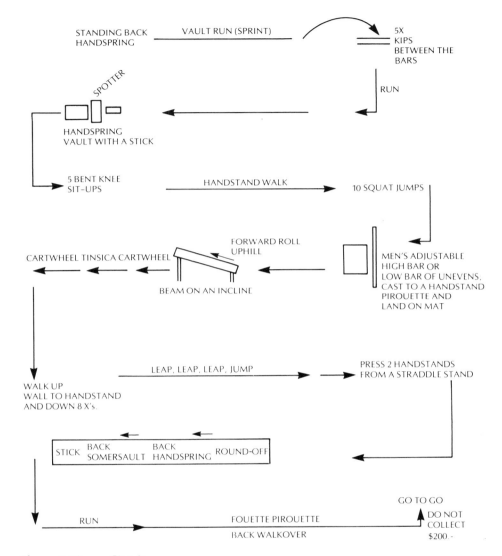

Figure 2.18 • Circuit

impression is poor." Parents and teacher/coaches have a responsibility to educate and counsel young gymnasts about the "weight problem." Unfortunately, once a girl has become an "Alice Adipose" weight loss is extremely difficult. Thus the objective should be to prevent weight gain from the beginning. Current nutritional information should be sought and applied. We know that Americans tend to overeat. We don't need to eat as much as we do. Gymnasts should try to limit their intake of carbohydrates and fats. Some gymnasts have successfully dealt with a weight problem by embracing vegetarianism, although this book does not necessarily advocate a vegetarian approach. Parents should not force children to eat whether they are hungry or not. The teacher/coach may have to educate the parents as well as the gymnast about proper diet.

To gain a better appreciation of the gymnastics weight hassle, let's review some recent information. The average college-age woman carries 20 to 22 percent of her total body volume as fat. The male distance runner generally carries 5 to 6 percent fat in total volume. A conservative goal for the female gymnast is between 10 and 14 percent body fat. The basis for this figure is the research of Sinning and Lindberg, who studied the physical characteristics of female gymnasts at Springfield College and compared this population with other populations of female gymnasts.[1] From these figures it is evident that the average college woman, whose body is 20 to 22 percent fat, could not perform as well as a woman carrying 10 percent fat. The closer the individual approaches lean body weight (0 percent fat), the more efficient her movements should be. It is not advisable for the female gymnast to carry less than 6 percent body fat.

Experience tells us that the only thing women lie about is weight (not necessarily age). If weight control is an important part of a gymnastics program, the teacher/coach should personally weigh in on a weekly basis and maintain an accurate record of each athlete's weight. The mental discipline of proper weight maintenance is a difficult variable to deal with, but it is one that the teacher/coach must help the gymnast to appreciate and control. Despite popular opinion, weight loss does not occur from exercise but from low food intake. A team of "mean and lean" gymnasts will accomplish and perform better than a group of "chubbies."

FEMALE PHYSIOLOGY

As the number of women participating in gymnastics and athletics increases, more and more information regarding the physiology of the female in sport becomes available. The old wives' tales predicting grave harm to a female athlete and particularly to her ability to bear children are no longer persuasive. No permanent damage can occur to the female reproductive organs from participating in sport, unless an implement ruptures the abdominal wall.[2] Many athletic achievements and records have been broken by menstruating females. Therefore menstruation should not hinder athletic performance. In a small and limited population of female gymnasts, the author found that amenorrhea (temporary cessation of menstruation) was common among the better, well-conditioned athletes, some of whom had lost weight during training. Evidently this is a

[1]Wayne Sinning and Gary Lindberg, "Physical Characteristics of College Age Women Gymnasts," *Research Quarterly,* May 1972, pp. 226–34.

[2]Clayton L. Thomas, "Special Problems of the Female Athlete," in *Sports Medicine,* ed. Allan J. Ryan and Fred A. Allman (New York: Academic Press, 1974), pp. 347–73.

temporary phenomenon and no cause for concern. This observation is supported by recent research.[3] Again, the reader should remember to seek the most current and accurate information regarding the female athlete.

[3]Dorothy V. Harris, "The Fat Factor," *Womensports*, August 1977, p. 52.

3

SELLING
floor exercise

Floor exercise is the most glamorous of the four Olympic events. The gymnast must "sell" herself, her ability, her talent, her expression, and her beauty of movement to the judges and an audience in a relatively short span of time. To accomplish this goal the gymnast and her routine should be in total harmony. She should present a picture of the very best of all things in life: vitality, health, the joy of effort, and so on. In reality, she is challenging her audience to buy her routine. Foremost of all the events, the gymnast must sell floor exercise (Fig. 3.1).*

Floor exercise provides, as no other sport activity does, an unlimited freedom of and for body expression through movement. The gymnast performs in an area approximately 40 ft. × 40 ft. (39 ft. 4½ in. × 39 ft. 4½ in. or 12 m × 12 m). The exercise should use all of this area and should last from one minute to one minute thirty seconds. The beginning and intermediate gymnasts' routines should not exceed one minute and a few seconds, for it is essential that the exercise finish as strongly as it began (a shorter exercise enables a novice gymnast to finish strongly). Music from a solo instrument accompanies the performer.

Basically, floor exercise consists of dance (ballet, modern, jazz, folk), acrobatics (movements of flexibility, such as walkovers) and tumbling combinations. Therefore, in this chapter, we will separately take up tumbling, dance, and acrobatics, as well as routine construction, coaching, performing, and training for floor exercise.

*Figure 3.1 is on preceding page.

Evident in the total composition of a floor exercise routine should be obvious changes in level, tempo, and direction. The exercise should convey a meaningful message. The gymnast should work toward proper form (legs straight, toes pointed, proper body alignment, composure, and balance) and amplitude (the bigness or completeness of each movement). Both the coach and gymnast should be as imaginative and creative as possible when choreographing a floor exercise.

SAFETY

The safety precautions for floor exercise include having a good floor exercise mat without any holes, separations, or unevenness. If a floor exercise mat is not available, a line or lines of regular gymnasium mats will suffice for learning acrobatic and tumbling skills. The mats should be carefully placed together in lines so that there is no overlapping or space between them. Ankle and knee injuries can occur if a gymnast lands on an uneven surface. The teacher/coach should be knowledgable regarding spotting techniques and should make provision for proper spotting. When using the trampoline as an aid in teaching certain tumbling skills the teacher/coach should insist on four spotters, one on each side of the trampoline. The spotting belt and/or overhead spotting rig can be very helpful in teaching certain skills for floor exercise, but only individuals who understand and can manipulate it should use it. Overuse of the spotting belt or rig can cause the gymnast to use it as a "crutch" or "security blanket."

TUMBLING

Tumbling is the basis for all gymnastics. In beginning gymnastics, it might be advantageous to spend a whole year learning to tumble properly. Tumbling skills require leg strength, something with which most women are not excessively endowed. Thus they must concentrate on tumbling with proper technique. Utilizing proper technique enables the gymnast to compensate for a moderate amount of strength. Because of their strength, male gymnasts sometimes don't have to be as concerned with such exact technique for success. Proper technique does not negate the necessity for leg strength, however, and women should work on increasing leg strength through tumbling and conditioning. The following tumbling skills are discussed in this section: rolls, back extension roll, handstand forward roll, roundoff, front handspring, side aerial, front aerial, back handspring, back somersault, front somersault, whipback, arabian, and back layout full twist.

Since tumbling skills require explosive leg strength, many gymnasts and their coaches erroneously think the length and dynamics of the run will improve or facilitate tumbling. Too much of a run with certain skills is counterproductive, however. The most effective approach to all tumbling seems to be three steps or less. The teacher/coach has a responsibility to gymnasts to stress this approach during tumbling practice. Female gymnasts must not believe that they are part 747 and need an airport runway from which to thrust their bodies into space. Skills such as aerials should be learned, practiced, and performed from a stand. The lunge position is extremely important and one the gymnast should assume prior to all tumbling skills (one leg bent in front, the other leg extended behind hips and shoulders in line: see Chapter 2).

All tumbling and acrobatic skills should begin and finish with a complete stretch—body extended and arms in the air. If the skill requires impetus from alternate legs, the free leg should be kicked into the air as high as possible prior to executing the skill. This extension gives amplitude (a judging category) to the sequence. All tumbling skills should be taught with light landings. A heavy landing is indicative of improper technique.

Forward Roll

This skill has been incorrectly labeled a "somersault." There is a vast distinction between rolls and somersaults. In a somersault, the body rotates 360° around its horizontal axis with no part of the body touching the floor from the time the feet push off, until they land. Obviously this is a very difficult skill and one that beginners should not attempt. In contrast, rolls are skills in which there is also a rotation about the horizontal axis, but the whole back is in contact with the floor throughout the rotation.

In the roll, the head is tucked (chin to chest), hands placed on the floor, fingers pointing forward (see Fig. 3.2). The back is rounded, and the legs lift the body up and over. The arms perform a reverse press (gently easing the body to the floor). Contact with the floor is made at the base of the neck (at the sixth cervical vertebra—C6) and top of the shoulders. The gymnast rolls on her rounded back and stands right up on her feet which are tucked in close to her body. At the completion of the roll, the body is stretched and the arms extended.

Teaching techniques and progressions:

1. Egg rolls are a progression for this skill. The girl sits on the floor, knees bent and apart, the arms held around the knees. She then begins to roll circularly from knee to knee up her arm to her shoulder, across the upper part of her back to her other shoulder, down the other arm to her knee.

Figure 3.2 • Forward roll

2. The forward roll can be attempted by going down a slight incline.

3. The gymnast can stand in a straddle position, and reach between the legs with the arms, continuing to reach back between the legs. Her head is brought back between the legs and she should be looking up toward the ceiling. As she further stretches and reaches back, her center of gravity is lowered and forced outside of its base support causing her to roll.

Corrections: The following problems should be noted and corrected.

1. Rolling over and sidewards (partial shoulder roll) can be corrected by performing the straddle roll as described in the techniques section.

2. Placing the head instead of the back of the neck on the mat.

3. A loud body slap or sound can be corrected by using the arms more in letting the body down on the mat and rounding the back so that it assumes a round wheel appearance and not that of a wheel with corners (flat back).

4. The inability to stand up at the conclusion of the roll can be due to a loose or open tuck, the feet not close enough to the body or too much adipose deposited in the general area of the center of gravity without proportional strength.

Spotting: Two techniques are effective for spotting the forward roll.

1. The spotter kneels or squats in front and to the side of the gymnast. As the reverse press begins, the spotter places her hand on top of the gymnast's shoulder and lifts her up to allow the roll to occur.

2. The spotter stands to the side and in front of the gymnast. As the roll begins the spotter places her hands on each side of the back of the gymnast's waist, lifts her so that the body does not slap the mat, and places the gymnast's body down. The spotter then releases her hands so the roll may be completed.

Combinations: 1. Jump, forward roll, jump.
2. Forward roll, jump half turn.
3. Turn, leap, forward roll, jump.
4. Chassé (step together step), forward roll.
5. Forward roll, back handspring.
6. Forward roll into a split.

Usually, the next skill presented in gymnastics is the back roll. A premise of this text, however, is that a back roll is not a skill that every girl should perform. It is difficult and is not a useful progression until the gymnast is proficient enough to attempt a back somersault because it can result in a stiff neck, unless performed correctly. "Alice Adipose" should not be expected to perform a back roll, for in this skill the body must be lifted off the floor to permit the head to pass between the hands and usually heavier girls lack strength that is proportional to their weight; thus attempting this skill is likely to force Alice's head into hyperflexion.

Handstand Forward Roll

This skill is an extremely important movement for the aspiring gymnast. It provides the proper method for the gymnast to utilize when she loses her balance in an inverted position. This is a skill that can add variety to movement because of its obvious change in level. The gymnast stretches upward and kicks a handstand (see Chapter 2) and from this position she overbalances her shoulders (forces her shoulders forward over her hands), as shown in Fig. 3.3. Once she has lost her balance, she reverse-presses (lets her body down by using her arms). As her nose approaches the mat, she tucks her head and, back rounded, completes a roll. A stretched stand completes the skill.

Teaching techniques and progressions:

1. The prerequisite for this skill is the successful performance of handstands and forward rolls.
2. The handstand can be kicked at the edge of a crash pad, hands on the floor, and the roll performed onto the crash pad with spotting.
3. A push-up performed in the handstand position with spotting (although difficult) is helpful in understanding the reverse press concept.

Corrections:

The common errors in this skill and their corrections are as follows.

1. Loose body can be corrected by STG.
2. The body of the gymnast collapsing directly on top of herself, possibly knocking the wind out of her, causing her to taste her breakfast for the second time, making a loud sound, or preventing a smooth roll can be due to:
   a. Not overbalancing the shoulders
   b. Not reverse pressing
   c. Not tucking tightly
   d. A banana back in handstand.

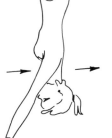

Figure 3.3 • (left) Handstand forward roll
Figure 3.4 • (below) The mat's view of a cartwheel

Spotting: 1. As the gymnast kicks the handstand, the spotter stands to the side and forward to catch the gymnast's legs. She holds the legs in the air once the shoulders have been overbalanced and the roll begins and slowly eases the gymnast to the floor. If the gymnast has difficulty overbalancing her shoulders, the spotter, while holding the legs, can place her knee in the gymnast's arm pit and then push the shoulders forward. This action causes the overbalance.

Combinations: 1. Scale (balance on one leg), handstand forward roll.
    2. Handstand forward roll, jump.
    3. Handstand forward roll, back handspring.
    4. Handstand pirouette (turn) forward roll.
    5. Handstand, straight-arm reverse-press forward roll.

Cartwheel

As a tumbling skill, this is one of the few moves in which the body proceeds through the side plane. The gymnast in lunge position places one hand on the mat and then the other while alternately kicking the legs into the air (the straight one first). The body passes through the handstand with legs straddled, then the feet alternately make contact with the floor. There is a distinct and even rhythm to the cartwheel: hand hand foot foot (Fig. 3.4). The body should stretch throughout the skill (pelvic tilt STG) with arms and legs straight (see Fig. 3.5). The head remains in a neutral position. Eventually the gymnast can start and finish a cartwheel facing sideways. The gymnast should be encouraged to cartwheel using either hand first.

Figure 3.5 • Cartwheel

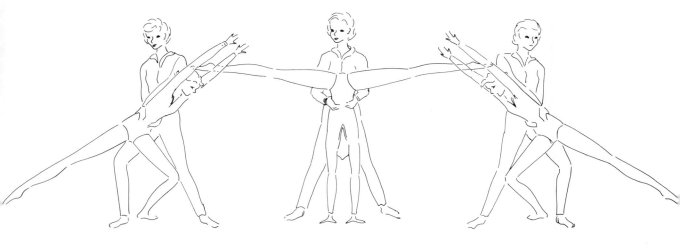

Figure 3.6 • Cartwheel with spot

Teaching
techniques and
progressions:

1. The performance of a tour jêté (see dance section). The teacher/coach explains that a cartwheel is a tour jêté on the hands.

2. The gymnast should place her hands on the mat next to her feet, step around her hands, and place one foot and then the other on the mat. The hips are piked; the legs are bent.

3. With each attempt, the gymnast takes more weight on her hands. Eventually she lifts her hips higher and higher so that they are over the shoulders. The gymnast is also encouraged to extend her legs more and more in each repetition.

Corrections:

1. Banana back (arching) or pancaking (hips piked) can be corrected by a spotter who catches the gymnast's legs in the straddle handstand and helps her to stretch her body into the proper alignment.

2. Pancaking can be caused also by the gymnast's reaching and placing her first hand behind rather than in line with her foot. The cartwheel should be performed in a straight line. Thus it is sometimes helpful to draw a chalk line on the mat or to find a seam in the mat and ask the gymnast to do her cartwheel on this line.

Spotting:

1. The spotter stands sideways and forward on the side of the gymnast's first hand or the bent knee in the lunge (see Fig. 3.6). The spotter crosses her arms with thumbs down. She places the arm closer to the gymnast on the gymnast's waist. With her free arm crossed over the other arm, she places her free hand on the other (further) side of the gymnast's waist. For example, if the gymnast's first hand is the right, the spotter stands on the gymnast's right side and places her left hand on the right side of the gymnast's waist. The spotter's right arm is crossed over her left arm. Her right hand behind the gymnast's back holds the other side of her waist. This spot is designed to give the most support to the

40

Figure 3.7 • Cartwheel with spot

gymnast when she is in the inverted position. As in all spotting, the spotter must be prepared to move with the gymnast (Fig. 3.7).

Combinations:
1. Cartwheel, cartwheel.
2. Cartwheel with the right hand first, then step and cartwheel with the left hand first.
3. Cartwheel, forward roll.
4. Leap or jump, cartwheel.
5. Turn, jump, cartwheel, leap.
6. Cartwheel on one arm—near and/or far (see Fig. 3.8).
7. Cartwheel to a split (the first leg moves past the hands into a split).
8. Cartwheel, tinsica (see acrobatics section).

Figure 3.8 • One-arm cartwheel

Roundoff

As a gymnastic skill, the roundoff is extremely important because it sets up and determines the failure or success of back and more advanced tumbling. After no more than a three-step run, from the lunge position, the gymnast puts her hands on the mat in a position similar to the one used in a cartwheel (quarter, or 90°, turn): hand, hand. She kicks her legs into the air and brings them together upon reaching the inverted position. Following another quarter turn (90°) in the hips, the legs are forcefully snapped down so that the gymnast finishes facing the direction from which she came. The placement of the hands is controversial. They can be placed:

1. As they are in a cartwheel (Fig. 3.9a).
2. With the fingers of the second hand placed on the mat and pointing toward the starting direction to gain more push from the mat (Fig. 3.9b). The push from the mat is a blocking of the shoulders (necessary for vaulting and back and front handsprings). Blocking in the shoulders is a very slight movement that changes the angle of the arms at the shoulders. The upper arms squeeze the front of the temples and quickly move backwards to the front of the ears. This action causes the body to rise and repulse the floor. In men's gymnastics, good results are achieved when the gymnast bends his arms slightly and then extends them. Are women strong and explosive enough in their movements for this technique to be effective? Or is the result the same as it might be if a woman placed her hands in quicksand? Experience indicates that the shoulder blockage is the most effective technique for the majority of females.
3. Both hands are placed so that the fingers point in the starting direction and blocking occurs in the shoulders (Fig. 3.9c).

Whichever hand placement technique appeals to the teacher/coach or is natural to the gymnast is acceptable.

The body should rebound with height and force from the mat. The purpose of the roundoff is to maintain the direction of the established floor pattern but to

Figure 3.9 • Roundoff hand and foot placement

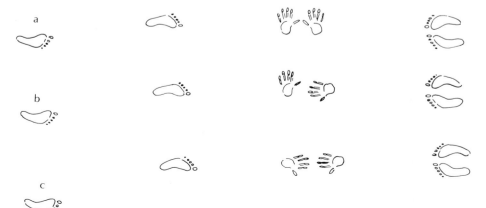

change the position the body is facing from forward to backward and to permit back tumbling with dynamic force.

Teaching techniques and progressions:

1. The prerequisite for the roundoff is a cartwheel.
2. The gymnast can attempt the skill in slow motion with a spotter using the cartwheel-spotting technique and helping the gymnast to do a cartwheel quarter turn.
3. The roundoff can be tried on a trampoline from a stand.
4. Standing on a reuther board or the edge of mats piled together to obtain a thickness of 4 to 6 inches, the gymnast places her hands on the lower mat and performs the roundoff. The spot is the same as the one used for the cartwheel.

Corrections:

Lack of vitality can result from several errors.

1. Placing the hands too close to the feet. The gymnast should reach and place her hands as far from her feet as possible. Otherwise the roundoff appears to go up and down rather than covering distance backwards.
2. Pancaking or banana-backing the skill.
3. Placing the hands behind the feet or in back of herself rather than in line with and in front of the feet.
4. Poor snap-down (piking in the hips and bringing the feet in and under the hips). The snap-down, ideally, should be so explosive and dynamic that the gymnast either falls on her glutes or does back tumbling. The snap-down can be aided by performing mule kick snap-downs, which involve kicking up into a handstand and piking the hips down forcefully. A spotter should stand behind the gymnast and catch her back as her feet land and she rebounds up from the floor. This spot prevents the gymnast from falling backwards from failing to block the shoulders, and from pushing off the mat with the hands.
5. Too long an approach. The run should be only three steps.

Spotting:

1. Once the gymnast has mastered the skill, the spotter stands slightly to the side of the area of the floor where the roundoff will be performed. As soon as the gymnast's hands touch the floor, the spotter moves in behind the place where the gymnast's feet will land, places her hands on gymnast's back (waist), and arrests the backward momentum. Eventually the gymnast will attempt to rebound from the floor with as much velocity and force as possible while the spotter catches her in a "tilt."

Combinations:

1. Roundoff, back roll.
2. Roundoff, back extension roll.
3. Roundoff, (half) pop turn, cartwheel.

4. Roundoff, back handspring.

5. Roundoff, back somersault.

Back Extension Roll

This skill is not a skill for everyone to learn. It is an important skill for students who aren't too fat, for it is the first kip. A kip is a skill in which the body moves from a lower position to a higher position through the force initiated by the unfolding of the body. The arms push or pull as the body is going from a tuck or pike to a layout position. The gymnast performs a back roll (in tuck or pike), and just as her hips are over or on top of her shoulders, she explosively extends her arms and body simultaneously upward (Fig. 3.10). As soon as her shoulders are off the mat she extends her head to the neutral position. The gymnast then walks out (foot, foot landing) or pikes her legs down—both feet at the same time—to the mat. The kip action is extremely explosive and forceful. This skill is the exact reverse of the handstand forward roll.

Teaching techniques and progressions:

1. The progressions for this skill are: roll backwards from a squat position in tuck (on a rounded back) to the shoulders and hands, which are placed over the top of the shoulders—thumbs pointing toward the ears, elbows bent and in—and then roll back onto the feet. This rocking action, shown in Fig. 3.11, is the progression for the back roll.

2. Next perform the back roll (Fig. 3.12). To begin the roll, move backwards from a squat, body in tuck position (back rounded, chin on chest, knees up to chest), hands on top of shoulders, and thumbs pointing toward the ears. Once the weight of the body is on the hands the gymnast pushes against the mat lifting her body up so that her head may pass between her hands. The spotter stands to the side, and as the hands of the gymnast touch the floor, the spotter places her hands on the waist of the gymnast with one arm around the gymnast's back. The spotter then lifts the gymnast up (not back) so that there is room for her head to pass between her hands. A common error in the back roll

Figure 3.10 • (right) Back extension roll
Figure 3.11 • (left) Progression for back roll

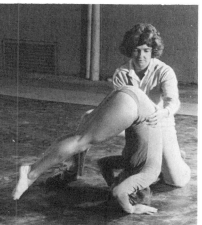

Figure 3.12 • Back roll

is opening from a tight tuck as the gymnast rolls backward. Another error is not getting the hands in the proper position to push.

3. Handstand push-up with spotting will aid the gymnast in the kinesthesis of the extension phase. (see Chapter 2).

Corrections:

1. A tight tuck in the roll will help make the handstand possible. The body must be tight, STG, throughout.

2. An explosive effort is necessary. The rhythm of the skill is "roll; BOOM; handstand."

3. The timing of extension should be noted:
   a. If the gymnast arches out and lands on the mat on her back, she has extended from the tuck too soon.
   b. If the gymnast lands on the front of her body on the mat, she has extended from the tuck position of the roll too late. This error is more common.
   c. Extension of the head once the arms are extended halfway can help with the lift.
   d. Some gymnasts can gain more lift by splitting their legs at the top of the extension.

Spotting: 1. The spotter or spotters (two) stand alongside the gymnast and grasp the gymnast's legs just above the ankles as the hips begin to come over the shoulders. The spot is to lift the gymnast's legs up and help her to obtain the handstand. This spot requires quick movement and an alert spotter (see Fig. 3.13).

Combinations: 1. Back roll, back extension roll.

2. Cartwheel, back extension roll.

3. Roundoff, back extension roll.

4. Back extension roll, front walkover. As the extension phase nears completion, the gymnast stretches and walks out of the skill as if finishing a front walkover (Fig. 3.14). The spotter lifts the small of the back as the gymnast extends into the walkover.

5. Handstand forward roll, back extension roll.

6. Back handspring, back extension roll.

Side Aerial   An alternate foot-foot takeoff, body rotation (hands don't touch the mat), and foot-foot landing typify aerial tumbling. The side aerial, or aerial cartwheel, is challenging to the gymnast, although it appears to be more difficult than it is. Poor technique and instruction cause many girls to perform this skill as if it were a "cranial perch." This is a leg skill (requiring power from the legs); therefore, from

Figure 3.13   •   Back extension roll with spot

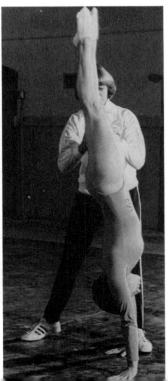

Figure 3.14 • Back extension roll, front walkover

the lunge position (stride position, first or front leg bent, second or rear leg straight, shoulders directly over the hips, arms relaxed at the sides), the gymnast lifts her rear leg up, then extends her bent leg to lift her body up and over (see Fig. 3.15). She passes through the side plane as if performing a cartwheel without hands. The gymnast then lands the skill foot after foot. There should be an obvious lift in the body as the rotation occurs.

Teaching techniques and progressions:

1. The gymnast stands in the lunge position and extends her rear leg and then front leg. She maintains the position of her shoulders over her hips while she lifts fore-upward from the floor.

Figure 3.15 • Side aerial with spot

2. From the lunge position, using her legs to get as much lift as possible without piking, the gymnast performs a cartwheel.

3. This skill can be performed either while standing on the edge of a reuther board or on the trampoline with spotting.

4. If necessary, the gymnast can touch the floor with her hands.

5. During all of the above steps, a spotter will help the gymnast feel the necessary lift.

Corrections:

1. Common errors in body position to be changed and corrected are:
   a. The arms extended up in the beginning of the skill. Throwing the arms down as the rotation begins forces the gymnast's body downward instead of upward. The result is a dumped aerial. This is a leg skill, and because the arms are not a necessary rotation aid, they usually create and exaggerate improper technique. Thus the arms should be loosely held at the sides.
   b. A tucked head will cause the rotation to be lower. Thus the head should be kept up.
   c. Piking at the waist (changing the position of shoulders over the hips) also causes a dumped aerial. Thus the torso should be prevented from piking.

2. Running prior to performing the skill also can cause a dumping. The aerial should be learned from a stand and performed from a step into the lunge position. This discipline on the part of the teacher/coach and gymnast must be encouraged and reinforced.

3. Throwing the skill off a straight front leg: erroneously the gymnast thinks she can get enough power and lift to rotate her body from ankle extension. To correct this mistake, ask the gymnast to jump as high as she can without bending her knees. A well-bent knee in the first, or front, leg of the lunge is essential. The gymnast must use all of the leg strength available. The quadriceps and hamstrings are the major muscle groups involved. This error often occurs if a run precedes the skill.

4. The hips continuing to move forward as the skill is initiated also causes a dumping. A blocking of the hips should occur. The spot for this skill can help the gymnast with the kinesthetic awareness of blocking.

5. A loose body in the air will cause the force from the impetus to dissipate and a dumped aerial will result. If the legs are bent (froggied) while inverted, the body isn't tight enough and possibly the gymnast did not completely push off with her legs.

Spotting:

1. The spotting for an aerial in the initial stages involves the spotter supinating (palms up) her hands, placing the little fingers together, as if to hold something in the hands. The spotter stands on the side of the gymnast's forward (bent knee) leg in the lunge and she turns her hands, keeping them together, to face

Figure 3.16 • Side aerial with spot

the gymnast. The hands rest on the front of the gymnast's hips. If the gymnast is large in proportion the spotter, the spotter can use her forearms to give more lift. As the gymnast pushes forward into the aerial, the spotter blocks her hips (prevents them from moving forward) and helps the gymnast move upward. The spotter's hands or arms actually provide an axis of rotation for the skill.

2. Once the skill has been learned, the spotter can place her hands on the gymnast as if spotting a cartwheel. A brief review of this spot follows: the spotter stands to the side and ahead of the front leg or bent knee in the lunge. The spotter's arm closer to the gymnast is placed with the thumbs down (supination), palm on the front of the hip (side of first leg) of the gymnast, as shown in Fig. 3.16. The spotter's free arm crosses over the other and reaches behind the gymnast to the other side of her waist, thumb down, palm on (pronation). In this spot, the spotter has more control over the landing but can't lift as much as the spotter using the first spotting technique.

Combinations: 1. Side aerial, pop (quarter) turn, cartwheel.
2. Cartwheel, side aerial.
3. Side aerial, side aerial.
4. Leap, step, side aerial.

Front Aerial   The front aerial, or aerial walkover, is more difficult than a side aerial because it requires more flexibility from the gymnast. The front aerial is initiated exactly as the side aerial. From the lunge position (hips and shoulders in line, knee of front leg bent, rear leg extended, and arms relaxed by the sides) the gymnast lifts or thrusts her extended (rear) leg into the air, then quickly extends the bent (front) leg (see Fig. 3.17). The hips are blocked and the body rises into the air. As the body

Figure 3.17 • Front aerial with spot

rotates around the horizontal axis, it moves through the front plane. The feet land on the mat in a walkout or alternately foot, foot. This skill looks like a front walkover (acrobatics) without hands. As in the side aerial, the body should rise.

Teaching techniques and progressions:

1. As in the case of the side aerial, the lunge and lift with proper shoulder-hip alignment is the first progression for learning an aerial.
2. The skill can be tried either while standing on the edge of a reuther board or on a trampoline.
3. Spotting during the preceding steps is necessary and will help the gymnast feel the necessary lift.

Corrections:

1. Common errors in body position to be changed and corrected are:
   a. The arms extended upward in the beginning of the skill. Throwing the arms down as the rotation begins causes the gymnast's body also to move downward instead of upward. The result is a dumped aerial. This is a leg skill, and because the arms are not a necessary aid to rotation, they usually create and exaggerate improper technique. Thus the arms should be held loosely at the sides.
   b. A tucked head will cause the rotation to be lower.
   c. Piking at the waist (changing the position of shoulders over the hips) also causes a dumped aerial.
2. Running prior to performing the skill also can cause a dumping. The aerial should be learned from a stand and performed from a step into the lunge position. The teacher/coach and gymnast must stress the "no-run" rule.
3. Throwing the skill off a straight front leg. Some gymnasts erroneously think they can get enough power and lift to rotate the body from ankle extension.

50

Figure 3.18 • Front aerial with three spotters

Asking a gymnast to jump as high as she can without bending her knees will demonstrate that a well-bent knee in the first (front) leg of the lunge is essential. The gymnast must use all of the leg strength available. The quadriceps and hamstrings are the major muscle groups involved. This error often occurs when a run precedes the skill.

4. The hips continuing to move forward as the skill is initiated also causes a dumping. A blocking of the hips should occur. The spot for this skill can help the gymnast with the kinesthetic awareness of blocking.

5. A loose body in the air will cause the force from the impetus to dissipate and the result will be a dumped aerial. If the legs are bent (froggied) while inverted, the body isn't tight enough and possibly the gymnast did not completely push off with her legs.

6. "Sitting down" at the end of the skill will not occur if the gymnast uses her "abominable abdominals" as her first foot touches the mat to pull her hips and then her chest up and over the base support. If the gymnast tucks her head, she will also "sit the skill down." Since the landing of this skill is a "blind" one the natural tendency is to tuck the head and look for the mat. To perform the skill the gymnast must do just the opposite and keep her head back, although she should be encouraged to maintain her head position (back) while looking down for the mat with her eyes.

Spotting:

1. An ill-advised spot that doesn't help the gymnast with the lift phase of the aerial is to place the gymnast in a spotting belt with one spotter holding each rope.

2. A spot that is quite secure and safe involves three spotters (see Fig. 3.18). Two spotters stand on either side and to the front of the gymnast. They each grasp

one of the gymnast's hands with the hand that is closer to the gymnast. The palms of the spotters' free hands are placed, fingers pointing down (pronated), on the top of the gymnast's shoulders. These spotters keep the gymnast in the air once she has inverted and help her with the landing. The third spotter stands beside the forward (bent) knee and places her hands on the gymnast's hip on that side. The objective of this spotter is to block the hips and lift or help the gymnast during the initial phase of the skill. This technique should be used only once or twice since it is very artificial. It might also help a girl who is dumping the skill to go back and try this progression.

3. The usual and best spot for a front aerial is for the spotter to stand in front and on the side of the forward (bent) leg of the gymnast. The hand of the arm closer to the gymnast is placed with the thumb down and the palm on the front of the gymnast's hip (supination). This arm helps with the lift. The spotter's free arm crosses over the other and the hand, palm facing and thumb down (pronated), supports the small of the gymnast's back. As the gymnast rotates, this hand maintains contact with the gymnast's back and rotates (supination) to help the gymnast stand at the end of the skill.

Combinations:
1. Front aerial, front walkover.
2. Front aerial, front handspring.
3. Front aerial, tinsica.
4. Front aerial landing on one leg keeping the other leg in the air, back walkover.
5. Front aerial, front aerial.
6. Front aerial, side aerial.
7. Front aerial, handstand forward roll.
8. Front handspring, front aerial.

Side and front aerials are skills that many girls can perform successfully if they are taught proper technique. Unfortunately, many teacher/coaches just explain the skill and never explain or teach how to accomplish it. Elementary-school-age children can learn aerials as quickly and as soon as they learn cartwheels.

Front Handspring

In front and back handsprings the gymnast springs from her feet to her hands to her feet making a complete rotation around the horizontal axis (Fig. 3.19). The front handspring is a tumbling skill in which, from the proper lunge position (shoulder and hips in line, head up, knee of front leg bent, rear leg extended), the gymnast places her hands shoulder width apart on the floor, fingers pointing straight ahead, as she kicks and lifts her rear leg into the air, then quickly and completely extends the front (bent) leg. The shoulders are blocked as the hips pass through the inverted position. This blockage of the shoulders causes the body to rise; the rise is

Figure 3.19 • (left) Front handspring

Figure 3.20 • (right) Front handspring with (a) incorrect shoulder positioning and (b) proper shoulder blocking from the spotter

a form of a kip. Blocking the shoulders necessitates extending and changing the angle of the upper arms at the shoulders (see Fig. 3.20). The upper arms press against the temples and, in a very brisk action, move to just in front of the ears. Blocking the shoulders converts the forward momentum developed through the three-step approach into upward momentum and causes the body to rise. The head remains back. The landing can be on both feet simultaneously or, alternately, foot after foot. The preferred landing is the walkout, for this kind of landing is usually lighter and thus appears to have more amplitude.

| Teaching techniques and progressions: | 1. A prerequisite to this skill is the performance of a handstand and cartwheel from a lunge. |
| | 2. This skill can be tried from a lunge position on the edge of a reuther board, on a trampoline, or in a spotting belt. |

Corrections:	1. Improper body alignment should be corrected by placing the head, shoulders and hips directly over each other, eliminating a banana back.
	2. Loose body can and should be eliminated by STG'ing.
	3. Frog legs when weight is on the hands can be corrected by completing the push from the floor with the legs and pointing the toes as much as possible (this remedy should automatically take the bend from the knees).
	4. Bending the elbows when the weight is on the hands can often be corrected by positioning the hands closer together so they are shoulder width apart. Also the hands should be on line, not one ahead of the other.

53

5. A handspring that doesn't rise can be corrected by:
   a. Blocking the shoulders.
   b. Eliminating a banana back by shortening, or tightening, the abdominals.
   c. Eliminating a long run—no more than three steps.
6. "Sitting out" the handspring can be corrected by:
   a. Not piking in the hips.
   b. Not pulling the head down (tucking to look for the mat).

Spotting:

1. The spotter stands to the side and slightly forward of the place where the gymnast will place her hands. When the gymnast's hands touch the mat, the spotter closer to the gymnast reaches down, hand supinated and thumb down, and grasps the gymnast's upper arm. The spotter's other hand is placed on the small of the gymnast's back.
2. For novice spotters or for spotters spotting a large girl: the spotters stand facing each other, holding hands or arms on each side and to the front of the area where the gymnast will place her hands (Fig. 3.21). The clasped arms closer to the gymnast cross the gymnast's back at shoulder blade level. The other clasped arms are placed across the small of the gymnast's back when she is inverted. The arms provide an axis of rotation and help lift the gymnast to a stand at the completion of the skill. The arms move and remain in contact with the gymnast's back from the time her hands touch the floor until she is standing.

Combinations:

1. Front handspring, front handspring walkout.
2. Front handspring (switch legs while inverted).
3. Front handspring to a straddle sit. To accomplish this skill the gymnast pikes in the hips after the kip or rise has occurred. The head should remain back until the sit. The heels and the back of the legs should absorb the fall. The first few times the gymnast should attempt this skill in a spotting belt, being held up and eased to the sitting position on the mat.

Figure 3.21 • Novice spot for front handspring

4. Front handspring walkout, front aerial.

5. Front handspring walkout, cartwheel.

6. Front handspring walkout, tinsica.

7. Front handspring walkout, roundoff, and so on.

8. Front handspring, front somersault.

Back Handspring

Pushing off from the feet, landing on the hands, and then the feet again to complete a 360° rotation, about the horizontal axis of the body is a handspring (Fig. 3.22). The arms and legs are straight and stretched and the skill should have athletic vitality. The back handspring is commonly called a "flip-flop" or, in Europe, a "flick-flack." As is evident by its name, in the back handspring the body moves in a backward direction. Some gymnasts have an inherent fear of moving backwards in a direction they cannot see. This psychological variable may affect

Figure 3.22 • Back handspring

the learning of a back handspring and the teacher/coach should have an awareness of and be prepared to deal with the fear (see chapter on coaching.)

Teaching techniques and progressions:

Since ability to perform the back handspring appears to be a significant indicator of a gymnast's metamorphosis from beginner to intermediate, teachers and coaches have many techniques and progressions for learning this skill. Therefore only a few of the most effective will be mentioned. As with all progressions and techniques, whatever works is the best progression.

1. The prerequisite for a back handspring is the ability to do a handstand and a cartwheel (to take the weight on the hands).

2. Two key concepts for the gymnast, regardless of teaching technique, should be emphasized and reemphasized:
    a. Locked elbows.
    b. Head back (extended).

3. Standing between two spotters, the gymnast extends her arms so that the upper arm is next to the temples (see Fig. 3.23a). The gymnast, her body absolutely tight (no banana) in stick position, leans backward until she loses her balance (Fig. 3.23b). Then she jumps. The two spotters face each other, standing behind and to the side of the gymnast, and hold hands. The joined arms closer to the gymnast cross her low back. These arms help to lift the gymnast up and over in the back handspring. The other joined arms cross the gymnast's back between the waist and shoulders. These arms form the horizontal axis of rotation for the skill. This technique provides extremely effective safety for the gymnast during the skill. The gymnast should understand

Figure 3.23 · Back handspring (progression #3)

Figure 3.24 • (left) Back handspring—spotter helping with the jump phase
Figure 3.25 • (right) Tilt, or jump, for back handspring

that by displacing her center of gravity she loses her balance and at that moment must jump backward forcefully.

4. The following technique is a classic in the world of gymnastics and should be done with spotting. There are basically three parts to the back handspring:

a. From a stand with the arms extended upward and the upper arms squeezing the temples, the gymnast sits back. This step can be practiced by sitting (without moving the feet) on the knee of a spotter or leaning against a wall with the knees and hips forming right angles. This phase is the "sit."

b. At this stage the gymnast loses her balance and jumps back, pushing with her feet against the floor as hard as she can. This is the "jump" phase. The jump should be performed without thrusting the hips forward. All momentum should be backwards. The back handspring should travel on the mat in a long, low path. Once the gymnast has performed the back handspring, if the teacher/coach thinks this phase of the back handspring is weak, she may have the gymnast place the arch of each foot in her spotter's hands while the spotter sits in a straddle position on the floor. As the gymnast begins her jump, the spotter lifts and throws the feet in the direction of the back handspring (Fig. 3.24). This technique increases the gymnast's awareness of the push she should be getting from her legs. A second spotter should spot the back handspring. This second phase, or "jump," can also be practiced as a "tilt." With the spotter behind her, the gymnast sits and jumps (head remains neutral) and, as shown in Fig. 3.25, the spotter catches her in the air or stops her backward momentum and puts her back down onto her feet.

c. The handstand is the third phase of the back handspring, although many authorities would argue that the third phase is the snap-down (forcefully piking the legs down from the handstand) and therefore should be taught. Experience has taught that many women pike too soon (prior to their bodies reaching the perpendicular in the handstand) and effect a weak "monkey jump" (similar to the back handsprings chimpanzees do, up, over, and under themselves, usually moving in a crooked direction). Emphasizing the snap-down reinforces this common error. Emphasis on the handstand will cause the snap-down to occur naturally without belaboring effort. When the hands touch the floor, there is a blocking in the shoulders (described under front handspring).

5. The back handspring can be performed on the trampoline, at the end of the reuther board, or on a slight incline (with the gymnast standing on the elevated portion).

6. Back handsprings should be learned from a stand and not with a run and roundoff. Series of standing back handsprings are excellent for conditioning and improving technique because by the third or fourth back handspring in a row the technique is usually better and the back handspring becomes correctly long and low.

7. There is a distinct rhythm to a good back handspring: evenly 1, 2, 3 or feet, hands, feet.

8. Eventually the arm throw can be taught. If taught before the gymnast has mastered the skill with arms by the temples, it can create a chain of errors. The arms are straight out from the shoulders, parallel with the floor. As the gymnast sits she pushes her arms down and back as balance is lost and she jumps backwards (Fig. 3.26). The arms are thrown up and back. With this technique the shoulders and hip alignment must be maintained—no piking or banana backing.

Corrections: Usually the errors in back handsprings are many and the teacher/coach should look for and correct them.

1. The back handspring that goes up and down or over and under (monkey jump) can be due to:
   a. Not sitting back far enough.
      i. The teacher/coach can force the gymnast to move the skill backward by facing the gymnast, nose to nose, and directing her to do a back handspring (Fig. 3.27). In the effort not to kick the teacher/coach the gymnast will jump backward.
      ii. The teacher/coach can place a chalk line on the mat four feet behind

Figure 3.26 • (left) Arm throw for back handspring
Figure 3.27 • (right) Correction for moving handspring backward

the gymnast's feet and ask her to place her hands on this line when she does the back handspring.

b. Not completely pushing off with the feet.

c. By piking (shoulders move forward) during the sit or banana-backing (thrusting the pelvis forward) at the beginning of the jump.

d. By piking before the body reaches the perpendicular handstand position. One spotter can use her arm to prevent the legs from snapping down too soon. A second spotter should be present for the back handspring.

e. Not blocking the shoulders. A spotter can kneel or squat beside the place where the gymnast will position her hands. The spotter then pushes the shoulders backward in the direction of the handspring when the body is inverted. Another spotter should be present for the back handspring.

2. A back handspring will lack vitality if the gymnast does not use her legs enough. Corrections for this error are given above.

3. The back handspring that prevents the performance of a series of back handsprings can be corrected by jumping more, as discussed above. Emphasis should be placed on explosively snapping the feet in and under, past the center of gravity.

4. There are several ways to correct a back handspring that looks like a "cranial perch":

a. Lock the elbows.

b. Keep hands only shoulder width apart.

Figure 3.28 • Novice spotters' positions for back handspring

       c.   Extend the head back (look for the mat).
       d.   Block the shoulders.
       e.   Tighten the whole body (STG).

Spotting:

1. The inexperienced spotters should stand to the sides and behind the gymnast facing each other hands clasped tightly (Fig. 3.28). The spotters cross the arms closer to the gymnast behind the gymnast's back at the gluteal fold to help lift the gymnast. The other arms cross the gymnast's back between her waist and shoulders and form the horizontal axis of rotation. Make certain the heads of the spotters are back so their noses don't get hit.

2. More experienced spotters take the same position to the back and sides of the gymnast, facing each other. The hand closer to the gymnast is placed on the back of her hips to lift her. The other hand is placed just above the small of the back and used to support the gymnast.

3. Eventually only one spotter is necessary and her hand placement is as shown in Fig. 3.29.

4. In any skill in which the gymnast is moving backward the spotter should stand behind her. To prevent the gymnast from turning her head and looking to see if her spotter is ready, the spotter can gently tap the gymnast's back. This signal says "go" to the gymnast and means the spotter is ready and will make *all* efforts to spot properly.

5. When the back handspring is combined with the roundoff for the first time, the teacher/coach may want to use a spotting belt. Beware, however, that continued use of the belt can cause it to become a psychological crutch for the gymnast.

Combinations:

1. Back handspring walkout, (alternate foot-foot landing).
2. Back handspring, back handspring.
3. Roundoff, back handspring.

Figure 3.29 • Back handspring with spot #3

4. Forward roll, back handspring.
5. Roundoff, back handspring, back somersault.
6. Cartwheel, back handspring.

Whip Back Somersault

The whip back, or alternate, is a skill that resembles a back handspring without hands. The whip back is usually performed during a series of back handsprings, thus the name, "alternate." The whip back is a low, relatively awkward-looking skill at the end of a tumbling pass. Because the whip back at the end of a series looks like a poorly executed somersault it should be followed by either a somersault or a back handspring. The skill added after an alternate is extremely difficult to do out of a whip back.

Teaching techniques and progressions:

1. The prerequisite for this skill is a back handspring.
2. This skill can be tried on a trampoline or from a slightly elevated area such as a reuther board.
3. This skill is usually accomplished more easily when it is done after a back handspring.
4. The last portion of this skill—mule kick and pike or snap-down phase—is quite important and should be practiced.

Corrections:

1. The snap-down is the part of the skill that requires the most effort. The gymnast should be encouraged to pull her legs around as quickly as possible after the feet leave the floor.
2. If the skill goes up and down, the gymnast needs to sit and go back more. This skill does not rise.

Spotting:

1. This skill is easily performed in a tumbling or spotting belt.

2. The hand spot is the same as that for the back handspring. Standing to the side and in back of the gymnast, the spotter places the hand closer to the gymnast on the gymnast's glutes and lifts. The other hand is placed just above the small of the gymnast's back and forms the point of rotation about the horizontal axis.

Combinations:

The whip back, or alternate, is really not a skill to be performed alone; it should be combined with other tumbling skills.

1. Roundoff, back handspring, alternate, back handspring.

2. Roundoff, back handspring, alternate, back somersault.

3. Roundoff, alternate, alternate, back somersault.

4. Roundoff, alternate, alternate, back handspring.

Back Somersault

A somersault occurs when a gymnast pushes off simultaneously with both feet, rotates 360° about the horizontal axis, and lands on her feet. Her hands do not touch the floor in this skill. The somersault can be done in a forward, backward, or sideward direction. The back somersault seems to be the easiest of the somersaults to accomplish. Progression-wise, the teacher/coach may want to teach youngsters (5–12 years) a back somersault prior to teaching a back handspring because the somersault is not as difficult technically as a back handspring, and the back handspring may be easier to learn after learning a back somersault. For older girls the better skill progression may be back handspring, back somersault because the fear element is less if the gymnast knows she may put her hands down as in a handspring. A somersault is a leg skill.

The gymnast lifts her arms from her sides into the air and positions them just in front of her ears so that her upper arms are adjacent to her temples. The arm lift and reach is extremely important to attaining height in the somersault, and it is performed with a dynamic and explosive thrust. As the arms are lifted the legs push off and up with as much power as possible. The body is kept tight (STG), and at the top of the lift the gymnast extends her head backward for the rotation. She then lands on her feet and absorbs the force of the landing by bending her knees.

Teaching techniques and progressions:

1. The gymnast tilts or jumps off both feet and lifts her arms with as much power as possible. The spotter stands behind her and places her hands on the gymnast's back to prevent her from falling backward. For a tuck somersault, the knees can be brought up to the chest after jumping up. This progression can be used as a preliminary to the somersault even after it has been learned.

2. On the trampoline, either in the overhead spotting rig or with competent hand spotting, the gymnast performs a standing back somersault. She may also

stand on the edge of a reuther board and do a somersault. She should have two competent spotters.

3. The standing back somersault can then be performed on the floor mat with competent spotting.

4. If the gymnast can do back handsprings, she can stand on the edge of the reuther board or mats about six inches high and perform a back handspring onto the floor mat and then do a back somersault, with good spotting.

5. Then the roundoff, back handspring, back somersault can be performed. It is preferable that during the first attempts at this skill the gymnast be in a spotting belt. If the belt is a nontwisting belt and the gymnast places her right hand down first in her roundoff, the rope on the gymnast's right side is placed and held by the spotter on the left side and vice versa with the other rope. If she places her left hand down first, the procedure is reversed. Thus, as she performs the roundoff, the ropes become untwisted and are ready to support the gymnast in her back tumbling.

6. When teaching small and/or younger girls, the reader may want to teach the somersault in layout position first. If the gymnast is rotating too slowly, then she should use the tuck position, for shortening the radius of rotation increases the speed of the rotation. Older girls who have a tight body concept will be able to do the somersault in layout initially and then learn a tuck or pike. If a girl can do a good, high layout, eventually she should be able to do a double back somersault in tuck. Girls who are relatively loose and need a somersault immediately for a routine should learn a tuck. A few girls will never successfully learn a good layout.

Figure 3.30 • Back somersault with walkout in layout

7. After performing a layout, the gymnast may want to use a walkout (foot-foot landing). At the top of the rotation (inversion), the gymnast splits her legs (see Fig. 3.30). Often, splitting the legs at the proper time causes a kipping action to occur and the body will actually appear to rise a bit.

Corrections:

1. Not reaching with the arms is a common error in performance of back somersaults.

2. Throwing the head back prior to reaching occurs frequently.

Numbers 1 and 2 the gymnast can correct by reaching and then rotating in two distinct steps.

3. The hips are thrown forward as the feet begin to lift off the ground.

4. Force dissipates during rotation and the somersault "stalls."

Numbers 3 and 4 the gymnast can correct by assuming a tight body (STG) throughout the skill. If the gymnast cannot accomplish the skill in layout, she should try it in tuck (shorter radius of rotation).

5. To correct a landing that is unbalanced and uncontrolled, the gymnast must attempt to stick her landing by bending her knees and not only squeezing her "glutes" but also grabbing the mat with her feet. The somersault skill order is: reach, turn, open, and land. The gymnast must complete rotation prior to landing in order to accomplish a stick.

6. The angle of the feet for the punch, or lift, may need correction. For a back handspring the feet should be blocked in ahead of the hips (Fig. 3.31a); for the back somersault the feet should be slightly behind the hips (Fig. 3.31b).

Spotting:

1. This skill is easy to perform in a tumbling or spotting belt.

2. The hand spot is the same as for the back handspring (see Fig. 3.32). Standing to the side and in back of the gymnast, the spotter places the hand closer to the gymnast on the gymnast's glutes and lifts. The other hand goes just above the small of the gymnast's back and forms the point of rotation about the horizontal axis.

Combinations:

1. Standing back somersault (eventually to be put on the balance beam).

2. Roundoff, back handspring, back somersault (layout pike or tuck).

3. Back somersault, walkout.

4. Back layout, half twist, walkout.

5. Back layout, full twist (and more twists).

6. Back somersault, back handspring walkout.

Figure 3.31 • (left) Punch for (a) back handspring and (b) back somersault

Figure 3.32 • Back somersault in tuck with spot

Front Somersault

The gymnast pushes off the floor simultaneously with both feet, rotates 360° about the horizontal axis in a forward direction, and lands on both feet. The gymnast's hands do not touch the floor. This seems to be a difficult skill for females to accomplish, possibly because considerable leg strength is necessary for the push-off. Although a plain front somersault in tuck is frequently part of men's floor exercise, it is unusual in women's floor exercise. More common in women's gymnastics is a front handspring, front somersault walkout, preferably in layout and pike rather than in tuck. Therefore, the front somersault will be explained as though it were preceded by a front handspring. The front handspring must allow for a good kip or rise of the hands from the floor. As the feet touch the floor, the gymnast immediately pushes off for the front somersault. The feet are in front of the hips (see Fig. 3.33). The angle of the feet with the floor is critical for the front somersault. The body is thrust into the air and the head tucks slightly at the top of the flight to aid with the rotation. The arms are stretched upward from the handspring and at the top of the flight the elbows are forcefully flexed (bent) and brought in and down to the sides to aid the rotation. As in all gymnastic skills, the body should be *tight*. Girls with good low-back flexibility will be able to perform this skill in layout; others will find more success in pike or tuck position. The landing should be balanced and controlled. A walkout is more conducive to a balanced landing since the landing is a blind one; it is difficult to do in control. Many girls place a forward roll after the front somersault in an attempt to cover up a front somersault done with poor technique that results in an unbalanced

Figure 3.33 • (left) Angle for punch in front somersault

landing. Judges, presumably, are aware of this strategy and look for the balance in the somersault regardless of what follows it.

Teaching techniques and progressions:

1. The prerequisite for this skill, as it is herein described, is a good front handspring, one that rises.
2. The front somersault can be learned on the trampoline with good spotting or with the gymnast in the overhead spotting rig. The steps in this skill are reach, rotate, land, or 1, 2, 3.
3. This skill can be done also by using a reuther board that is next to a crash pad. Good spotting is important whether it comes from spotters' hands or spotting belt.
4. The gymnast can then add the front handspring prior to the somersault on the trampoline or off the edge of a reuther board and somersault into a crash pad, with spotting.
5. Using a spotting belt for the first few attempts, the gymnast does a front handspring, front somersault.

Corrections:

1. A poor front handspring may be due to:
   a. A banana back so that the feet come in and past the hips, providing a poor angle for take-off and a weak body;
   b. Hands too far apart in the front handspring;
   c. No kip in the handspring from not blocking the shoulders.
2. A low (dumped) front somersault may result from:
   a. Punching for the somersault too late. The punch should be initiated before the gymnast sees the floor.
   b. Loose body dissipating the force. The gymnast should STG.
   c. Rotating the somersault too soon, before the lift occurs.
   d. Rotating too slowly. If in tuck, the gymnast can punch off with more strength and shorten the radius of rotation, thus tightening the tuck. If in layout, the gymnast should drive her heels faster around and behind herself or perform the skill in pike or tuck.
3. An improper landing has several possible causes:
   a. Tucking the head on landing. The head should be slightly back upon landing and the eyes should be looking down.
   b. Failing to anticipate the landing. Knees should bend upon contact with the floor.
   c. Not enough height in the somersault.

Spotting:

1. The spotter stands sideways and slightly in front of the gymnast and places the forearm closer to the gymnast on the front of the gymnast's waist (providing the horizontal axis for rotation). The spotter places her other hand on the small of the gymnast's back to help with rotation.

Figure 3.34 • Front handspring, front somersault with spot

Combinations: 1. Front handspring, front somersault (layout, pike, tuck with a two-feet landing or in walkout); see Fig. 3.34.

2. Front handspring, front somersault, forward roll.

3. Front handspring, front somersault, front walkover.

4. Front handspring, front somersault, front handspring.

5. Front handspring, front somersault walkout, front aerial.

Side Somersault   For aesthetic purposes in women's floor exercise, it is wise to perform this skill in layout position. A side somersault in pike or tuck is common in men's floor exercise. Some would call this skill a back aerial or a back somersault from one leg. Unlike most other tumbling skills, the side somersault is a beautiful skill that fits in a very "light" or "soft" portion of the music. The side somersault is preceded by a hybrid cartwheel-roundoff. The feet most typically are placed one slightly ahead of the other, as shown in Fig. 3.35. The skill can be initiated with both feet pushing off the floor simultaneously (somersault) or with an alternate foot push-off (aerial). As the feet begin the push from the floor the arms are forcefully thrust upward and the body turns sideways, moving as in a side aerial backwards. The feet land in walkout facing diagonally between sideways and forward. This landing position prevents landing sideways, which creates force, strain, and trauma in the knee joints.

Teaching techniques and progressions: 1. This skill is relatively easy to learn if the gymnast can do a back somersault walkout in layout, as well as a side aerial.

2. The cartwheel-roundoff is done on the mat with the feet landing next to a crash mat. The somersault is thrown over and into the crash pad. Spotting is necessary.

Corrections: 1. In the cartwheel-roundoff the feet should land in the proper direction and just behind the hips.

2. The push-off of the feet should be powerful.

3. The lift of the arms may need improvement.

4. Body tightness is important.

5. The direction of the feet should face the proper way upon landing.

Spotting: 1. The spotter stands sideways and to the side, slightly behind the point where the gymnast's feet will land after the cartwheel-roundoff. The spotter should stand beside the area where the gymnast's back will be in the somersault. The

Figure 3.35   •   Foot position for side somersault punch

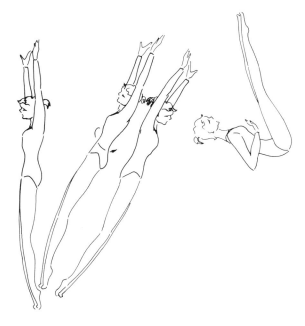

Figure 3.36 • Arabian somersault in pike

spotter uses the hand closer to the gymnast to help block her hips by stopping backward momentum on the side of the gymnast's waist. This blocking converts the backward momentum to upward momentum. The spotter's other hand reaches up and clasps the other side of the gymnast's waist as inversion occurs, aiding with the landing. This spot is the same as the spot for the side aerial, except that the gymnast is moving backward through the side plane.

Combinations:

1. Cartwheel-roundoff, side somersault.
2. Cartwheel-roundoff, side somersault, pop turn cartwheel.
3. Cartwheel-roundoff, side somersault, pop turn roundoff, and so on.
4. Cartwheel, cartwheel-roundoff, and so on.

Arabian Somersault

The term "arabian" refers to the 180° (half) twist about the longitudinal axis that precedes a front somersault. The somersault can be performed in tuck, pike (Fig. 3.36), or layout position, and usually the landing is in walkout. Upon landing a roundoff or back handspring, the body is stretched as the jump from the floor occurs, and a 180° twist is initiated. (A description of the front somersault appeared earlier in this chapter.)

Teaching techniques and progressions:

1. The prerequisites for this skill are a good bounding roundoff or back handspring and a front somersault.
2. A standing stretched jump with a 180° (half) twist, landing on the feet.

3. The gymnast than jumps into the air, performs a half twist and lands in the spotter's arms or in a front drop on the trampoline. When a spotter is present, she uses her arms, one placed just above the front of the waist and the other on the mid-front of the thighs, to catch the gymnast in midair. The spotter is on the side toward which the gymnast is turning.

4. The gymnast adds to skill number 2 a front walkover or handstand forward roll at the end, with spotting, on the trampoline, from the edge of a reuther board, or on the mat.

5. Then a jump (half) twist front somersault (arabian) in a prescribed position is performed on the trampoline. Spotting is essential.

6. In a twisting tumbling belt (for the first attempts), the gymnast performs a roundoff, arabian, or roundoff back handspring arabian.

Corrections:

1. The jump turn must be high and powerful.

2. A tight body is essential.

3. All the corrections that apply to the front somersault are also applicable to this skill.

Spotting:

1. The spotter stands to the side and slightly behind the point where the arabian will be initiated (see Fig. 3.37). The spotter stands on the side toward which the gymnast will twist. The spotter places the arm closer to the gymnast at about mid-thigh; the other arm holds her just above the waist. As the gymnast turns, the arm across the front of the thighs slips up to the waist and forms the horizontal axis of rotation for the somersault. The other arm disengages and the hand moves to the back of the gymnast's shoulders and pushes to help

Figure 3.37 · Arabian somersault in tuck with spot

with rotation. As the landing occurs, the same arm (further from the gymnast initially) slips to the front of the gymnast's waist to help the landing and to arrest forward momentum.

Combinations:	1. Roundoff, arabian in tuck, pike, or layout with a walkout.
	2. Back handspring, arabian in tuck, pike, or layout with a walkout.
	3. Back handspring, arabian, forward roll (can be overused as a balance crutch).
	4. Arabian, front handspring.
	5. Arabian, front aerial.
	6. Arabian, roundoff, and so on.

Back Somersault with Twist (180°, 360°, 720°)

Refer to the section on twisting in Chapter 2 before reading this section. Some people call this skill "twisting backs." Unfortunately, this terminology is confusing to the gymnast and her coach because it emphasizes the twist and not the somersault. The gymnast must have a strong back layout (see earlier description of the back somersault) in order to add a twist. The twist in this skill is a combination of the classic and modern twist.

As the gymnast's feet leave the floor in the somersault, a slight initiation of the classic twist is accomplished with the feet. As the hips reach their maximum height, a *slight* pike and extension—the modern twist—should complete the rotation about the longitudinal axis of the body. This skill is very difficult because the body must rotate about the horizontal as well as the vertical axis. The amount of twist the gymnast can accomplish depends on the height of the somersault, the body's tightness, the shortness of the radius of rotation, and the gymnast's ability to cerebrate and then coordinate all the necessary changes and adjustments that must be accomplished in what seems to be a millisecond. Although the full twist (360°) is a skill to which most gymnasts and their coaches aspire, the half twist (180°) is a particularly beautiful skill in women's floor exercise, for the landing can be in walkout, which gives the illusion of lightness, grace, and control. Certainly a double full twist (720°) is an amazing accomplishment.

Teaching techniques and progressions:

1. The gymnast must be able to do a high, body-tight back layout as a prerequisite for this skill.
2. The gymnast should do a jump 360° turn about the longitudinal axis of the body and land on both feet. This skill should be explained as the classic twist.
3. Hanging from a set of rings (feet off the floor), the gymnast should begin to twist (spin) by slightly piking and extending her hips. This skill should be explained as the modern twist.
4. The teacher/coach explains that the twist with a somersault is a combination of the classic and modern twists.

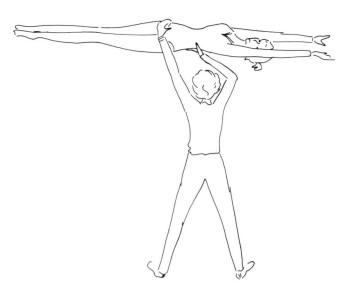

Figure 3.38 • Full twist and spot (progression #6)

(Note: Because the spotting techniques are the same as for the progressions, they will be explained here. Thus the spot and the skill can be learned simultaneously.)

5. The gymnast does a jump half turn (180°). The spotter identifies the direction toward which the gymnast is turning. The spotter than stands to that side and in back of the gymnast. She places her arm closer to the gymnast around the back of the gymnast's thighs; the hand is supinated, thumb down. The spotter's other arm reaches around the gymnast's back just above the waist. Therefore the gymnast twists in contact with the spotters arms.

6. The gymnast then does a jump half twist front layout to be caught in the spotter's arms (Figs. 3.38 and 3.39).

Figure 3.39 • (left and middle) Full twist and spot (progression #6)
Figure 3.40 • (right) Full twist and spot (progression #8)

7. The gymnast does the skill number 6 and from it goes into a handstand forward roll. This progression is performed with the same spotting.

8. The gymnast does a jump half twist, landing on both feet and placing the hands down on the mat, and goes into a roundoff in the opposite direction from her twist (Fig. 3.40). If the gymnast twists to her right, she places her left hand down first; if she twists to her left, she places her right hand down first in the roundoff.

9. The gymnast next does a jump half twist, front layout into the spotter's arms, hands down on the mat and roundoff.

10. Eventually, the hands do not touch the floor and the result is a "barani" (roundoff without hands), a popular trampoline skill. At this stage, or progression, the whole skill is easily accomplished on the trampoline with the exact same spotting. During the second half of the twist (barani) the gymnast continues to twist around the arm of the spotter that was further from the gymnast initially. If the jump is high enough, the skill will be done over the shoulder and upper part of that arm.

   When the hands are placed on the mat as in progression 9, this skill looks like a half twist in one direction followed by a half twist in the other direction. It is a full twist, however. When the hands do not touch the mat, the skill looks like a back somersault with a full twist.

11. The arm movement is explained in Chapter 2.

12. The whole skill can then be performed on the trampoline.

13. Standing on a reuther board, the gymnast should do a back handspring, back layout as a review and then do the same skills with the twist added to the somersault. Good spotting is important.

14. Finally, a three-step or shorter approach, roundoff, back handspring, back somersault full twist is performed in a twisting belt or with good, experienced spotting.

15. Some teachers and coaches advocate teaching a back somersault with a full twist by having the gymnast do a half twist (180°) and adding more and more of a twist with each repetition.

Corrections:

1. The most common error associated with this skill is a poor back layout (see section on back somersaults for corrections). The gymnast must lift and twist.

2. In learning this skill the gymnast occasionally panics because there is so much to be done in a short period of movement time. As a result, the body becomes loose. Symptoms of a loose body are low "sommie" (somersault), legs bent and/or apart, sloppy landing, and incomplete twist. A loose body readily dissipates the force of the skill. STG, or body tightness, is essential for a successful full-twisting back somersault by a female gymnast.

3. When tumbling skills are done in a series, each skill depends upon the

preceding skill. Therefore the corrections for a "full" often will include improving the preceding somersault, back handspring, roundoff and/or approach.

4. This skill requires a 110 percent commitment on the part of the gymnast. It must be a skill *she* wants to learn and accomplish. It is a move that requires explosiveness, tightness, and cerebration.

Spotting:

1. Two spotters using a twisting spotting belt ensure a safe, controlled spot for this skill. The hand-spotting technique for a full is as described under "teaching techniques."

2. The spotter stands on the side of the gymnast toward which she is twisting (see Fig. 3.41). The objective of this technique is to keep the gymnast in the air during her back somersault so that she can complete the twist. Therefore the spotter lifts and helps initiate the somersault. The arm of the spotter closer to the gymnast reaches across the back of her mid-thighs. The spotter's other arm reaches across the gymnast's back just above the waist. As the gymnast is performing the skill, the spotter moves backward with her, shifting her arms, especially the one that was orginally on the gymnast's back so that, as the skill is completed, this arm is once again behind the gymnast. In this way the spotter aids the landing by preventing the gymnast's momentum from continuing to carry her backward (see Fig. 3.41). All spotting requires good and constant footwork in the direction of the gymnastic skill. The gymnast will eventually be going up and over the arm and shoulder of the spotter's second arm (initially the arm further from the gymnast). This spotting technique can be learned as the gymnast goes through the suggested progressions.

3. Some spotters are effective starting on the opposite side of the gymnast than herein described. By spotting in yet another fashion some spotters aid the gymnast in twisting. For the novice "full twister," however, the spot described in detail is preferable.

Combinations:

1. Roundoff back handspring(s), back somersault full twist.
2. Roundoff back handspring, back somersault half twist walkout (this is a particularly beautiful skill for floor exercise because of the landing).
3. Roundoff back handspring, back somersault full twist, back handspring.
4. Roundoff, back handspring(s), back somersault full twist, back handspring, back somersault.
5. Roundoff, back handspring, whip back, back handspring, back somersault full twist.
6. Roundoff, back handspring, double full twist (720°).

Figure 3.41 • End of roundoff, back somersault full twist with spot

DANCE   The form of dance associated with women's gymnastics is a hybrid, a combination of the dynamic movements gleaned from ballet, modern, ethnic, folk, and jazz. In international competition, the gymnasts of the Western world are not as strong or as adept at dance skills as gymnasts from the Communist countries. Acquiring dance skill and proficiency requires as much training, time, and effort as acquiring an equal level of skill on the unevens, in vaulting, in tumbling, and on the beam. In our culture we are often concerned with instant success and rewards; we have a fascination with "quick and easy" methods. The instant gymnast, like instant potatoes or pudding, is not a reality. Since many Americans erroneously believe that dance is only a small part of floor exercise and balance beam, the hours and effort that dance requires do not receive the same emphasis that learning a new "trick" does. Yet American gymnasts and coaches could learn from the way Soviet and Eastern European gymnasts are trained. A critical part of their training involves the dance. Dance has as much emphasis in their programs as each event. The beginning gymnast could effectively spend her first year in gymnastics dancing and tumbling only. As a gymnast improves and grows in the sport, continued dance training is essential. It is therefore advisable for the teacher/coach of gymnastics to have or to obtain an appreciation of and a strong background in dance. The serious gymnast should seek the additional teaching of a well-trained and qualified dance specialist. The area of gymnastics dance has a few self-acclaimed "specialists" whose training and accomplishments are nebulous, so ask questions before investing money and time—get quality dance help!

Ballet as a dance form provides an excellent background for gymnastics (Fig. 3.42). Proper body alignment and balance will accrue from ballet training. A few years ago football players were encouraged to take ballet for the purpose of improving their balance. The sport of gymnastics utilizes the dynamic locomotor forms of leaps, jumps, and turns from ballet. In certain combinations, these skills receive credit as difficulty on the beam and in floor exercise (for specific ratings of value see the *Code of Points*). Locomotor movements are movements in space, usually from one point to another, and thus utilize and move the base of support.

75

Figure 3.42 • (left) Dance
Figure 3.43 • (middle) Split leap
Figure 3.44 • (right) Split leap

In dance, the moving base is usually the feet; often the base in gymnastics is the hands. Lightness of locomotor movements is important and can be accomplished through proper technique. When the base is the feet, movements should be performed with ankle flexion (plantar while in the air, dorsi upon landing), moving on the outer edge of the foot, with the knee in line with the big toe in flexion. A major contrast between mediocre and good gymnasts is that good gymnasts are constantly on the balls of their feet. Their heels rarely touch the floor or beam while dancing. This distinction has implication for the beginning gymnast and her teacher/coach; both should be striving to see and do work on the toes. The positioning for performing locomotor movement is a stretched torso (separating each rib), the shoulders down, head up as if one were a puppet with a string attached to the top of the head holding it and the spine uprightly.

The *split leap* is a transfer of weight from one foot to the other (as in a walk or run) with as much height as possible (Fig. 3.43). The legs should both be parallel with the floor and absolutely straight. This position is quite difficult to achieve but should be a goal. The hip flexors of the first leg in the air must be strong and the hamstrings flexible; the hamstrings of the second or rear leg must be strong and the hip flexors and quadriceps flexible to accomplish a proper split leap. At any skill level, it is important for the rear leg to be as high as the front leg (Fig. 3.44). Often the gymnast is not aware that the rear leg is dragging (lower) because she can see only the front leg. The rear leg lower can often be corrected by increasing the hip flexors' flexibility of that leg. A mirror, videotape, and evaluation from the coach can also help in the correction. The illusion of greater height can be accomplished by taking a breath, lifting the chest, and extending the head backward as the body leaves the floor. Changes in arm position can add character, expression, and variety to the movement. Changing the position of the legs turns a split leap into another type of leap.

76

Figure 3.45 · (left) Completion of scissors leap
Figure 3.46 · (middle) Abstract leap
Figure 3.47 · (right) Turning leap

The *switch leg,* or *scissors leap,* begins as a split leap, but as the foot of the rear leg leaves the floor the legs switch position in the air so that the forward leg becomes the rear leg and the rear leg becomes the forward leg. This is a beautiful and difficult leap (Fig. 3.45). It requires strength and great explosion from the gymnast. Again, arm changes add variation.

In the *abstract leap* the gymnast bends the forward, rear, or both legs while in the air during a split leap (see Fig. 3.46). The common name for the leap in which the forward leg is bent is "the stag." Changes in arm positions add variation.

The *turning leap* is a difficult one in which the gymnast turns or opens the hips toward the rear leg when in the air during a split leap (Fig. 3.47).

Alternately bringing each leg straight up either in front or in back of the body while leaping (transfer of weight from one foot to the other) results in a *hitch kick.* Height of the legs is important. This step is a fundamental dance form of historic significance. It is part of the polonaise, a court form originally danced by men, and it has athletic connotations. A cat leap is a hitch kick with bent knees. Variations in these leaps can be accomplished by varying arm position and turning.

The *tour jêté* is a leap (transfer of weight from one foot to the other) with a half turn. The gymnast thus changes the direction she is facing in the air. The emphasis is on lifting the rear leg (see Fig. 3.48).

Teaching techniques and suggestions:

1. The body should be held upright without any piking at the waist.
2. If the prescribed posture of the legs in the air is straight, there should be no knee bend (not even the slightest); if the legs are to be bent in the air, then there should be an obvious knee bend.
3. The chest and head should be lifted as the top on the leap occurs.
4. Variations in leaps can be accomplished by changing:

a. Leg position.
b. Focus and head position.
c. Arm position.
d. Direction.
e. Levels.
f. Force.
g. Torso position.

5. Landings should be light with control and balance. A light landing results from proper body alignment—center of gravity (hips) over base support (feet), shoulders in line with hips, head upright—tight body, and bending the knees upon contact with the floor.

6. Only one or two steps should precede a leap.

7. Ideally, leaps in a series should be done without any steps between them.

Jumps are skills in which the performer usually leaves the floor from both feet simultaneously and lands on both feet simultaneously. Leg strength, proper body alignment, hips and shoulders over the base support (feet), and proper technique are the prerequisites to artistic yet athletic jumps. Many female gymnasts do not jump naturally and need help acquiring this skill. One of the basic problems is not using the quadriceps (muscles of the front of the thigh) efficiently by bending and extending the knees explosively. Increasing flexion of the ankles (both dorsi and plantar) will increase jumping height. As in leaping, extension of the head, separation of the ribs, and breathing as the feet leave the floor should increase the amplitude. Repetitions of jumps in drill form should aid jumping ability. Maximum height should be the objective in jumping.

Figure 3.48 • (left) Completion of a tour jêté
Figure 3.49 • (middle) Straddle pike jump (Dutchman)
Figure 3.50 • (right) Dramatic jump

The basic jump is the hollow jump. The gymnast jumps into the air from both feet, legs straight, back and head arched, arms out to the side, and the body in layout position. The same jump can be performed in tuck position (squat jump) or pike position (jackknife). Another variation, commonly called a "Dutchman," is a very dynamic jump performed in straddle pike position (Fig. 3.49).

An often used and dramatic jump is one in which, after leaving the ground, the gymnast brings one leg behind her, knee bent and touches the back of the head with her foot (Fig. 3.50). A variation of this jump is to bring both feet up to the back of the head; somehow this jump is not as aesthetic as the other one.

Jumping with one leg either in front or to the side of the body is a common movement. The higher the jump and the leg in arabesque position, the more amplitude and credit the jump will receive. Jumps with turns are often performed in floor exercises. These jumps are prime examples of the classic twist (turning is initiated from the floor). The extent of the turn (180°, 360°, 450°, etc.) depends upon the gymnast's talent and need for direction in her floor exercise.

Teaching techniques and corrections:

1. If the prescribed leg position is straight in the air, then there should be no knee bend at all (Fig. 3.51); if bent in the air, there should be an obvious knee bend; if together in the air, there should be no space between them.

2. The chest and head should be lifted and extended at the top, or peak, of the jump.

3. Variations in jumps involve changing:
   a. Leg position (see Figs. 3.52–3.54).
   b. Focus and head position.

Figure 3.51 • (left) Jump with straight leg in back
Figure 3.52 • (middle) Jump with straight leg to side and other leg abstract
Figure 3.53 • (right) Jump with straight leg in front and other leg abstract

Figure 3.54 • (left) Jump with both legs abstract
Figure 3.55 • (right) Completion of a turn

    c.   Arm position.
    d.   Direction.
    e.   Level.
    f.   Force.
    g.   Torso position.
4.   Landing should be light and in control and balance. This feat requires proper body alignment—base support under center of gravity, tight body in the air, and the knees bent upon landing.
5.   No more than one step should precede any jump.

Turns are an essential part of floor exercise and balance beam routines. They demand frequent, regular practice on the floor exercise mat because its surface increases the difficulty of turning. All turns should be performed on the toes and balls of the feet. Proper body alignment and focus provide balance in the turn (Fig. 3.55).

A *tour* is a circular movement, or turn. A pirouette is a turn on one foot or in the air. Pirouettes can be executed in two directions: outward (backward) and inward (forward). The free leg in a pirouette may execute different movements or positions. One of these variations is a fouetté pirouette, or a whip turn. In a fouetté turn, the free leg sweeps out (or in) in the horizontal plane, helping to turn the body. There is a swing with a snap at the end. The fouetté pirouette is similar to the rond de jambe for historically the fouetté is a turn performed by males and the rond de jambe is performed by females. A relevé consists of a pirouette on one leg while the free leg is bent with its foot in back, in front, or to the side of the supporting leg's knee. The chaîné tour involves turning on alternate feet. Each tour is half a turn.

Teaching techniques and corrections:

1.   Proper body alignment is essential to the performance of turns in balance. The hips and shoulders (down) should be square and in line with and over the base support (feet).

2. Turns should be done on the toes and balls of the feet.
3. The head turns and the eyes focus on the wall at a point at eye level for balance.
4. Variations within given turns involve changing:
    a. Leg position.
    b. Arm position.
    c. Torso position.
    d. Head position.
    e. Degree of the turn.
    f. Force.
    g. Direction.
    h. Tempo.

The ability to leap, jump, and turn are essential in gymnastics. The teacher/ coach must continually correct body alignment. The gymnast should work in front of a full-length mirror so that she can constantly make self-corrections. Many gymnastic authorities consider these dance skills connectors, which relegates them to a lesser role than they actually have. Some girls who possess "dynamite" tumbling ability never earn scores in the 9s because they have not learned leap, jump, and turn difficulties or they perform them without expression and amplitude. Generally, Americans don't dance as well as they should or could with

Figure 3.56 • Modern dance

Figure 3.57 • Forward contraction

Figure 3.58 • Beginning of a forward contraction

greater emphasis and training. Leaps, jumps, and turns in combination with tumbling and/or acrobatics form the "glue" that seals the exercise together and unifies it.

Fluid use of the arms and torso and movements on the floor, which are basic to the discipline of modern dance, also enhance women's gymnastics (Fig. 3.56). Body waves, or contractions, are successive bodily movements that progress in order segmentally throughout a limb, limbs, and/or torso and head (Figs. 3.57 and 3.58). These successive contactions should be performed in the front and back plane as well as through the side plane (Fig. 3.59). Today floor exercises contain an increasing number of torso movements. Movements of any kind provide interest,

Figure 3.59 • Side contractions

expression, and change of level in floor exercise. The percussive and angular movements of the limbs and torso effect different expressions and, in small doses, should be part of an exercise. Since these movements are not specifically prescribed or described, there is much room for creativity. Practicing in front of a full-length mirror is very helpful because it shows the gymnast how she looks while performing a movement to which she is unaccustomed. Freedom to be oneself in movement is another contribution of modern dance to gymnastics.

Falls like the ones in modern dance are quite effective in floor exercise. Gymnasts should be able to do front, back, side, and spiral falls (Fig. 3.60). The theory of falls is to let oneself down to the floor without getting hurt or causing a sound. A "body slap," the term applied to the sound that occurs when the body hits the floor, lowers a gymnast's score. It is an indication of poor control, balance, and alignment. To avoid slaps the gymnast must counterbalance her falls by leaning in the direction opposite to that of the fall. Each segment of the body in succession takes up the force of the fall. A currently popular fall is a side slide onto the mat.

Jazz as a musical form had its birth in our culture. Consequently, jazz movements should be natural for Americans. Jazz dance skills effect punctuation and expression although these movements should not dominate an exercise.

Folk dance steps are popular connectors in a floor exercise, particularly as and if they relate to the music. The basic folk steps that are primary to most folk forms are the schottische, polka, mazurka, and waltz. Jazz may be considered an American folk form.

Runs, walks, skips and gallops are basic locomotor movements in floor exercise. An elegantly elongated run in which the arms are in opposition to the legs and feet are pointing straight ahead and in which the gymnast displays torso movements is most effective in an exercise.

Figure 3.60 • Side fall to supine position

Teaching
techniques and
corrections:

1. The floor pattern can be straight or curvilinear.
2. These locomotor movements should be performed on the toes and balls of the feet.
3. Variations involve changing:
   a. Levels.
   b. Tempo.
   c. Force.
   d. Magnitude.
   e. Direction.
   f. Arm position.
   g. Leg position.
   h. Torso position.
   i. Focus.

Beginning gymnasts often feel uncomfortable about their arms and hands. "What should I do with my arms?" is a common question. Arm and hand positions should be natural. A basic position is: shoulders down, arms out to the sides, elbows slightly bent, and hands visible peripherally (slightly to the front). The novice can imagine she is holding an apple between her thumbs and first three fingers (Fig. 3.61). The little finger can be slightly extended. Arm positions should be practiced in front of a mirror.

Mimetics is a technique the teacher/coach may use to help the novice move in a manner to which she is unaccustomed and might feel inhibited doing. The coach presents an image to the gymnast; the gymnast forms a mental image and acts it out. The following are suggestions for imagery and their purposes.

To assist with
body alignment:

1. Your spine is a tall skyscraper.
2. Point your ears as a rabbit does when it hears someone approach.
3. Jump up and down as though you were a tight spring.
4. Place an extra vertebra in your neck.
5. The string attached to the top of your head is drawn up very tightly.
6. Your body, except your arms, is in a complete girdle.

To assist with
fluid movements
as in body
waves, or
successions:

1. Fall to the floor as syrup pours from a bottle.
2. Ripple your arm as though it were a flag on a flag pole.
3. Zip up and down your full-length robe. There are zippers in the back, front, and on the sides.
4. Unfold and grow as though you were a flower.

Figure 3.61 • (left) Hand position

5. Move as though you were seaweed.

6. Be a folding door opening and closing.

7. Move to the floor as through you were water draining from a sink.

8. Roll your head on your shoulders as though your neck were an elastic band.

9. Bounce a balloon on your stomach.

To assist in changing level:

1. Walk on clouds.

2. Fly.

3. Move in a low tunnel.

4. Be a yo-yo.

To assist in changing direction:

1. Be a ball in a pinball machine.

2. Be a spinning top.

To assist in changing tempo and force:

1. Punch your way out of a paper bag.

2. Move as through you were in molasses.

3. You are a mechanical doll.

Another technique the teacher/coach can use with beginning inhibited gymnasts is to have them perform a sport skill without the equipment. Then they should perform the skill in slow motion. Examples are:

1. A dribble and lay-up shot in basketball.

Figure 3.62 · Acrobatics

2. A serve in tennis and movement to the net.
3. A volleyball bump, set, and spike in sequence.
4. A javelin throw.
5. The instep kick in soccer.

The sport skills can also be done in twos; for example, try one on one in basketball or a boxing match.

Artistic and creative combinations of all forms of dance are essential to floor exercise. The gymnast is inhibited only by her own or her coach's lack of imagination. Sometimes combinations of movements that feel strange and weird at first can be very effective in certain parts of the exercise and can compliment or contrast effectively with the music. Dance, its importance and the practice of it cannot be overemphasized, for its contribution to the total effect of the gymnast is invaluable.

ACROBATICS

Acrobatics is a distinct school of movement from which the sport of gymnastics has borrowed a group of skills. Avoid pure acrobatics in floor exercise, especially skills that appear to be contortionist or that use bent knees, bent elbows, or extreme low-back flexibility. The acrobatics in floor exercise can be classified and grouped separately from tumbling skills, which require leg strength, and dance skills, which are primarily movements involving the feet as the base support. Acrobatics require flexibility (Fig. 3.62).

For many years, low-back flexibility was all-important in gymnastics. Currently, flexibility in the upper back and shoulder girdle is as important, if not more important, than low-back flexibility in terms of proper technique for women's gymnastics. The development of low-back flexibility should accompany an increase in abdominal strength. Low-back flexibility without abdominal strength marks a weak, mediocre gymnast. The implications for the training and conditioning of a female gymnast are obvious.

When learning or teaching acrobatics for gymnastics, emphasis should be on straight legs, straight arms, and use of the upper back as well as the low back.

It appears that a disproportionately high number of gymnasts, compared to the general population, have well-developed scolioses. Scoliosis is a lateral curvature of the spine that is noticeable in that one hip and the opposite shoulder are higher than the other. It is the author's belief that a possible cause of scoliosis among gymnasts is the performance of walkovers with the same leg always leading. If this conclusion is correct, the teacher/coach has a responsibility to encourage the gymnast to learn to perform splits, walkovers, and cartwheels with either leg leading. This proficiency will also help the gymnast in compulsory exercises. There are very few accomplished gymnasts who don't suffer from low-back syndrome (pain). Again, quite possibly "one-sidedness" could be one of the causes. Other possible causes are not bending the knees upon landing and poor body alignment, particularly a banana back.

Back Walkovers A gymnast must be stretched in the hamstrings, low back, and upper back prior to attempting a back walkover. Some teachers and coaches teach a limbre prior to a back walkover. It is a contention of this book that as an acrobatics skill, a limbre does not relate nor is it a useful progression for the back walkover.

The gymnast stretches her arms up from her shoulders. One leg is extended by hip flexion and lifted as high as possible (amplitude) (Fig. 3.63a). From this position, the gymnast's hips move backward and just before her hands touch the floor the gymnast kicks off with her support leg. The head is extended and looking backwards. The hands touch the floor in shoulder width position with the fingers pointing directly backwards. As the full weight is taken upon the hands, the hips and shoulders are in alignment, the legs are forcefully split so that they are parallel with the floor (Fig. 3.63b). The shoulders are blocked and do not move forward but help to keep the body moving in a backward direction. As the foot of the first leg touches the mat, the hands push the body up and away. The knee of this leg bends slightly for balance. The second leg is kept in the air, in arabesque position, for amplitude.

Teaching techniques and progressions:

1. The skill, as described, should be tried with spotting.
2. The skill can be attempted from the edge of a mat or a reuther board.
3. Encourage using either leg first.

Corrections:

1. The gymnast getting "stuck" in the bridge position can be caused by:
   a. Not kicking off soon enough, just prior to the hands touching the mat.
   b. Not pushing or kicking hard enough with the legs.
   c. Arms too far apart, causing elbow bending and cranial perching. Hand placement should be shoulder width.
   d. Weak abdominals.
   e. Not using upper-back flexibility. The walkover should cover distance and not be in and under itself (using only low back).
2. The gymnast not being able to stand up at the skill's conclusion can be caused by:

Figure 3.63 • Back walkover

Figure 3.64 • Back walkover with spot

    a.   Not blocking the shoulders.

    b.   Not pushing away from the mat with the hands.

Spotting: 1.   For novice spotters, two girls stand behind and to the side of the gymnast facing each other. The spotters clasp the hands of their arms further from the gymnast to provide an axis of rotation. The free hands aid in lifting the hips up and over initially.

    2.   The spotter stands slightly to the back and on the side of the gymnast's first leg in the air. The spotter uses the arm nearer the gymnast to support the gymnast's extended leg by placing her hand under the back of the gymnast's thigh. The spotter's other arm reaches around and behind the gymnast's waist to provide an axis of rotation. Once the hips of the gymnast have passed over her supporting arms and shoulders, the spotter shifts her hands so that the arm under the thigh is in front of the gymnast's waist. The spotter's other arm shifts to support the front of the thigh of the extended leg. The spotter helps to stretch the extended legs as well as to provide balance and support (see Fig. 3.64).

Combinations: 1.   Back walkover, back walkover.

    2.   Vary leg position: both abstract (bent), one abstract.

    3.   Switch legs in the air during the back walkover.

    4.   Back extension roll, back walkover.

    5.   Side aerial, back walkover.

    6.   Back walkover, back tinsica (vice versa).

One-arm Back Walkover   This skill is a variation of the back walkover that is worthy of a brief description. The key to performing a one-arm back walkover is the realization and awareness of the change in the base support and the resultant consequences. In the back walkover, the base support comes from the hands, shoulder width apart; in the one-arm back walkover, the base support is one arm instead of two and thus must be moved into the midline of the body. Therefore the hand of the supporting arm is placed directly above the head so that the base support will be below the center of gravity. The free arm is dramatically held out to the side from the shoulder.

The teaching suggestions, progressions, corrections, and spotting for this skill are the same as those for the back walkover. The prerequisite for a one-arm back walkover is the back walkover.

Combinations:
1. Back walkover, one-arm back walkover.
2. One-arm back walkover (right arm), one-arm back walkover (left arm).

Back Tinsica

Another variation of the back walkover is the back tinsica, once referred to as an arab wheel. The tinsica concept is controversial. The approach presented here is based on logical progressions and nomenclature. In the tinsica the hips continue to move either through the front or back plane as they do in a front or back walkover. Therefore the most direct relative of the tinsica is the walkover. Another approach dictates that the hands are placed on the floor as in a cartwheel (front or back) so that the hips move into the side plane with a quarter turn. As the skill is completed, the hips again quarter turn. The hips move from the front or back plane into the side plane and again into the forward or backward plane. Done this way, the tinsica would be more closely related to the cartwheel. The first approach is the basis for the following description.

In the back tinsica, the hands come in contact with the mat alternately, one

Figure 3.65 · Completion of front walkover

after the other, as though the gymnast is taking steps with the hands in the direction of the skill. The legs are kicked into the air alternately also, and the first leg leaves the mat just prior to the first hand touching the mat. The fingers point directly backwards. The rhythm of the skill is hand, hand, foot, foot.

The teaching progressions, techniques, corrections, and spotting are the same as for the back walkover. The prerequisite for the skill is a back walkover.

Combinations:
1. Back walkover, back tinsica.
2. One-arm back walkover, back tinsica.
3. Back tinsica, back tinsica.
4. Cartwheel, back tinsica.
5. Back tinsica, one-arm back walkover.
6. Aerial cartwheel, back tinsica.

Front Walkover The front walkover requires more back flexibility than the back walkover. This skill is begun by stretching the arms into the air, kicking the second leg in the walkover into the air, stepping on the foot of that leg, and pushing the knee forward into a lunge with the shoulders over the hips in alignment. The rear leg in the lunge is lifted up and over as the hands touch the mat shoulder width apart with the fingers pointing straight ahead. The second leg is pushed off the mat. When in a handstand position, no banana back, the legs are completely split, stretched and straight, and parallel with the mat. As the foot of the first leg approaches the mat, the gymnast pushes off the mat with her hands. The head remains extended. Once the foot of the first leg is on the mat the gymnast attempts to pull her center of gravity (hips) up and over this leg, which is the base support. Ultimately, the second leg in the walkover is kept in the air as high as possible with arms stretched for amplitude (Fig. 3.65). The ability to keep the leg in the air is related to abdominal and hip flexor strength as well as the ability of the gymnast to balance on the support leg.

Teaching techniques and progressions:
1. Stretching and warm-up is necessary prior to attempting a front walkover.
2. With spotting, this skill can be attempted from standing on a reuther board or any other slight elevation.
3. The skill should then be performed on the mat with amplitude and again, with spotting.
4. Encourage the use of either leg first.

Corrections:
1. Inability to complete the skill may be due to:
    a. Lack of sufficient upper- and low-back flexibility.
    b. Improper use of the legs for initial lift. The correct lunge position including shoulders over hips without leaning forward (piking) while initiating

the skill will help solve this problem. The legs should lift or push off with authority.

c. Hands placed too far apart on the mat thus causing elbow bending.

d. Not blocking the shoulders (preventing shoulders from moving forward when the hands are on the mat) or not pushing off the mat with the hands to aid in standing up. A spotter can assist in the blocking by pushing the shoulder backwards with a hand on the shoulder blade. The concept of pushing off with the hands needs to be explained to some novice gymnasts for they tend just to pull their hands away from the mat rather than push their body up from the floor with their hands.

e. The novice gymnast frequently just drops her feet onto the mat rather than placing one foot down, grasping the mat and pulling with her legs and abdominals to help her stand up.

f. Discontinuous movement. The skill must move in a continuous, forward direction, except the blockage, and the teacher/coach should look for this feature.

g. The gymnast tucking her head and sitting out the skill near its completion, thereby preventing her from standing up. The head should be kept back even though the landing is blind, and the body should remain stretched throughout.

Spotting:

1. Beginning spotters should stand slightly in front and to the side of the gymnast facing each other. They clasp each other's far hands to provide the axis of rotation. The hands nearer the gymnast rest on the gymnast's shoulder blades when her hands are on the mat and aid her in standing up.

2. Once the walkover has been accomplished, one spotter can stand on the side

Figure 3.66 • Front walkover with spot

of the gymnast's raised leg with the arm closer to the gymnast's back placed around her waist (Fig. 3.66a). The other arm supports the upheld leg under the thigh. The spotter releases the upraised leg and it is placed on the mat. Then the spotter moves forward with the gymnast, supports both legs in the handstand, and helps the gymnast get complete leg stretch (Fig. 3.66b). The spotter continues to move sideways as the gymnast moves forward, and at the end of the walkover she helps the gymnast stand up by placing the arm closer to her back behind the gymnast's waist. The other arm supports and keeps the second leg in the air for amplitude.

Combinations:	
1.	Front walkover, switch leg (in the air) front walkover.
2.	Front walkover, handstand forward roll.
3.	Front aerial, front walkover.
4.	Front walkover, front aerial (more difficult).
5.	"Tick-tock" (gymnast does first part of front walkover until the first foot touches and then changes directions and does the last half of a back walkover).

One-arm Front Walkover   This skill is performed as the front walkover with a few adjustments to compensate for the fact that one arm takes all of the body weight. The gymnast executes the kick, step, and lunge of the front walkover, then places one hand on the mat toward the midline so that the head and body's center of gravity will pass over it (the base support). The free arm extends dramatically out to the side, at shoulder level (Fig. 3.67). The skill is then completed as though it were a front walkover.

Teaching techniques and progressions:
1. The prerequisite for this skill is a front walkover.
2. The skill should be performed initially with spotting.

Figure 3.67   •   One-arm front walkover

Corrections: 1.   The corrections for this skill are the same as those for the front walkover, except that for proper hand placement the hand should be on the mat with the upper arm directly in front of the forehead.

Spotting: 1.   The spotting is the same as for the front walkover.

Combinations: 1.   Front walkover, one-arm front walkover.
2.   One-arm front walkover, (opposite or same) one-arm front walkover.

Front Tinsica   The front tinsica (arab wheel) is just like the front walkover except for the hand placement. After the stretch and kick, step, and lunge, the hands touch the mat one after the other, as though the gymnast were walking on the hands. Fingers point directly forward. The rhythm of the skill is an even hand, hand, foot, foot while the body moves through the forward plane. The skill is completed as if it were a front walkover. The proper way to do a front tinsica, as we saw in the description of the back tinsica, is controversial. The approach presented here follows logical progressions and nomenclature. In the tinsica the hips move either through the front or back plane, as they do in a front or back walkover. Therefore the most direct relative of the tinsica is the walkover.

Corrections: 1.   The corrections applying to the front tinsica are like those for the front walkover with the addition of the alternate hand placement and the finger placement in a forward direction.

Spotting: 1.   The spotting for this skill is the same as for a front walkover.

Combinations: 1.   Front walkover, front tinsica.
2.   Cartwheel, front tinsica, cartwheel.
3.   Front tinsica, one-arm front walkover.

Figure 3.68 • Butterfly

4. Front tinsica, front walkover.

5. Front aerial, front tinsica.

6. Front tinsica, front aerial (requires good lunge and power for aerial).

Butterfly

The butterfly is a lovely, quite flighty skill that, according to movement, is neither a pure tumbling nor a pure acrobatic skill (Fig. 3.68). Since the butterfly is a skill originally performed by acrobats, it is usually considered part of the acrobatics repertoire. For the sake of balance, a turn usually precedes and follows the butterfly. The butterfly is a horizontal tour jêté, a turn in which one leg pushes off the floor and a landing occurs on the other leg. As the turn is occurring, the body is at least in a horizontal position.

Teaching techniques and progressions:

1. The gymnast stands with her feet shoulder width apart. She is piked at the waist so that her back is parallel with the floor. Arms extend out from the shoulders.

2. From this position the gymnast sways to her right and left, bending her knee on the side toward which she is turned (see Fig. 3.69). The back remains parallel with the floor.

3. The butterfly is attempted from the above position by extending the straight leg up and behind and then forcefully turning and pushing off with the bent leg. Once airborne, the leg is stretched up and behind. The gymnast then lands on the leg that was the first one in the air.

4. During each attempt the gymnast lifts and stretches her legs more. Surprisingly, this skill is not that difficult and can be attempted by beginners.

Corrections:

1. The most common error in a butterfly is poor height and lift in the chest. This problem can be corrected with greater push from the legs.

2. The legs should be completely stretched and the toes pointed when they are in the air.

Figure 3.69 • Butterfly progression

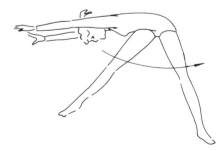

3. This skill should not be confused with an aerial cartwheel. The aerial cartwheel is a skill that travels in the vertical plane, while the butterfly travels in the horizontal plane.

Spotting:

1. This skill is one of the few for which this book does not recommend a spot.

Combinations:

1. Turn, butterfly, turn.
2. Tour jêté, butterfly, turn.
3. Turn, butterfly, butterfly, turn. (This combination is particularly effective because it creates a curvilinear floor pattern, which is unique and necessary for an artistic floor exercise.)

Illusion

This skill is a full turn on one leg as the other leg passes through the vertical position (Fig. 3.70). Standing on the leg that will be the base support, the gymnast kicks her other leg into the air in front of her. She then swings this leg down and past the support leg while piking at the waist. The head and shoulders pass by the inside of the support leg—on which the turn is occurring—while the other leg continues up through the vertical and down again at the turn's completion.

Teaching techniques and progressions:

1. The gymnast should complete a full turn (360°) on the ball and toe of one foot. This foot will be the support leg during the illusion.
2. Standing to the front and on the swing leg side of the gymnast, the teacher/spotter takes the gymnast's hand in her hand (loosely so that the gymnast's hand will turn in the spotter's hand). The spotter's other arm supports the

Figure 3.70 · Illusion

upper back during the turn and particularly helps the gymnast to stand at the skill's completion.

3. Once the gymnast understands the skill, she performs it alone, with straight legs and pointed toes.

Corrections:

1. The most frequent error in the performance of an illusion occurs when the gymnast does not remain on the toes and ball of the foot of the support leg.

2. This skill requires excellent leg flexibility, the lack of which can cause the leg to pancake (be semihorizontal rather than vertical).

3. Occasionally, grave embarrassment for the gymnast occurs when she swings into the illusion so forcefully that she actually picks up her support leg and ends the attempted illusion with a loud and obvious seat drop.

Spotting:

1. The spotting technique described in the section on progressions is used only to establish the kinesthesis of the skill for the gymnast and is not necessary after that.

Combinations:

1. Turn, illusion, turn.
2. Cartwheel, illusion, cartwheel.
3. Butterfly, illusion, butterfly.

Shoot Through   Skills from a handstand position moving into a split are an important means of changing levels in floor exercise. This particular skill begins in the handstand position and requires leg flexibility. The legs are split so that the forward leg is on

Figure 3.71 • Shoot through with spot

the front side of the body. The forward leg is brought down between the hands into a split (Fig. 3.71). In order to accomplish this movement, the gymnast overbalances the shoulders in a forward direction.

Teaching techniques and progressions:

1. The prerequisite for this skill is good leg flexibility, a deep split, and the ability to control a handstand.

2. While a spotter standing beside the gymnast clasps her waist, the gymnast is lowered slowly into the split and encouraged to push her shoulders forward as the foot begins to pass through the hands. The spotter may gently push her knee into the armpit of the gymnast to help her "feel" the shoulder lean, the overbalancing that this skill requires. Once the foot has passed between the hands without touching the floor, the shoulders are moved back into proper alignment.

3. When the gymnast can perform the skill without any lifting from the spotter, she should perform the skill alone.

Corrections:

1. The most obvious correction is to increase the gymnast's leg flexibility.

2. If a gymnast cannot become more flexible (an unlikely problem), then increasing shoulder and upper-chest (pectoral) strength will facilitate greater overbalancing.

3. Body slaps (loud sounds produced upon contact with the floor) can be avoided by lowering the body to the floor more slowly and overbalancing the shoulders.

Spotting:

1. The spot for this skill involves holding the gymnast by the waist and lowering her into the split as described in the teaching techniques section.

Combinations:

1. Back walkover, shoot through.
2. Handstand pirouette, shoot through.

Stoop Through

This skill is like the shoot through except that both legs come between the hands simultaneously and the skill ends in a sitting position on the floor (Fig. 3.72). The stoop through is a more difficult stunt than the shoot through because it requires more leg flexibility and shoulder girdle strength for overbalancing. The teaching progressions, techniques, corrections, and spotting are the same as for the shoot through.

Combinations:

1. Handstand, stoop through.
2. Back walkover, stoop through.
3. Handstand pirouette, stoop through.
4. Stoop through, back extension roll.

Figure 3.72   •   Stoop through with spot

Cutaway

The cutaway appears to be a shoot through, but it is an easier skill than the shoot through because it does not require as much flexibility. In a handstand position, the legs are split. The forward leg in the split is brought down, and as it approaches the hands, it is circled to the outside of the arm opposite the front leg in the split. The hand of this arm is picked up (cut away) so that the leg can pass under it and into a split.

Teaching techniques and progressions:

1. The prerequisites are a split and a controlled handstand.
2. The gymnast identifies her forward leg in the split and then the arm of the opposite side of the body. From a front support position on the floor the gymnast circles the leg that will be forward in the split in front of her other leg and continues to circle it to the side and front. She then cuts, or picks up, the arm on that side so that her leg can pass under it into a split position.
3. The gymnast assumes a split handstand position. The spotter stands on the side of the leg that will be forward in the split and supports the gymnast's thighs with her arms (Fig. 3.73a). The spotter quickly circles to the front of the gymnast's body and the gymnast turns her legs (Fig. 3.73b). As the spotter approaches the other side of the gymnast, she lowers her into a split by continuing to support her legs (Figs. 3.73c and d). The gymnast must "cut" the appropriate arm.
4. When the gymnast can perform the skill without much help from the spotter, she can perform the skill alone.

Corrections:

1. The gymnast must learn to lean, or overbalance, her whole body over her supporting arm and shoulder as the "cut" occurs. Greater overbalancing, which requires more flexibility, will reduce the intensity of the body slap.
2. The gymnast must circle her leg more if she lacks flexibility.

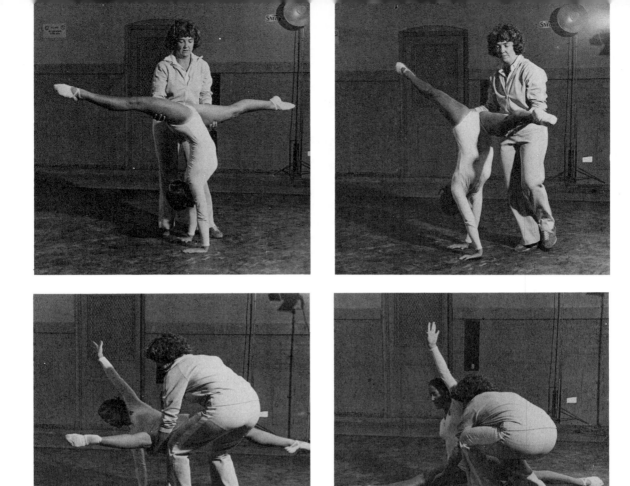

Figure 3.73 • Cutaway with spot

Figure 3.74 • Handstand side fall into a split

Spotting: 1. The spotting for this skill is described as a teaching technique and is necessary only when learning the skill.

Combinations: 1. Handstand, cutaway.

                 2. Back walkover, cutaway.

                 3. Handstand pirouette, cutaway.

Handstand Side Fall to a Split

From a handstand split position, the gymnast falls to her side into a split (Fig. 3.74). If her right leg is forward in a split, she falls over her right arm, cutting her left arm. Again the gymnast must overbalance the shoulder of the support arm.

Teaching techniques and progressions:

1. The prerequisites are a split and a controlled handstand.

2. The spotter, standing on the side of the gymnast's leg while in a handstand that will be forward in the split, supports the thighs with her hands. The spotter gently brings the gymnast toward her into the split.

3. When the spotter can feel very little of the gymnast's weight in her hands, the gymnast can attempt the skill by herself.

Corrections: 1. The correction for the most common error in this skill—insufficient over-balancing—is to have the gymnast lean way over to overbalance the shoulder of her support hand. The more the gymnast is able to overbalance, the easier the fall, the less intense the body slap, and the more control she will have.

Spotting: 1. The spotting for this skill is discussed in the teaching techniques section as well, because spotting is useful only as a means of improving the gymnast's kinesthesis. The spotter stands on the side of the forward leg in the split. The spotter holds the gymnast's thighs in her hands and the gymnast falls toward the spotter, turning her thighs in the spotter's hands so that the spotter's hands will be under the legs of the gymnast to ease the fall as the gymnast goes into the split.

Combinations: 1. Handstand, side fall to a split.

                 2. Back walkover to a handstand, side fall to a split.

                 3. Cartwheel to a handstand, side fall to a split.

                 4. Split handstand pirouette, side fall to a split.

Front Walkover into a Split

In this skill, as the first leg over in the walkover approaches the mat, the foot is forcefully plantar-flexed so that the top of the foot makes contact with the mat first. As the walkover ends, the gymnast rolls down the front of the flexed leg, which becomes the rear leg in the split, to break the fall (Fig. 3.75a). The roll proceeds

Figure 3.75 • Front walkover into a split

from foot to shin to knee to thigh while the other leg continues forward into the split (Fig. 3.75b).

Teaching techniques and progressions:

1. The gymnast must be extremely flexible in her low back to perform this skill. The prerequisite is a controlled front walkover and a deep split.

Corrections:

1. The gymnast must be encouraged to use the front of the first leg over in the split to break the fall and prevent a forced split.
2. The gymnast should lean backward as much as possible to counterbalance the force of the fall.

Spotting:

1. The spotter, standing to the side of the gymnast, can help the gymnast by holding her waist at the top of the walkover and easing her into the split.

Combinations:

1. Front walkover to a split.
2. Front walkover, front walkover to a split.
3. Front aerial, front walkover to a split.
4. Forward roll into a split. This skill is performed from a forward roll rather than a walkover, but the technique of going into the split is the same.

The techniques for getting up from or out of a split are more varied than those for going into a split. These skills are limited only by the imaginations of the gymnast and her teacher/coach. Experiment. The more unique or creative you can be, the better. Experimentation should take place in front of a mirror.

ROUTINE COMPOSITION

Compulsory exercises are not as common as they should or could be in the United States and Canada. Too often we expect a 10.00 performance from a year of gymnastics. This desire for instant results and success often hurts the gymnast's progress at the higher levels. If our gymnastics is to improve at the international level, we must begin to train ourselves to delay gratification by insisting upon good basics. Compulsory exercises can provide a good foundation for gymnastics, the basics, that can be taught through compulsory exercises.

A compulsory exercise is one designed for a particular event and skill level. The ideal progression is a year of dance and tumbling followed by a year of compulsory exercises. It is advisable that gymnasts perform either USGF or NAGWS compulsories or compulsories choreographed by the teacher/coach prior to work on optional exercises or routines.

In teaching and learning the skills of floor exercise, it is equally important to practice combinations of skills rather than just practicing new skills as the gymnast learns them. The effective teacher can have a whole class moving across a floor exercise mat in groups of four or five and performing combinations of tumbling, dance, and acrobatic skills. The selected combinations should include tempo changes, direction changes, level changes, and force changes.

When composing an optional floor exercise, it helps the gymnast to write down her floor exercise vocabulary or all of the various skills she can perform. The teacher/coach can keep this record and add to it as the gymnast progresses.

The selection of appropriate music is critical to the success of the floor exercise. The only requirement is that the music be provided by a solo instrument. The music should complement the somatotype as well as the movement qualities of the gymnast. The Soviet gymnastics teams are noted for this. It would be trite to select overly dramatic music for a cute, bouncy gymnast or to select a snappy, cutesy tune for an elegantly moving gymnast. The character of the music is dependent upon the character of the gymnast; in other words, an eight-year-old would appear foolish attempting sensuously flowing movements that would be more suitable for an eighteen-year-old.

There are currently many records of floor exercise music available. If a record is selected, an audio tape of the record should be made and used for practices and competition because records are easily damaged with use. Furthermore, nothing is more unsettling for the gymnast than to be on the floor ready to begin an exercise and to have someone put on the wrong band or skip into the band of the music. Whether to use cassettes, individual reel to reels, or one master reel containing the music for an entire team depends upon fidelity, availability, and feasibility.

A willing pianist can be a distinct advantage and beneficial addition to a gymnastic team. It is helpful if the pianist can play "by ear." (although this can be painful for one's ear). Experience indicates that the most efficient and pleasant way to communicate with a pianist is for the coach to act as the liaison between the gymnast and the pianist. Since the gymnast is expected to effect changes in level, tempo, direction, and force it is helpful if the music reflects these changes. The music should be tasteful and not necessarily taken from the current top ten because its popularity lends a certain interpretation that might be limiting. Music that is native to a girl's culture can help to keep the exercise in character. Thus it should be easier for the American gymnast to move to jazz since the origins of jazz and its movements are American. This ethnic influence should not dominate the exercise, however.

In the Soviet Union and East European countries, a much used method of integrating music and routine is to develop an exercise that incorporates the best possible movement qualities and combinations for the gymnast and then to have a highly trained pianist either compose or arrange music to suit the exercise. In the United States, more often than not, we select the music and choreograph the exercise for the music. These contrasts reflect the differences in importance of

Table 3.1   Choreography Checklist for Floor Exercise

Tumbling
　　Minimum of 4 tumbling passes　　　　　　　　　　　　　　　_____
　　Preferably including 1 forward aerial (somersault)　　　　_____
　　And at least one backward aerial (somersault)　　　　　　_____
Difficulties (number)　　　　　　　　　　　　　　　　　　　_____
　　　　　　　　　　Superior_____
　　　　　　　　　　Medium_____
Dance
　　Leaps　　　　　　　　　　　　　　　　　　　　　　　_____
　　Jumps　　　　　　　　　　　　　　　　　　　　　　_____
　　Running steps　　　　　　　　　　　　　　　　　　　_____
　　Trunk movements with steps　　　　　　　　　　　　_____
　　Turns on feet　　　　　　　　　　　　　　　　　　　_____
　　Balances　　　　　　　　　　　　　　　　　　　　　_____
　　Dance steps　　　　　　　　　　　　　　　　　　　_____
Difficulties (number)　　　　　　　　　　　　　　　　　　_____
　　　　　　　　　　Superior_____
　　　　　　　　　　Medium_____

Acrobatics
　　Minimum of 4 acrobatic passes　　　　　　　　　　　　_____
　　Turns on hands　　　　　　　　　　　　　　　　　　_____
　　Movements on floor　　　　　　　　　　　　　　　　_____
Difficulties (number)　　　　　　　　　　　　　　　　　　_____
　　　　　　　　　　Superior_____
　　　　　　　　　　Medium_____
General
　　All movements with amplitude　　　　　　　　　　　　_____
　　Arm movements and head positions considered in
　　　　whole composition　　　　　　　　　　　　　　　_____
　　Connectors between elements well chosen for gymnast　_____
　　Movement, music, and gymnast in harmony　　　　　　_____

sport—in particular, gymnastics—between countries and also the fact that a gymnastic accompanist is an honorable and highly sought after position among extremely well-trained pianists in Eastern Europe.

Regardless of the source of the music, it is important for the coach's sanity that the selection please both the gymnast and the coach, for it will be heard thousands of times in a given season. It also makes sense for a gymnast to keep the same music as long as it affords her the flexibility to make changes in the exercise. A year is the minimum amount of time to keep the same music. Two years is the ideal.

The shorter the routine, the better the opportunity the gymnast has to perform it with perfection and to finish it as strongly as she began. The timer will start the watch when the gymnast begins to move, but the gymnast and the music must end together. The time limit is one minute to one minute thirty seconds. Prior to final selection, the coach should time the selection (length of play designations on records have been known to be inaccurate) so that a gymnast will not incur a penalty for her music being under- or overtime.

The composition or choreography of the exercise should provide opportunities for the gymnast to cover or reach the whole area (40 ft. × 40 ft.) in straight-line and curvilinear floor patterns as she performs artfully combined tumbling, dance, and acrobatics. The current trend is to have a greater concentration of tumbling in an exercise. Gross movements are more typical of floor exercise: subtle and small movements and expressions are unnoticeable on a floor exercise mat. Not only the music but also the movements within the floor exercise should suit the gymnast and her style. If a gymnast is a beginner, her teacher/coach can help her to develop her style by taking into account the gymnast's size and potential for movement, as well as those movements she feels comfortable doing.

A mirror is a must for a gymnasium. Regardless of skill level, gymnasts often need the reassurance that they don't "look weird" doing a new or different movement and, often, seeing it in a mirror helps to provide security and self-confidence.

A skeletal framework that may assist the coach in choreographing a floor exercise appears in Table 3.1. A general rule of thumb is that the exercise should begin and end with difficulty, usually of a tumbling nature.

The coach's role in routine composition is that of advisor. The gymnast should make up her own routine, but some girls need lots of help and guidance. It is important that a coach not compose each team member's routine because the coach's routines reflect her and her style rather than the gymnast's. Unfortunately this is too often the case with the result that a whole team's floor exercises look alike and have the same character. Each girl is unique; she moves and expresses herself differently and her personality should be evident in each exercise.

Expression will be enhanced if the gymnast feels comfortable about what she is doing and if she feels good about herself and about what she is attempting to say to the audience through her movement. An exercise should have one main theme or quality and myriad variations. Any body part that moves is capable of contributing to the expression. The obvious ones are the arms, hands, and legs. In addition, though, the torso, the facial expression, and the head position are potentially dynamic and dramatic means for expression.

The contractions, successions, or body waves of modern dance aid in the use of the torso. At one time in women's gymnastics the "plumb line" of the torso, a term borrowed from the ballet discipline, was a popular concept. Gymnasts are now liberated in terms of torso movement and these skills are encouraged and required in routines. Isadora Duncan, a pioneer in a free, uninhibited form of movement in the early 1900s, believed that all expressive movements should emanate from the heart or mid-torso area of the body. Duncan was not a highly skilled technician of the dance, but she had the ability to bring tears to the eyes of the great dance masters and directors of the time, including Fokine. She expressed herself from the heart by dramatically moving her torso.

Many coaches in the United States and Canada have neglected the potential of the face as a mode of expression in gymnastics. The effectiveness of the performances of Eastern European gymnasts has been enhanced by drama. These athletes have a well-designed plan of specific facial expressions for each part of their exercise. It is time for us to leave the era of the perpetually excruciating smile or grimace that many Western gymnasts wear and learn to punctuate some very expressive body movements with well-calculated facial expressions.

The head and its position are generally neglected by a majority of gymnasts. Beginning with the novice gymnast, the coach must help her gymnasts to accentuate and exaggerate the head position. Gymnasts could learn a great deal about head positioning from figure skaters. Obviously the skater with a heavy skate at the end of her leg cannot perform with the leg amplitude of a gymnast, but the skater uses her head so well that she creates an illusion of greater amplitude. Dramatic, exaggerated head positions are essential in gymnastics. Nothing projects more joy, youth, forthrightness, and vibrance than an upraised face and an extended head.

As part of the head and its positioning, the hair—its movement or lack of movement—should be well planned for its overall effect on the routine. Often female gymnasts practice with their hair one way and then style it differently for competition; others don't even consider their hair. This should be a coaching consideration. Long bangs tend to shadow or cover the eyes when a gymnast is on the floor or beam because the lighting in most gymnasiums is overhead. The eyes are an important source of expression and the gymnast cannot afford to lose their effect in a shadow. A good "do" suited to the individual is most helpful. The judging deduction for fixing the hair during a routine is further incentive for coaches to instruct gymnasts in appropriate grooming.

During the teaching of all gymnastics skills, the coach should emphasize proper technique and form. Proper form includes pointed toes, straight legs (no knee bends except on landings), completely stretched or tightly tucked body or

Figure 3.76 • Proper form and amplitude

body parts (amplitude), proper body alignment, balance throughout, movements on the feet performed up on the toes, and composure (Fig. 3.76). After the routine has been composed, the coach must continue to "harp" on amplitude and form to prevent gymnasts from reverting to laziness and sloppiness, which render the ultimate goal of perfection unattainable.

TRAINING AND CONDITIONING

Training and conditioning for floor exercise should be as specific as possible. Therefore nothing can replace routines. Routines aren't fun except for that important minute during a meet (if performed well), so the gymnast must discipline herself, with the coach's help and insistence, to practice routines. By mid season the gymnast should easily be able to throw two consecutive routines, including all tumbling. Three complete, consecutive routines are ideal. After she has practiced the routines, the gymnast can and should work on parts or sections. If, in the beginning of the season, the gymnast's endurance is such that she can't execute whole routines, the routine can be divided into thirds and then halves. Eventually she will be able to perform the whole routine. If the gymnast does practice in parts, the coach should emphasize the last part because the gymnast will be tired and will have to push herself more. Since floor exercise requires endurance, the coach can help the gymnast improve her endurance by applying the "overload" principle. There can never be too much stress on routine practice because the ability to do all of the skills and "tricks" in gymnastics does not make a routine or a good score.

To determine the appropriate conditioning or training for floor exercise it is necessary to evaluate the demands of the event. Tumbling and dance require explosive leg strength. This quality increases through repetitions of tumbling and dance skills. At the end of a practice, the team might line up across the edge of a floor exercise mat and, moving across to the other side, together do passes of:

1. Series of back handsprings (4) from a stand
2. Series of aerials, sides, or fronts (3)
3. Roundoff, pop turn, roundoff, and so on.
4. Back handsprings, back somersault
5. Leap, leap, leap, leap
6. Leap, step, leap, step, leap
7. Dance fall, recovery jump, fall, and so on

These skills should be repeated without rest. For a slight break, a pass of acrobatics, such as repeated back walkovers can be performed excruciatingly slowly with amplitude and balance. Acrobatics require flexibility. Therefore extensive stretching (see Chapter 2) can also be a part of the conditioning that follows practice. Body parts that must be flexible for floor exercise are the wrists, upper back, low back, hamstrings, quadriceps (thighs), gastrocnemius (heel cord), and the dorsi and plantar flexion in the ankles. Since knee, ankle, and wrist injuries are the most common in floor exercise, proper conditioning, strengthening, and flexibility in these areas are important.

Endurance increases by doing complete routines as well as by tumbling at the end of practice. Some general conditioning exercises that may increase endurance for floor exercise are running (one or two miles on one day and wind sprints for one mile on alternate days), stair running, 60 half-squat jumps, 20 straddle pike jumps, 40 jump squat half back roll to shoulders jump, rope skipping, 80 low-high jumps (alternating with push from ankles, low and push from knees, high), and a circuit (see Chapter 2).

THE PSYCHOLOGY OF COACHING AND PERFORMING FLOOR EXERCISE

The body is the primary medium in floor exercise. For this reason the gymnast must feel comfortable about herself in order to perform effectively. Part of this comfort comes from confidence in self, confidence in her teacher/coach, a good feeling about her body, and the knowledge that she can do everything in her routine.

The development of self-confidence is aided by positive reinforcement from peers and coach. Thus the coach is responsible for providing a compatible workout atmosphere where goals are attainable and realistic. A gymnast should never be ridiculed. Each improvement and growth should be recognized and rewarded. What could be more difficult than to walk out onto a floor exercise mat, alone, to do an exercise? All excuses stop at this point and no one can "bail" the gymnast out; her abilities are truly being tested. Regardless of the skill level, just getting out on the floor requires guts. How many people in the general population could or would expose themselves to either instant success or failure? Certainly the performer in floor exercise is worthy of respect. The coach's confidence in the gymnast's ability should increase the gymnast's self-confidence.

Body image is extremely important on the floor. A gymnast who has a positive body image won't feel self-conscious in a leotard. She will be able to express her self-worth and positiveness in her routine. The grave implication for the coach is to help the gymnast to control her weight through diet counseling.

Confidence in the coach will develop if the gymnast likes her music and her floor exercise routine and, in general, feels good about participation in the event. Therefore skills that the gymnast has not mastered do not belong in the routine. Also, the coach should know what the event regulations and difficulties are.

The coach should help the gymnast with her presentation. A girl's appearance, carriage, and demeanor can make quite a difference in her score. The gymnast should walk out onto the floor with an air of confidence (even though her stomach is doing flip-flops), as though she owned the floor, the gym, the meet, the world: "Hey, look at me! I want to talk to you with my body, through this exercise, with this music." The gymnast is attempting to sell the judges and audience the idea that she is the best at that moment. The gymnast should not only begin the exercise with this attitude but also finish it with pride, regardless of how she performed, and walk off the mat looking like she just won a gold medal in the Olympics.

Prior to beginning her exercise, the gymnast walks with dignity to a spot, off the mat, as close as possible to where her exercise begins. Assuming a relaxed attention position, she patiently waits until the head judge acknowledges her and grants permission for her to mount the floor exercise mat (apparatus). With class and dignity the gymnast walks onto the floor mat to her starting place. It is advisable to start the exercise in a standing position because trying to hold a pose while waiting for the music is difficult, tiring, and can result in loss of balance. Also, in the final position or pose the gymnast might count to five mentally after the music has ended, to exhibit complete control, composure, and balance. At the end of the exercise, the standing gymnast raises both arms into the air and acknowledges the judges by facing at least two corners of the mat.

The most glamorous of the women's gymnastic events is floor exercise. The glamor evolves from "selling."

4

FLYING:
side horse vaulting

Side horse vaulting is a significant part of women's gymnastics, both as one of the all-around events and as one of the Olympic events. It comprises one-quarter of the all-around score as well as one-quarter of the team score. Unfortunately, most coaches and teachers do not spend sufficient time with the gymnast or team analyzing and practicing vaulting. In this event, the objective is for the gymnast to jump over the side horse covering as much height and distance in flight as possible (Fig. 4.1). The hands must touch the horse and are the only part of the body permitted to contact the horse. The hands should be used only for balance and direction. Since the body is orbited into the air by and through the power of the legs, this event can be both exciting and fun for the performer. By defying gravity and becoming airborne, the gymnast can experience a great feeling of accomplishment and success. The whole vault, including the run, occurs in a matter of seconds. For the easiest and the most complex vaults alike, proper running, jumping, and vaulting techniques are essential to the gymnast. In the initial stages, emphasis on proper technique facilitates learning and execution as the vaulter improves her skill and increases her vault difficulty.

Vault difficulties can be found in the *FIG Code of Points* and the *NAGWS Rule*

* Figure 4.1 is on preceding page.

Book. Generally, the closer the gymnast comes to flying and the more often her body rotates through the horizontal plane (somersaults) and/or vertical plane (twists), the higher the value of the vault.

In competition, the gymnast or her coach must inform the judges of the vault to be performed. The judges know the established difficulty or value of the vault (highest possible score a gymnast can receive for that particular vault) and the judges evaluate the gymnast's vault according to the way in which it was executed. Generally, the judges look for complete body stretch in preflight, balance, and control in landing. The gymnast may do two vaults; she will receive the higher of the two scores. Normally the gymnast may perform the same vault twice or do two different vaults. During meets at the highest national or international level, however, a gymnast who "makes finals" (by being one of the top ten or twelve gymnasts in the preliminary competition of the meet) must perform two different vaults, one of which must contain a twist. As a coaching suggestion, beginning and intermediate gymnasts should concentrate on perfecting one vault and should perform that one vault in competition. As the gymnast's ability increases, more difficult vaults can be learned. In a meet, the gymnast should perform her regular vault first and ask for the score from the judges; if she and her coach are satisfied, she should then try a new or alternative vault. However, if the score for the first vault is unsatisfactory, the gymnast should repeat the more practiced vault.

Three pieces of equipment and apparatus are necessary for this event. They are the side horse without pommels (handles), a carpeted board (wooden or metal), and proper mat coverage.

This chapter discusses and categorizes vaults by family according to preflight and consequently do not represent a ranking from easy to difficult (handsprings, quarter twists, half twists, full twists, somersaults, and hechts). Some girls find it easier to rotate about the horizontal axis (somersaults) than the vertical axis (twists) and vice versa, so ranking vaults according to learning ease is debatable. In terms of progression, the following suggestions may be modified to fit the gymnast's ability (the slash separates the action in the preflight from that in the afterflight).

1. Handspring (a prerequisite for all inverted vaults)
2. Handspring/half twist
3. Yamashita
4. Quarter on/quarter off
5. Yamashita/half twist
6. Half twist/handspring
7. Quarter twist/three-quarter twist and (or) half twist/full twist
8. Handspring/full twist and (or) half twist/full twist

The following vaults are extremely difficult because they require somersaulting and twisting in combination: quarter twist/one and a half back somersaults and (or) half twist/one and a half back somersaults, Tsukaharas. Twists can be added to somersaults in the off-flight. Other extremely difficult vaults involve blind landings on the horse or when dismounting. They include: handspring/one and a half front somersaults (twists can be added); and one and a half front somersaults/any combination of somersaults or twists.

SAFETY TIPS

Mats should be placed behind the horse, where the gymnast will be landing. Proper mat placement requires: mats flush with each other; no spaces between mats; and no overlapping areas to cause ankle or knee injuries. Double mat thickness is recommended. It is preferable to sandwich landing, dismount, or crash pads (very thick mats) between two regular mats.

The height of the horse should conform to the most current USGF age-level recommendations. At the time of this book's writing, the height specification is 1.2 meters or 3 ft. 11¼ in. To determine the height (since the sides of the horse are rounded), place a clipboard flat on the center surface of the horse and measure the vertical distance from the floor to the edge of the clipboard.

Once the height has been established, a check should be made to insure that all handles are properly tight and other adjustments adequately prevent the horse's movement when a gymnast vaults.

Knowledgeable, capable spotters should *always* be present for this event. The priority (#1) spotter should stand behind and to the side of the horse. Her responsibility is to aid the gymnast's landing. An additional spotter (#2) can stand next to the horse, slightly to the side of the board in front of the horse. Her responsibility is to help the gymnast over the horse, if necessary. In the beginning and intermediate stages in gymnastics there is no such thing as overspotting.

The gymnast should fully understand the proper technique for the vault prior to attempting it.

All vaults performed should be landed with the gymnast squarely facing in the direction of the run or the horse. Sideward landings are prohibitive because of the potential for serious injury to the knees and ankles: *they should not be performed.*

BEGINNING VAULTING

Vaulting is a jumping skill. Jumping skills require the efficient use of the legs. The run and vault approach are important factors in an efficient jump. A beginning vaulter should take a few easy running steps, take off on the last step before reaching the board. Bringing both feet together on the board, she should perform a two-foot takeoff and jump up and over the horse, touching it only with her hands. The landing on the mat should be completely controlled.

This preliminary exercise gives the gymnast a feeling of the board and an awareness of her jumping potential. A low Swedish box or a low bench that is stabilized is placed between the board and the mats. The task for the girl is to run easily, execute a two-foot takeoff from the board to a standing position on the box or bench, and jump down to a controlled landing. This task gives the girl a feeling that she can jump. A spotter should be present to stop the girl's forward momentum on the box. A horse is then substituted for the box, and the girl is told to climb over the horse.

Squat Vault

Next, she should run and perform a bent-hip squat vault. The squat vault requires a two-foot takeoff, body immediately brought into tuck position (knees up to chest, back rounded, heels close to body); hands are placed on the horse in shoulder width position, the body of the vaulter passes between her hands, and she lands in a balanced standing position on the other side of the horse (see Fig. 4.2). The only part of the body to touch the horse is the hands and they are used for balance and for a push off or away from the horse.

Teaching techniques and progressions:

1. The teacher must believe the girl can do it and must show this.
2. A large or heavy girl who has little strength proportionally should be encouraged to get over the horse in any manner she can.
3. The horse does not have to be lowered for the average girl to perform a squat vault.
4. When the gymnast can perform the squat vault, she should work on proper running technique. Proper running technique will be discussed in detail a little later in this chapter.
5. Other basic vaults, including the flank, face, thief, wolf, and fence, have been taught in the past and are described in other gymnastics texts. Even if these vaults are considered important for the vaulting unit, it is best that very little

Figure 4.2 • Squat vault

time be spent on them, for they are not the best progressions for learning more difficult and currently recognized vaults.

Corrections:

1. A good vault requires a smooth approach, a two-foot takeoff from the board, and a good jump.

2. A tight tuck position with knees up to chest insures that the "glutes" rather than the shins pass closest to the horse.

3. Elbows should be locked while the hands are on the horse.

4. The vaulter should avoid arching her back to complete passage over the horse because it causes an unsatisfactory landing and back strain.

5. The board must be approximately three feet from the horse; otherwise the vaulter will crash and burn into the horse.

Spotting:

1. The prime spotter (#1) stands sideways behind the horse, slightly to the side of the spot at which the vaulter will pass over the horse. While reaching over the horse, she grasps the vaulter's *upper* arm with both hands. She holds the vaulter until she has landed in complete control.

2. If desired, another spotter (#2) can stand sideways in front of the horse, close enough to the vaulter to help lift her up and over the horse. This is a quick spot because the spotter must place the arm that is closer to the horse on the front of the vaulter's waist and use her other hand to help lift the glutes when the tuck begins. She must accomplish all of these moves between the time the vaulter leaves the board and when she begins to pass over the horse.

The squat vault is a challenging skill for a beginner. Therefore it is an accomplishment that the teacher/coach should recognize. This skill might be the maximum vaulting requirement in a short basic introductory unit in gymnastics.

Straddle Vault

Once a gymnast has successfully accomplished the squat vault, she can learn the straddle vault. The bent hip straddle vault requires leg flexibility; therefore everyone in a physical education class may not be able to perform this skill. A girl who has a good run and jump, however, can compensate for her lack of flexibility. The vaulter approaches the horse with a controlled run, uses a two-foot takeoff from the board, and lifts her hips in a pike as high as possible while straddling her legs (Fig. 4.3). Only her hands touch the horse in a shoulder width position to help push the body up and away from the horse; the body passes over the horse and the legs are brought together for a controlled and balanced landing.

Teaching techniques and progressions:

1. A preliminary run, piking of the hips and straddling of the legs at the horse may be attempted.

Figure 4.3 • Straddle vault

Corrections: There are five keys to the successful performance of this skill.

1. Good power from approach and jump will enable the gymnast to lift her hips as high as possible in pike position.
2. The legs should be straddled equally.
3. Elbows must remain locked while the hands are on the horse.
4. A stable pelvic girdle will prevent hyperextension of the lower back at the end of the vault and the uncomfortable landing that it can cause.
5. The board should be at least three feet from the horse.

Spotting: 1. The spot for the straddle vault requires the spotter to move her feet. She begins by standing behind the horse and facing the vaulter. As the vaulter leaves the board the spotter reaches over the horse and grasps the vaulter's upper arms. She continues to move with the vault by backing up and helping the vaulter land properly.

Handspring Vault   One of the premises of this book is that the proper progression for all competitive vaults (those vaults listed in the *FIG Code of Points* or *NAGWS Rule Book)* is performing a handspring vault. The handspring vault is a prerequisite to layout or inverted vaults (whether through the side plan quarter on or cartwheel, front plan handspring, or rear plane half on). It is more difficult to teach and learn proper techniques on inverted vaults after learning layout vaults. A correctly performed layout vault is actually the first part of a handspring vault. A proper layout vault is more difficult than a handspring, for once the layout position on the preflight has been accomplished, the gymnast must completely change and redirect her momentum and movement rather than allowing her body to continue over the horse in the same direction. Any vault will be successful if the vaulter's body reaches the horse at an inverted angle of approximately 120° to 150°. Therefore the ability to do a handspring vault in women's gymnastics is essential to the correct performance of the other competitive vaults. The prerequisites for performing a handspring vault are: the ability to perform a handstand (see Chapter 2) and having successfully jumped over the horse in a squat vault.

The handspring vault and all other vaults have two distinct phases: the preflight, or onflight phase, and the afterflight, postflight, or off-flight phase. The preflight lasts from the time the body leaves the board on the front side of the horse until the hands touch the horse. The afterflight begins when the hands leave the horse and continues until the feet touch the mat on the far side of the horse.

Approach

The preflight phase of side horse vaulting for women is a most critical part of the vault. The approach to the horse is extremely vital. Although the run itself is not judged, its dynamic power and quality provide the impetus for the vault. Therefore the vaulter needs to develop as much velocity as possible before she reaches the board. To accomplish this objective, the vaulter should run on the balls of her feet, hips and shoulders moving in a forward direction (not swinging from side to side). At the beginning of the run, the gymnast lifts her knees high and points her feet directly toward the horse; as she nears the horse, her strides should become longer and lower. The vaulter should be running as fast as possible with complete control when she reaches the board. This type of run should look like a track sprint. By forcefully moving, or pumping, the elbows in a forward-backward direction the performer can increase her velocity. The body should be as upright as possible by the time the vaulter reaches the board. The vaulter's eyes focus upon the board and the horse throughout the run.

The distance of the board from the horse and the length of the run vary from vaulter to vaulter. The run should be just long enough to attain maximum velocity. The runs of most women are too long. Generally, maximum speed can be attained in fifty feet. Sixty-five feet is more than sufficient for any vaulter. The distance of the board from the horse should be five to seven feet initially. The practice of placing the board at a distance from the horse equal to the height of the vaulter (determined by having her lie down between the board and the horse or by using a tape measure) seems illogical because this space should relate to the speed of the run, the takeoff, and the inverted angle of the body required for a given vault. Once the correct distance has been determined (by trial and error), it should be measured and recorded. Each time the gymnast vaults, the run and takeoff should be the same. Pacing the run backwards from the horse is also inaccurate because the vaulting run is dynamic and the step distances are different from those of pacing. The tape measure is an invaluable tool for the conscientious coach.

Takeoff

The last step of the run occurs approximately five to eight feet from the board. The vaulter takes a long step, called a "scoot step," onto the middle of the board. The scoot step is analogous to the skimming of a stone on the water. The smaller the angle as the stone reaches the water, the greater the height and length of the rebound the stone makes as it ricochets off the water. This last stage is usually referred to as the "hurdle." This designation is not the best choice because the vaulter quite often confuses this skill with the hurdle that precedes spring board diving. The action recommended differs greatly from what is commonly considered a hurdle, however, because the second, or rear, leg quickly follows the first leg onto the board and neither knee goes any higher than it did during the run. This action, performed correctly, allows for a long, low, scoot step. A high, short hurdle is a common error of bad vaulters.

The correct body position on the board is a slight back lean in which the body forms less than a 90° angle with the board so that proper rotation off the board can occur. The feet are forced together slightly in front of the hips, blocking out. This approach stems from the principle of parallelogram of forces (the angle of the body on the board will be similar to the inverted body angle on the horse). Further, this blocking of the forward momentum of the run converts this force to both vertical and horizontal thrust.

When both feet arrive on the board, the knees are only slightly bent, thus allowing for a two-foot takeoff. The knees and ankles forcefully extend in an explosive action. As soon as the feet touch the board the extension must occur quickly: there is no pause. In the coaching of gymnastics it is quite often necessary, for brevity and clarity, to develop key phrases or gymnastics clichés. A common gymnastics term that describes getting off the board as quickly as possible is "pop." In reference to the uneven bars, coaches talk of "popping" off the bar in an eagle catch or hecht dismount.) A pop is an explosive action that is really a simple way of stating Newton's third law of motion: for every action there is always an equal and contrary reaction.

Preflight

As the pop off the board for height and distance is being executed by the legs, the arms are strongly thrust fore-upward to aid with lift. The action of the arms is like that of the legs. Thus the body should be forced into a completely straight, *tight,* and stretched position: STG.

The body should arrive on the horse in a completely stretched (not arched), tight position. The upper arms should be held just in front of and touching the ears, still seen in peripheral vision, with the elbows extended.

Three primary arm delivery techniques have been developed for women's vaulting. The coach must carefully match the style and needs of each gymnast with an appropriate arm delivery.

The first arm delivery is not as popular as it once was. The arms are circled low, around and behind the body, and then brought up and over the shoulders. This technique often results in tilting or rotating the body early, sometimes prior to reaching the horse. This action can cause a distinct shortening of the onflight, and thus of the offflight, for the vaulter and severe heart palpitation for the coach.

The second arm delivery is accomplished by bringing the arms up from the waist, bringing the hands to the shoulders and then extending the arms. According to the principles of physics and, more specifically, mechanics, this technique should and can be most effective, for it is an action-reaction movement. (*Caution:* the arm delivery occurs in a very limited amount of time—about a second. Therefore, often the arms never become completely stretched at the elbows or shoulders. This incomplete or incorrect angle of the shoulders and arms shortens the onflight and prevents the blockage and repulsion of the horse necessary for off-flight. An incorrect angle at the shoulders is a common error among female vaulters, who cannot compensate as males do with greater strength.) A variation of this technique utilizes a "Russian lift" (quite different from the "Danish lift"). To perform the Russian lift as a vaulting arm delivery variation the gymnast holds her hands a bit higher (nearer the shoulders). When contact with the board occurs, she explosively forces her elbows backward in a very limited range and then extends her arms upward. This technique has been used successfully, but, again, it is important to establish whether proper arm position occurs.

The third arm delivery is especially useful for the individual learning inverted vaulting, as well as for intermediate and advanced vaulters who do not have their arms in the appropriate position upon landing on the horse. During the run, as the vaulter approaches the horse, the hands are held high so that when the vaulter scoots onto the board the hands are already shoulder high, elbows in. When the vaulter leaves the board, she forcefully extends her arms directly upward. Thus the ears and upper arms are in alignment and the vaulter can be reminded to squeeze her ears with her upper arms. This technique insures proper shoulder angle as well as proper hand position, often a vaulter's hands are too far apart and, as a result, her elbows bend on the horse. This technique does not take advantage of the action-reaction principle, yet the thrust from the arms in this phase of the vault is unnecessary, for the power for the lift stage of the vault is developed by and through the run and takeoff from the board. This third arm delivery is that which is advocated in this book.

As the body of the gymnast leaves the board it moves upward and slightly forward and must become very tight and extended (not arched)—STG. Rotation occurs as the feet leave the board. The integration of forward linear motion with rotary motion will produce the best results. Stretching and tightening the body in the preflight phase of the vault allows the preflight to be as high and long as necessary for the specific vault. The direction of the body in the air is determined by the direction of the resultant of the forces that set it in motion.

When the hands arrive on the horse, the body should be straight, stretched, and tight. The elbows should be well extended and locked; the hands should be approximately shoulder width apart when they touch the horse. This placement of the hands provides the strongest position as the base support for the body's center of gravity and thus establishes equilibrium and should eliminate elbow bending. There is a judging deduction for bent elbows because they reflect improper vaulting technique. The body angle on the horse, depending upon the specific vault, should be between 130° and 160°.

Afterflight

The moment the hands contact the horse the afterflight phase of the vault begins. The hands should be in contact with the horse for less than a second. Two techniques are currently employed to increase afterflight. The first is successfully accomplished by male vaulters as well as a number of female vaulters and is the one that some coaches recommend: the shoulders relax slightly as the hands touch the horse (similar to a shrug); then the shoulders and wrists are forcefully extended and stretched to send the body in an upward direction, in accordance with Newton's third law of motion. The gymnast should pop off the horse. The sooner and faster the pop, the better the afterflight.

Unfortunately, most girls and women are not strong, powerful, or explosive enough to be able to sink into their shoulders and then push up and away in an extremely short period of time. Therefore the second proven technique for achieving afterflight is the one this book recommends. Blocking the shoulders while the hands are on the horse permits the body to rise and sail during off-flight. Blocking is the pushing, or repulsing, of the horse. The upper arms are in a position slightly in front of the ears so that they appear in the gymnast's peripheral vision, the head is upright—neither tucked nor extended—the body is straight (not arched), and the hips are in a forward pelvic tilt (STG). From this body position, the hands then push backwards explosively and travel about eight to ten inches so that the upper arms cover the ears; this is the blocking of the horse. This technique is also useful in eliminating common errors that females make in the performance of a front handspring and/or a back handspring in floor exercise. Again, blocking changes the body flight or direction. Errors that prevent blocking are: bent elbows, improperly angled shoulders, (shoulders in front of the hands on the horse), head tucked or extended, and arched body on the horse. The most desirable and ideal effect in a vault is the longest and highest off-flight (Fig. 4.4). Achieving this effect requires body tightness, no arch, and quick blockage of the shoulders to cause repulsion of the horse.

Figure 4.4 · Off-flight

Landing

When the feet contact the mat at the end of the vault, the knees bend to absorb the force, the feet are hip width apart and point straight forward, the arms are extended up and to the side, palms facing forward. The hips are high. For stability the center of gravity is lowered as much as is consistent with the given vault for stability. To stop quickly when the body is in rapid motion, the gymnast spreads the base (feet) and drops the center of gravity as low as possible. Then the feet are slid together as the legs extend and the vaulter comes to an upright standing position. Landing, or "sticking" (landing a dismount without taking steps), a vault must be practiced separately as well as while performing *every* vault. Sticking requires mental discipline. The great international gymnasts appear to have giant suction cups for feet and toes, for when they land vaults or dismounts, they always stick. Many American gymnasts lack this discipline, which requires consistent and regular practice. The teacher/coach should demand a good stick.

The landing of a handspring vault is a blind one. Therefore the vaulter must anticipate the landing and not tuck the head to see the mat. Tucking the head prevents a stick. The vaulter should look down with her *eyes*, not her head, and take a "sneak peek."

Summary

To reiterate briefly and succinctly, the essentials of the handspring vault, which are applicable to all women's side horse vaulting are:

1. A fast, hard run; high knee lift in the beginning.
2. Long scoot step onto the board; blocking the feet in slightly in front of the hips.

Figure 4.5 • Arm delivery (a) correct and (b) incorrect

3. Quick action off the board; body tight and extended (STG).
4. Arms extended, shoulder width apart; upper arms slightly in front of the ears (Fig. 4.5).
5. STG—form is essential.
6. Blocking the shoulders for off-flight.
7. Anticipated landing, knees bent; focus on spot in front of, not on, the mat.
8. *Stick* the way an octopus would hold the mat.

These are the keys to the handspring vault and other vaults are accomplished using these techniques.

Teaching techniques and progressions:

1. A front handspring on the floor is a prerequisite.
2. The gymnast stands sideways on a side horse, cartwheels into a handstand with a tight body and lots of spotting (two on the back side of the horse). The vaulter repulses the horse by blocking her shoulders and sticks the landing. This move gives the gymnast the kinesthetic awareness of the position her body will pass through during the vault.
3. The gymnast runs as though vaulting, jumps off the board with body stretched, arms extended, legs straight, and lands on a low Swedish box, folded mats, or secured bench. Then she jumps down, sticking her landing on the mats. This progression gives the gymnast the kinesthesis of a stretched body off the board and landing a vault as well as the use of the board. The height of the mats or box is gradually raised to competitive height and

Figure 4.6 • Tilt

Figure 4.7 • Tilt

eventually a horse is substituted. This progression is an excellent warm-up and review for advanced vaulters also. Two spotters stand to the side at the back of the apparatus with hands raised so the gymnast can reach for them if she needs balance. Straight legs (except upon landing), control, and stick are important. This skill is not as difficult as it first appears to the vaulter.

4. The tilt is a technique in which the gymnast takes a short and easy run and delivers her arms as she leaves the board with a tight body. The spotter, who stands between the board and horse facing the gymnast, catches her by placing her hands on the gymnast's hip bones (Figs. 4.6 and 4.7). This technique demonstrates to the gymnast the need to go up and avoid reaching for the horse or rotating too soon. The spotter should be strong enough to catch the gymnast, but this is not a difficult spot.

5. If a trampoline is available, the horse may be placed flush with one end. Mats should be next to the horse and should cover the springs or cables of the tramp. The gymnast kicks a handstand onto the horse from the trampoline (Fig. 4.8a) and repulses the horse, as previously explained, by blocking her shoulders with a tight, straight body: there should be no arch in the back because it will cause a forced hyperextension of the back upon landing resulting in a stiff, aching back the next day. Two spotters standing on the off side of the horse, as in the handspring vault, carry the gymnast to the floor (Figs. 4.8b and c). Then, on the trampoline, the gymnast is encouraged to take one step to a two-foot takeoff, handspring onto the horse and dismount with off-flight and spotting. The takeoff should be far enough from the horse so that piking in the hips does not occur. This technique takes the gymnast through the vault in a fairly realistic way, the only difference being that rotation comes from the trampoline rather than the run and takeoff.

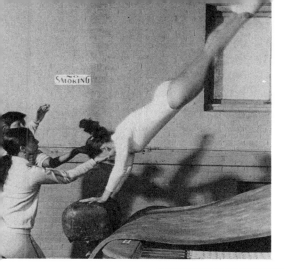

Figure 4.8 • Trampoline vaulting (progression #5)

6. This technique takes the gymnast, in a controlled and very safe way, through the handspring vault. It requires seven or nine spotters (see Fig. 4.9). Four or six spotters stand sideways between the board and the horse, two or three on each side of the board facing each other (group A). The prime spotter (B) stands between the board and the horse and faces the gymnast. The two second-best spotters (group C) stand facing each other behind and to the side of the horse where the gymnast will place her hands. The gymnast stands on the board, body stretched and tight. Group A spotters lift the leg of the gymnast on their respective sides up and into B, whose hands grasp the gymnast's hip bones. Group A continues to lift and rotate the girl about B's point of rotation onto the horse. As the vaulter reaches the inverted position on

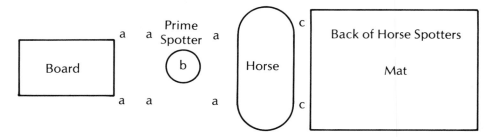

Figure 4.9 • Handspring vault (progression #6)

the horse, the group C spotters grasp her upper arms with the hands that are closer to the horse. Their free hands are placed in the small of the girl's back. These spotters try to prevent hyperextension of the gymnast's back and hold her until she has landed and lost all momentum. If the gymnast is large, she may be asked to jump up from the board. Once the gymnast has completed this progression, she takes three or four steps of an easy run, scoot step and the spotters carry her through the vault as before. Eventually the run can be increased and the spotters decreased. Members of group A and finally all of group A can be eliminated, followed by one from group C, so that only one spotter remains in front of the horse. This is the proper spotting for the handspring vault.

7. The trampoline is very helpful for teaching body tightness and positioning during postflight after the gymnast has learned to invert herself onto the horse. The horse is placed next to the trampoline with a board in front of it and mats covering the cables of the trampoline. The vaulter runs, takes off from the board, inverts onto the horse, repulses the horse by blocking her shoulders, and lands in a perfectly tight layout position on her back on the trampoline (Fig. 4.10). All of the vaulter's body parts should strike the trampoline simultaneously if she is in the proper position (STG).

Figure 4.10 • Handspring vault (progression #7)

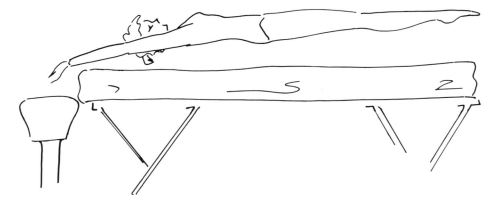

Corrections:

1. The approach and run are critical to the vault itself; thus the coach should listen closely to the rhythm of the run. Any unevenness, heavy flat-footed running, or smaller/shorter steps close to the horse should be corrected. Some girls run as though they were working in a vineyard and were paid according to the number of grapes they trampled on the runway. Other girls look like they are out of step in a marching band, and try as they may, they cannot get on the proper foot as they approach the horse. Sometimes vaulters think they are sprinting, but in reality, they are just chugging along. The coach or spotter can race them back to their starting position with surprising results.

2. Try to keep the scoot step relatively long and low. It may help to place a chalk line or a piece of tape on the runway six feet or so from the board to indicate the placement of the last step prior to the scoot step. The gymnast should be encouraged to get off the board as fast as possible so as to get the benefit of the limited and quick action of the board. It should be noted where the feet hit the board. Some girls lose power because they are too far back on the board. Slipping off the end of the board tends to smart the feet. The ideal placement of the feet is in the upper middle of the board.

3. Low onflight can occur if the gymnast does not block her feet in ahead of the hips and consequently leans forward off the board (Fig. 4.11), if arm delivery or reach for the horse from the board is incomplete, piking in the hips occurs off the board, the run is poor, the board is too close to the horse, or the gymnast has a loose body (in other words, the legs separate and a banana back is obvious).

4. Signs that the gymnast is staying on the horse too long include: a loose body, arched back, and bent elbows; and no repulsion of the horse by blocking the

Figure 4.11 • Correction #3 (a) correct and (b) incorrect

shoulders. A technique that might help the vaulter feel the blocking she needs to do in her shoulders can be accomplished by the two spotters. The shoulders of the vaulter will be ahead of her hands and the spotter should use the hand closer to the horse to push backward near the top of the shoulder. By applying force to prevent the gymnast's shoulders from moving forward, the spotter artificially blocks the shoulders so that the gymnast's body will rise up and out on the off-side of the horse (See Fig. 4.12).

5. An improper landing, the inability to stop momentum in control or in balance or to stick a vault can be due to: arching the body in flight; not bending the knees upon landing; tucking the head; piking at the waist; not anticipating the landing; and lack of discipline in sticking. The discipline of sticking can be practiced by standing on the horse and jumping down onto the mat—STICK! Twenty repetitions of this exercise at the end of practice will prove helpful. The same skill should be done from the beam, trampoline, and low bar of the unevens. The coach cannot compromise; she must expect and demand the execution of a perfect stick every time during warm-up vaults (squats), practice of inverted vaults, practice sticking, and so on. In order to do a stick vault in competition it is necessary to perform it consistently enough in practice so

Figure 4.12 • Correction #4

that it is rote. The effort to stick every time requires much discipline on the part of the coach and gymnast. (See Fig. 4.13).

Spotting: The spotting positions for all vaults are basically the same. The necessity for good spotting cannot be overemphasized.

1. One spotter stands between the horse and the board and faces the vaulter. Her task is to see that the gymnast goes up and rotates; she is responsible for the gymnast until her hands touch the horse. The spotter places her hands on the gymnast's hips when she reaches the board and lifts, or directs, the gymnast's body up and over herself (spotter). After a few such vaults, the spotter can move to the side of the board and, standing sideways, reach in to lift the front of the hips. As the gymnast and coach become more confident about the performance, this spotter can continue to move further and further away (Fig. 4.14). According to FIG rules, a spotter may not stand between the board and the horse during competition. Perhaps this rule should be suspended locally in competition involving beginning and intermediate teams for the safety of the gymnasts. Suspension of the rule does not give coaches carte blanche to encourage unethical lifting.

   The spotting technique discussed initially may help experienced vaulters who are reaching for the horse and have low onflight. Having the spotter stand in front of the horse encourages the gymnast to go up and over the spotter; if she does not, both the gymnast and the spotter will become integral parts of the horse. Accomplished vaulters need this spotter only in warm-up and review during practice.

Figure 4.13 • (left) "Stick"
Figure 4.14 • (right) Front handspring vault onflight with spot

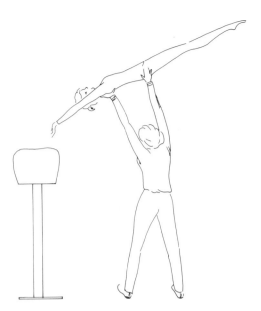

Figure 4.15 • (left) Afterflight spot
Figure 4.16 • (right) Front handspring vault afterflight with spot

2. The other spotter stands sideways behind the horse but in close enough proximity to be able to comfortably place the hand closer to the horse on the upper arm of the vaulter (see Figs. 4.15 and 4.16). Her other hand is placed in the small of the gymnast's back; once the feet of the vaulter have touched the mat this hand is quickly shifted to the front of the waist to help arrest forward movement. The need for this spot lessens as the gymnast becomes more proficient but is usually employed during the warm-up and practice. Gradually the spotter steps back further and further away from the vaulter.

The main objective of spotting this event is to see that the feet of the vaulter are under her. Again, any girl who is relatively strong, has kinesthetic awareness, and the ability to tighten her body can perform inverted vaults with proper coaching, which partially entails the coach's belief that the girl can do it. The handspring can be a gorgeous vault when the gymnast flies through the air, for the whole vault continues from beginning to end in the same visual path. For this reason, the handspring vault is relatively easy to judge and one can readily identify errors. Therefore, the learning process should encourage and emphasize proper form and technique.

Yamashita

Many skills in gymnastics are named for the individuals who introduced them. This vault is named after an excellent Japanese male gymnast who first performed it in competition.

The yamashita vault is a handspring vault with a pike and opening in the

130

Figure 4.17 • Yamashita

off-flight (Fig. 4.17). The approach and takeoff for this vault are the same as for the handspring vault, the only difference being a lower onflight or a smaller angle of the body with the floor while on the horse (approximately 135°). A slight piking in the hips occurs as the stretched body leaves the board so that the gymnast assumes a slight pike as the hands reach the horse. The gymnast should think of this piking as a lifting of the chest to the knees. The pike assumed as the body passes over the horse should be less than 90°, approximating 45°. Shoulder blocking is the same as in the handspring, and as repulsion of the horse occurs, the back is parallel to the floor. The body is forcefully laid out, or extended, without arching. The gymnast should concentrate on lifting her chest. Her back should be parallel to the floor when she assumes the layout position. She lands her body (completely open) at the vertical, utilizing vaulting landing techniques (see handspring vault). The piking and extending of the body at the proper time causes the body to rise (as in a kip on the bars) so that the height and distance of the off-flight exceed that of a handspring vault. Again, proper form and technique include: straight arms and legs, legs together, and straight back. The head position throughout the vault is neither tucked nor extended but remains neutral. The judges are looking for good flight, good pike, complete opening, and a controlled landing.

Teaching techniques and progressions:

1. A handspring vault is the progression, or prerequisite, for a yamashita, although there are gymnasts who will be able to perform a yamashita better than a handspring.

2. The gymnast assumes a supine position on the mat. She pikes by lifting her chest and legs simultaneously and then extending without slapping the floor

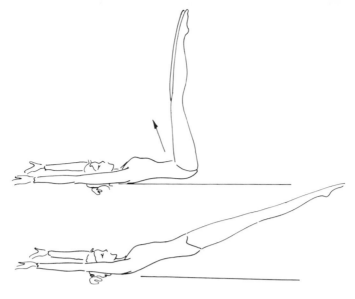

Figure 4.18 • Yamashita (progression #2)

(Fig. 4.18). The pike and extension should be done very quickly to give the gymnast the kinethesis of the yamashita action. This exercise also is appropriate as a general conditioner for the abdominal and back muscles.

3. The vault can then be attempted by trampoline vaulting for both on and postflight with good spotting (see handspring vault). When working on the postflight, the gymnast must strive for an opened and stretched body just prior to landing in layout on the trampoline.

Corrections:

1. Corrections 1 through 5 for *handspring vault* (see previous corrections list) also apply to the yamashita.

2. Common errors in the performance of the yamashita are: starting the pike too

Figure 4.19 • Yamashita with spot

late, taking too much time to complete the whole yamashita action (it should be over very quickly), and not opening the body prior to landing.

Spotting:

1. One spotter stands between the horse and the board facing the vaulter. Her task is to see that the gymnast goes up and rotates; she is responsible for the gymnast until her hands touch the horse. The spotter places her hands on the gymnast's hips when she reaches the board and lifts or directs the gymnast's body up and over herself (spotter). After a few such vaults, the spotter can move to the side of the board and, standing sideways, reach in to lift the front of the hips. As the gymnast and coach become more confident about the performance, this spotter can move further and further away.

2. The other spotter stands sideways behind the horse but in close enough proximity to be able to comfortably place the hand closer to the horse on the upper arm of the vaulter (Fig. 4.19). Her other hand is placed in the small of the gymnast's back; when the feet of the vaulter touch the mat, this hand is quickly shifted to the front of the waist to help arrest forward movement. The need for this spot lessens as the gymnast becomes more proficient but is usually employed during the warm-up and practice. Gradually, the spotter steps back further and further away from the vaulter.

3. A spotting technique that will help the gymnast feel the opening or extension phase of the yamashita vault calls for the two spotters standing on the back side of the horse to place the hands closer to the horse on the gymnast's shoulder blades (scapula). Their other hands push up on the gymnast's back

Figure 4.20 • Yamashita with spot #3

just on and above the glutes (Fig. 4.20). This force suspends the gymnast in the horizontal position, back parallel to the floor and forces her to extend or open the vault.

Yamashita with Half Twist, Full Twist, or More

When the gymnast can perform the yamashita vault, she can add a twist to the vault in the off-flight just as the body is completing the extension, or yamashita, action. The twist is primarily a modern twist initiated through the extension in the hips and then the shoulders. (For a detailed explanation of the twisting action, see Chapter 2). It is important to complete both the opening of the yamashita vault and the twist before landing the vault.

Teaching techniques and progressions:

1. The progression or prerequisite for a yamashita vault with a twist is a yamashita.
2. The gymnast assumes a supine position, pikes by lifting her chest and legs simultaneously, and extends without slapping the floor. As she is completing the extension, the gymnast does a half turn into a facedown position.
3. The vault can then be attempted from a trampoline with good spotting (see handspring vault). In the postflight trampoline work, to practice a half twist the vaulter should open, half twist, and land in a front drop on the trampoline.

Corrections and suggestions:

1. The run and approach given in detail for the yamashita and handspring vaults apply to this vault. The coach should briefly evaluate:
   a. The dynamics of the run.
   b. The scoot step.
   c. The angle of the body on the board.
   d. Body tightness off the board.
   e. Angle of the body on the horse.
   f. Shoulder repulsion.
   g. The length of time in pike position.
2. Common errors occurring in the afterflight with the twists can be identified and corrected by noting:
   a. The quickness of the yamashita.
   b. The angle of the pike in the hips (must be at least 90° flexion).
   c. Whether piking occurs early enough.
   d. Whether the twist is complete; correct:
      i. Late initiation of the twist.
      ii. A twist that is too slow due to loose body—legs apart and arms outward (this error defies the principle of increasing rotation by shortening the radius of rotation).
3. Encourage the landing of the vault with a stick.

Spotting:

1. The spotting for this vault is the same as the spotting for the yamashita until the twist occurs. One spotter in front of the horse lifts the gymnast by the hips onto the horse.

2. To spot the twist, one of the spotters behind the horse at the side away from the direction of the twist reaches with the hand closer to the horse under the vaulter's hips and grabs the hip that is further from her. Her other hand grabs the hip closer to her. The spotter then helps the gymnast twist by pulling with the hand that is under the hips and pushing with the hand on the near hip. If the gymnast is twisting toward the spotter, the hand positions are the opposite, with the arm and hand closer to the horse on the near hip of the gymnast. The other arm and hand reaches in front of the gymnast to the far side of the hip. The outstretched arm pulls while the near arm pushes away, twisting the gymnast. The twist should be either a half or one full turn. The spotter must know the intended direction of the twist.

3. The third spotter helps with the landing by positioning herself behind and on the opposite side of the mat from the spotter who is twisting the gymnast. If the gymnast is doing a half twist she will land facing the horse, so this spotter's arms must be in front of and behind the gymnast's waist to prevent her from falling backwards. If the gymnast is doing a full twist, the spotter's arms must be in the same position, but the gymnast will be facing away from the horse and the spot usually prevents a forward fall upon landing. This spotter can and should also make sure the half or full twist has been completed so that no sideward landing occurs.

Handspring with Half Twist, Full Twist, or More

The techniques used in the handspring vault apply to the preflight for this vault. As the action of the shoulders and wrists of the vaulter repulse the horse, the twist is initiated through the hips and shoulders in a combination of the classic and modern twists (see discussion of twisting in Chapter 2). The twist should be completed before the feet touch the mat. (Fig. 4.21).

Teaching techniques and procedures:

1. The handspring with half twist is a relatively easy vault to do. As a matter of fact, a gymnast who "chickens out" of a handspring vault will often perform this vault. The consequence of this action is a "pancaked" twist, which looks somewhat like a poorly done roundoff on the floor. Therefore a suggested progression is for the gymnast to perform a slow handspring, pushing her body up and away with a half twist on the mat, or she may kick a handstand at the edge of a crash pad and, as she passes the perpendicular, she twists while falling into the mat. She should land on her front for a half twist and on her back for a full twist.

2. A handspring vault is the prerequisite for either vault.

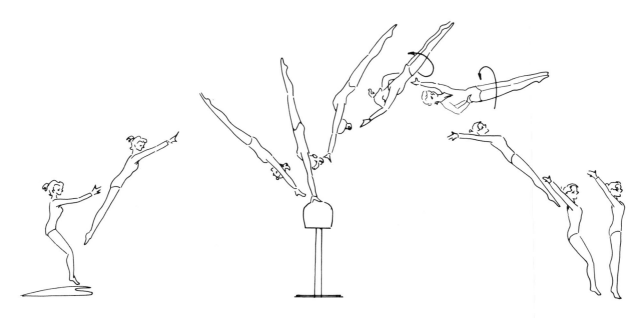

Figure 4.21 • Handspring with half twist, full twist, or more

      3.   The vault can be attempted by trampoline vaulting with good spotting (see handspring vault). When practicing the postflight, the gymnast should land in a front drop on the trampoline for a half twist.

Corrections: 1.   The same corrections apply for the preflight on this vault as for the handspring and yamashita. Briefly evaluate:
    a.   The dynamics of the run.
    b.   The scoot step.
    c.   The angle of the body on the board.
    d.   Body tightness off the board.
    e.   Angle of the body on the horse.
    f.   Shoulder repulsion.

     2.   Common errors occurring in the afterflight with the twists are:
    a.   Twisting too early or while still on the horse. Look for:
       i.   No repulsion
      ii.   A pancake twist.
     iii.   Hands leaving the horse alternately resulting in an obvious bent elbow of the last arm to leave the horse.
    b.   Incomplete twist. Look for:
       i.   Late twist initiation.
      ii.   No repulsion for off-flight.
     iii.   A twist that is too slow due to loose body, legs apart, or arms outward in defiance of the principle of increasing rotation by shortening the radius of rotation.

     3.   Landing the vault with a stick.

Spotting:

The spotting for these vaults is the same as the spotting described for the yamashita with a half or full twist. To review:

1. The spotter on the front side of the horse lifts the gymnast onto the horse by placing her hands on the front of the gymnast's hips.

2. One of the spotters on the back side of the horse twists the gymnast away from her by placing one arm behind the gymnast with her hand on the hip further away from herself. The other hand goes on the side of the hip closer to herself. The outstretched spotting arm pulls while the arm closer to the spotter pushes away. This motion twists the gymnast. To twist the gymnast toward the spotter, the hand positions are the opposite; the arm further from the horse reaches in front of the gymnast and pulls her toward the spotter while the hand closer to the horse pushes the other hip away. Obviously, the spotters must know the intended direction of the twist.

3. The third spotter helps with the landing by positioning herself behind and on the opposite side of the mat from the spotter who is twisting the gymnast. If the gymnast does a half twist, she will land facing the horse, so the spotters arms must be in front of and behind the gymnast's waist preventing her from falling backwards. If the gymnast does a full twist, the spotter positions her arms the same way, but because the gymnast will be facing away from the horse, the spot usually prevents a forward fall upon landing. This spotter can and should also make sure the half or full twist has been completed so that no sideward landings occur.

Handspring/ One and a Half Somersaults

This is an extremely *difficult* vault and should be attempted only by a good, talented, and experienced vaulter (one who scores consistently in the range 8.8 and up) with two or three well-skilled and experienced spotters. The vaulter uses the same approach as for the handspring vault, although the angle of her onflight onto the horse is less than that of a handspring. The repulsion from the horse is quite early and powerful so that the afterflight will have as much height and distance as possible. The vaulter then completes one and a half rotations of a front somersault in tuck (shorter radius of rotation) or pike (Fig. 4.22). The vault is landed back to the horse, in balance, with a stick.

Teaching techniques and procedures:

1. The prerequisite for this vault is the ability to do a front handspring, front somersault on the floor. The tumbling combination is quite similar in movement and movement path to the vault, the major differences being that the somersault in the vault is initiated from the handstand and is one and a half rotations whereas in a front handspring, front somersault the initiation is from the feet and only one rotation occurs. (For a description of the front handspring, front somersault tumbling combination, see Chapter 3.)

2. The gymnast should understand and be able to attain good afterflight by repulsing the horse as in other vaults.

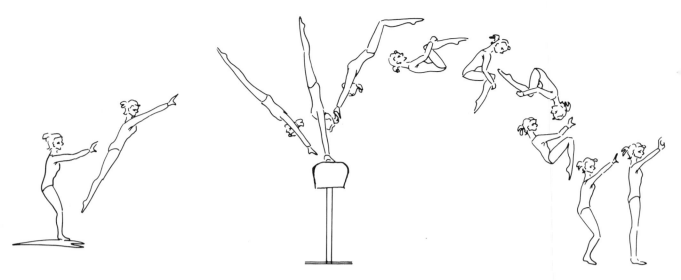

Figure 4.22 • Handspring with one and a half somersaults

3. The vault can be attempted by trampoline vaulting for both on- and off-flight (see handspring vault). It is further suggested that the trampoline be placed under an overhead spotting rig and that the gymnast be placed in a spotting belt attached to the rig. Good spotting is essential for this vault. The postflight practice should include horse repulsion and rotation to landing on the feet (180°), then a front drop (almost 360°), and then to a backdrop (almost 540°). When a vaulter can accomplish the last rotation, she will easily perform the skill during the vault.

Corrections:
1. The same corrections apply for the preflight phase of this vault as for the previous vaults. The coach should briefly evaluate:
   a. The dynamics of the run.
   b. The scoot step.
   c. The angle of the body on the board.
   d. Body tightness off the board.
   e. Angle of the body on the horse.
   f. Shoulder repulsion.

2. Specific corrections for this vault include insuring:
   a. Lower onflight.
   b. Repulsion of the horse, beginning the rotation early (just prior to reaching a perpendicular position on the horse).
   c. A tighter tuck and more height in the off-flight if rotation is incomplete (to increase rotation and shorten the radius of rotation).
   d. The opening and stretch of the body at the completion of one and a half revolutions.
   e. A stick landing (no tucked head).

Spotting:
1. The spotting described for this vault can be used during the mimetic progression with the trampoline and for performance on the actual horse vault.

a. The spotter (#1) on the preflight side of the horse assures that the gymnast reaches the horse by lifting the gymnast onto the horse without increasing the angle of her preflight.

b. One of the spotters (#2) on the back side of the horse stands sideways close to the horse and gymnast and quickly reaches in as the gymnast's hands touch the horse to lift up under the shoulder of the gymnast and give her as much height and lift in off-flight as possible. This spot provides the gymnast with more time in flight to accomplish the rotations necessary to the vault.

c. Another spotter (#3) stands sideways, behind and on the opposite side from spotter (#2). She aids the vaulter's rotation by helping to keep her in the air and quickly placing and moving her hands from the back to the hips. If she can reach in, the spot then becomes similar to the spot for the front somersault. The arm closer to the gymnast and horse reaches in front of the gymnast's waist to become the axis of rotation. The other hand reaches for the upper mid-back and turns the gymnast so that her glutes (at least) or feet are under her.

d. A fourth spotter (#4) on the same side as spotter #2 but further away from the horse assists with the landing of the gymnast by stopping forward momentum as the gymnast's feet touch the floor.

e. While practicing on the trampoline with overhead spotting rig, an experienced handler of the ropes and rig should be involved. Only *accomplished* gymnasts and coaches should attempt this vault. To increase the difficulty of this vault, add a twist (half or full) to the somersault during the off-flight.

Cartwheels

In the next family of vaults the body sails through the side plane in the onflight. These vaults are commonly called "cartwheels" or "quarter ons." This form of vaulting requires a twist (turn about the vertical axis of the body). Emphasis again is on preventing the gymnast from landing in the side plane and thereby decreasing the potential for knee and ankle injury. It is for this reason that the following vaults are not discussed or recommended in this text: cartwheel; quarter twist (cartwheel), half twist; quarter twist (cartwheel), full twist; and quarter twist (cartwheel), one and a half side somersault.

Quarter Twist/Quarter Twist or Three-quarter Twist

The approach to the horse is the same as that for the handspring: a good powerful run, knees high in the beginning; proper scoot step onto the board; arms delivered so that the body is completely stretched and tight as it leaves the board. The quarter twist on is primarily a classic twist; the three-quarter twist off is a classic and modern twist. (See Chapter 2 for an explanation of twists.) Therefore the quarter twist begins as the feet leave the board. As the gymnast's body rotates and lands on the horse, the body angle with the floor is between 135° and 160° (Fig. 4.23). There should be an alternate hand placement in which the fingers of the hand face sideways on the horse (as in a cartwheel on the floor). The repulsion is

Figure 4.23 • (left) Quarter onflight
Figure 4.24 • (right) Quarter off

accomplished by blocking the shoulders as in the previously described inverted vaults. As the body leaves the horse, the wrists extend and initiate the quarter twist (or three-quarter twist), as shown in Fig. 4.24. The flight is directed up and out so that the rotation and twist occur prior to the vertical ascent of the body for a balanced stick landing in which the gymnast squarely faces the direction of the run with her back to the horse.

Teaching techniques and progressions:

1. A cartwheel with a quarter twist (easier) or three-quarter twist out performed on the floor is a progression to the performance of the vault. This progression provides the gymnast with the kinesthesis of body positioning throughout the vault.

2. The gymnast may perform a cartwheel with a quarter twist or three-quarter twist out at the edge of a "crash pad" so that she finishes in a back drop into the mat. The whole body should strike the mat at once if her body is completely stretched (not arched or piked).

3. The vault can be attempted by trampoline vaulting for on- and off-flight with good spotting (see handspring vault). The postflight includes landing on the back on the trampoline.

Corrections:

1. The same corrections and techniques apply for the run and scoot step in this vault as in the handspring. Briefly evaluate:
   a. The dynamics of the run.
   b. The scoot step.
   c. The angle of the body on the board.
   d. Body tightness off the board.

140

     e.   Angle of the body on the horse.

     f.   Shoulder repulsion.

2.   The most frequent errors in this vault are:

     a.   An incomplete twist in the onflight because of lack of flight or because the gymnast reaches for the horse too soon.

     b.   A shortened on- and off-flight caused by dropping the first hand onto the horse. As in the handspring, the upper arms should remain in contact with the head just slightly in front of the ears.

     c.   Incorrect hand placement. Alternate hand placement is considered proper technique for this vault.

     d.   Incorrectly pointed fingers. Fingers of the hands should point sideways while in contact with the horse. The hands should be placed directly in the middle of the horse at a midpoint between where the pommels would be. If the gymnast chalks her hands prior to vaulting, she will leave an accurate indication of her hand placement on the horse.

     e.   Turning the head down to look for the horse in the onflight. The head position should remain constant, as in a cartwheel or side handstand.

     f.   Improper passage over the horse. The gymnast's body should be perpendicular to the horse during flight. A coach or other gymnast should stand squarely and way behind the horse to evaluate this portion of the vault. Common causes of this error include:

       i.   Arching the back.

      ii.   Pancaking the vault (Fig. 4.25) by piking in the hips or by reaching, changing the angle of the shoulders and placing the hands to the side of the horse (hand placement should be in the middle of the horse).

Figure 4.25 • Pancaking a quarter on

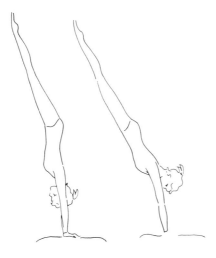

Figure 4.26 • (left) Spotter's hand placement for twist (spot #1)
Figure 4.27 • (middle) Quarter off with spot #2
Figure 4.28 • (right) Three-quarter off with spot #2

3. Flat, low, and short off-flight and an incomplete twist upon landing. Corrections are:
   a. Repulsion of the horse.
   b. Blocking the shoulders.
   c. Alternating wrist extension (hand release), which causes the body to rise while the gymnast completes the quarter or three-quarter twist; elbow bending of the arm of the second hand to leave the horse indicates poor and improper shoulder repulsion.

4. Uncontrolled landings, caused by:
   a. A loose body, which prevents completion of the twist (whether quarter or three-quarter).
   b. Tucking the head to see the landing area.
   c. Lack of height in off-flight, which inhibits a vertical landing with proper body alignment, knees bending upon landing, and STG.

Spotting:
1. The spotter (#1) stands on the preflight side of the horse, places her hands on the front of the gymnast's hip bones, and turns her a quarter of a twist as she helps lift her in the preflight onto the horse (Fig. 4.26).

2. The next spotter (#2) to touch the gymnast aids in the off-flight by positioning herself on the back side of the horse (Fig. 4.27 and 4.28). Standing sideways, she places her hands on the gymnast's sides just below the waist. This is a difficult spot. The spotter must reach up quickly. Since the body is in the side plane as it leaves the horse, one hand will be up and the other hand down. The spotter helps the vaulter to twist a quarter or three-quarters of a turn. She supports the gymnast's back and makes certain that the vaulter will land facing forward and not sideways, thus preventing injury. Just as the gymnast's feet touch the mat, the spotter shifts one of her arms to the front of the

142

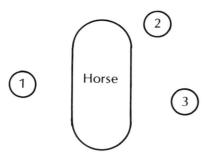

Figure 4.29 • Spotter's placement during quarter on

gymnast's waist; the other hand remains behind her waist to help eliminate and prevent further forward movement.

3. A third spotter may be assigned to aid with the landing. She stands to the side at the approximate landing place (see Fig. 4.29) and reaches in naturally at this final stage of the vault.

Quarter Twist/One and a Half Back Somersaults (Tsukahara)

Like the half twist, one and a half back somersaults and handspring/one and a half front somersault, this vault is an *extremely difficult* vault that only a good, talented, and experienced vaulter (who scores consistently in the range 8.8 and up) should attempt with two or three well-skilled and experienced spotters. The vaulter uses the same approach as that for the other quarter twist on vaults. The body is completely stretched leaving the board, although the angle of the preflight onto the horse is less than that of a pure quarter twist, quarter twist. The repulsion from the horse is quite early and powerful so that there is as much height and distance

Figure 4.30 • Quarter twist with one and a half back somersaults

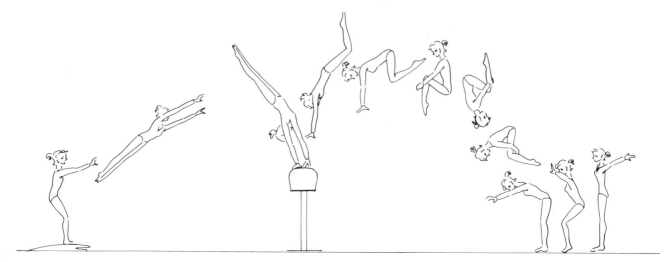

in the afterflight as possible. As she leaves the horse, the vaulter completes one and a half rotations of a back somersault in tuck (easier) or pike or layout position and lands facing the horse, in balance, with a stick (Fig. 4.30).

Teaching techniques and progressions:

1. The prerequisite to performing this vault is the ability to do a roundoff high back somersault on the floor (see Chapter 3). This tumbling combination is quite similar in movement and movement path to the vault. The major differences between these skills are that the somersault in the vault is initiated from the hands and is one and a half rotations whereas in the tumbling combination the somersault is initiated from the feet and only one rotation is accomplished.

2. The gymnast should understand and be able to attain good afterflight in other vaults through repulsion of the horse.

3. The vault can be attempted by trampoline vaulting for both on- and off-flight (see handspring vault). The off-flight practice involves the gymnast eventually landing in a seat drop (almost 360°) rotation on the trampoline. Then a crash pad can be placed on top of the trampoline: if the gymnast can still land in a seat drop, she can probably do the vault. It is also advisable to place the trampoline under an overhead spotting rig and the gymnast in a twisting spotting belt attached to the rig. Good spotting is essential for this vault.

Corrections:

1. The same corrections apply to the preflight phase of this vault as apply to the other quarter twist on vaults. Observe:
    a. The dynamics of the run.
    b. The scoot step.
    c. The angle of the body on the board.
    d. Body tightness off the board.
    e. Angle of the body on the horse.
    f. Shoulder repulsion.

2. Specific corrections for this vault include insuring:
    a. Lower onflight.
    b. Repulsion of the horse and early rotation (just prior to the moment when the body reaches the perpendicular on the horse).
    c. Height in the off-flight and a tighter tuck or pike if rotation is incomplete (to increase rotation, shorten the radius of rotation).
    d. The opening and stretch of the body at the completion of one and a half revolutions so that a vertical descent occurs.
    e. A stick landing.

Spotting:

The spotting described for this vault can be used during the mimetic progression with the trampoline or the actual horse vault.

1. The spotter (#1) on the preflight side of the horse assures that the gymnast accomplishes the quarter twist and reaches the horse by lifting and twisting

the gymnast onto the horse without increasing the angle of her preflight (see Fig. 4.26).

2. One of the spotters (# 2) on the back side of the horse stands sideways close to the horse and gymnast. She quickly reaches in as the gymnast's hands touch the horse and lifts up under the shoulder of the gymnast in order to give her as much height and lift in the off-flight as possible (thereby providing more time in flight to accomplish the rotation necessary to the vault).

3. Another spotter (# 3) stands sideways opposite spotter # 2 but further away from the horse on the back side. She helps the gymnast to complete the rotation by keeping her in the air and spinning her by quickly placing one arm in front of her waist and moving her other hand from the gymnast's hip to her back. The arm closer to the horse is in front of the waist; when the rotation is almost complete, the other arm is in back of the waist finishing the rotation so that the gymnast's feet are under her.

4. A fourth, optional spotter stands on the same side as spotter # 2 but further away from the horse to assist with the landing.

5. During use of the trampoline and overhead spotting rig an experienced handler of the ropes and rig should be present.

Only *accomplished* gymnasts and coaches should attempt this vault. For increased difficulty, the gymnast can add a twist (half or full) to the somersault in the off-flight.

The next family of vaults is similar to the cartwheels except that the body in the preflight makes a half twist (a turn about the vertical axis of the body) moving from the frontal plane through the side plane (cartwheel) into the back plane. These vaults are commonly referred to as half ons/half offs, half ons/full offs, or half ons/one and a half back sommies.

Half Twist/Half Twist or Full Twist

The approach to the horse is the same as in the handspring: good powerful run, knees high in the beginning; proper scoot step onto the board; arms delivered so that the body is completely stretched and tight as the gymnast's feet leave the board. The half twist onto the horse is primarily a classic twist (see explanation of twists in Chapter 2); therefore the twist begins with the push-off the board from the feet. As the gymnast rotates and lands on the horse, the body angle with the floor is approximately 135° to 160° (Fig. 4.31). The half twist is completed as the hands touch the horse in an approximation of a straight handstand. The repulsion of the horse by blocking in the shoulders is the same technique used in all inverted vaults and described in detail in the section of the handspring vault. As the body lifts up and into the air on the off-flight due to the shoulder block, the half twist or full twist off is initiated from the hands and through the hips in a combination of the classic and modern twists (Fig. 4.32). The afterflight is directed up and out so

Figure 4.31 • (left) Half twist on
Figure 4.32 • (right) Half twist off

that the rotation and twist can be accomplished in the air, allowing for a vertical descent of the body for a balanced or stick landing. With a half twist in the off-flight, the vaulter lands with her back to the horse. With a full twist in the off-flight, the vaulter lands facing the horse.

Teaching techniques and progressions:

1. Standing on a crash pad, kicking a handstand with the hands on the floor, and then falling back on the crash pad and doing a half twist and landing in the crash pad on the back with the body perfectly straight will provide the gymnast with the kinesthesis of the twist in the off-flight (Fig. 4.33). The whole body should strike the mat at once if it is completely straight.

2. The gymnast can take a step and do a facsmile of a roundoff but complete a half twist as the hands touch the floor (as in a handstand) next to the crash pad. Then the gymnast falls into the crash pad after completing another half twist to land on her back. The body is totally stretched tight and straight. The whole body will strike the mat at once if it is completely straight. This progression helps the gymnast appreciate the twists that will occur in the vault.

3. Both on- and off-flight techniques for this vault can be attempted on the trampoline with good spotting (see handspring vault). The postflight practice should include landing in a back drop on the trampoline.

Corrections:

1. The same corrections and techniques apply to the run and scoot step in this vault as apply to the handspring. Observe:
   a. The dynamics of the run.

Figure 4.33 • Half twist (progression #1)

      b.   The scoot step.

      c.   The angle of the body on the board.

      d.   Body tightness off the board.

      e.   Angle of the body on the horse.

      f.   Shoulder repulsion.

2. The most frequent errors in the performance of this vault are:

      a.   An incomplete half twist onto the horse due to lack of onflight, loose body off the board, or reaching for the horse too soon.

      b.   Shortened onflight, which results in an incomplete twist. The cause may be that the gymnast is either looking for the horse by turning and/or tucking her head prior to completing the half twist. The head should be kept in alignment with the upper arms and the gymnast should not look at the horse after the twist is begun until the body has twisted and the hands are within proximity of the horse.

      c.   Uneven hand placement, which could be caused by reaching or dropping one arm onto the horse prior to the other, an incomplete turn, or not enough onflight. The gymnast can chalk her hands prior to vaulting so that the imprints left on the horse by her hands will be evidence of her hand placement.

      d.   Passing incorrectly over the horse. The body of the gymnast should pass directly over the middle of the horse and through the vertical. Someone can stand way behind the horse or at the end of the runway and note the following:

          i.   If the gymnast's body is pancaking, her twist is incomplete prior to reaching the horse.

          ii.   If the onflight is too low, completion of the half twist may not be possible.

      e.   Low and flat off-flight and incomplete twist in off-flight. The gymnast may not be repulsing the horse through the shoulders.

      f.   Elbow bends, which may indicate that the gymnast has not pushed off the horse and twisted but has attempted to twist prior to complete repulsion.

      g.   Uncontrolled landings, which may be due to a loose body and/or not allowing for completion of the twist, whether half or full; tucking the head during the completion of the half twist in off-flight can also cause additional forward momentum or no stick. A lack of repulsion from the horse will cause flat and low off-flight, which, in turn, will prevent the feet from landing under the center of gravity (vertical landing) and force the gymnast to take steps.

Spotting:

1. Standing on the preflight side of the horse, the spotter (#1) places her hands on the front of the gymnast's hip bones and turns her through half a twist as she helps lift her in the preflight onto the horse.

2. The next spotter (#2) aids with the off-flight by positioning herself on the back

side of the horse and standing sideways. She places her hands on the gymnast's sides just below the waist. This is a difficult spot; the spotter must stretch up quickly. Since the body is in the back plane as it leaves the horse, this spotter can reach up and over her own shoulders with her back slightly to the horse. She helps the vaulter to twist either a half twist or a full twist. She supports the gymnast as she helps her twist. If the gymnast is doing a half twist off, the spotter continues to support the back with one arm; with the other arm she reaches in front of the gymnast to help arrest forward momentum. If the gymnast is doing a full twist off, the spotter continues to support the back (waist) with one arm. The other arm is in front of the gymnast's waist and helps arrest backward momentum upon landing.

3. A third spotter (# 3) can be assigned to aid with the landing. She stands to the side at the approximate landing place and reaches in naturally at the final stage of the vault. This spotter should try to insure that the vaulter lands either facing the horse or with her back to the horse rather than sideways. A sideways landing can occur as a result of an incomplete twist in the afterflight.

Half Twist/One and a Half Back Somersaults (tuck or pike)

This vault is an *extremely difficult* one that only a good, talented, and experienced vaulter (who scores consistently in the range 8.8 and up) should attempt. Two or three well-skilled and experienced spotters should be present. This vault is very much like the quarter twist, one and a half back somersault (Tsukahara) vault. All of the techniques are the same except that the preflight includes a half twist instead of a quarter twist. The decision to perform a half on or a quarter on depends upon which twist is more natural for the gymnast, which twist will allow the maximum repulsion from the horse, and which twist is easier to follow with a somersault. This decision is purely an individual one. However, it is important for the coach to correctly announce the vault to be performed so that the gymnast does not incur a penalty for performing a vault that was not announced. The

Figure 4.34 • Half twist with one and a half back somersaults

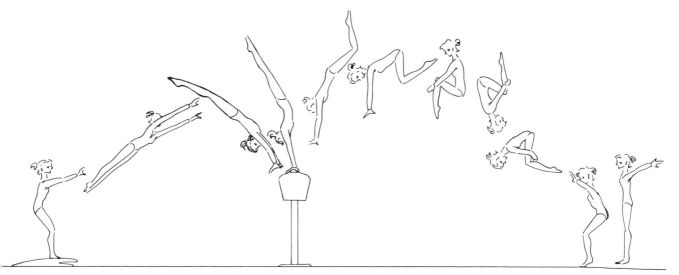

detailed description for this vault can be found in the description of the quarter twist, one and a half back somersault. The progressions and teaching techniques, corrections, and spotting are the same, except that the gymnast twists a half turn about the vertical axis of the body rather than a quarter twist (Fig. 4.34).

Teaching techniques and progressions:

1. The prerequisite to performing this vault is the ability to do a roundoff high back somersault on the floor (see Chapter 3). This tumbling combination is quite similar in movement and movement path to the vault. The major differences between these skills are that the somersault in the vault is initiated from the hands and is one and a half rotations, whereas in the tumbling combination, the somersault is initiated from the the feet and the gymnast executes only one rotation.

2. The gymnast should understand and be able to attain good afterflight in other vaults by repulsion of the horse.

3. Both on- and off-flight techniques for this vault can be attempted on the trampoline (see handspring vault). To practice off-flight the gymnast strives to land in a seat drop (almost 360°) rotation on the trampoline. Then a crash pad can be placed on top of the trampoline; if the gymnast can still land in a seat drop, she can probably do the vault. It is further advisable to place the trampoline under an overhead spotting rig and the gymnast in a twisting spotting belt attached to the rig. Good spotting is essential for this vault.

Corrections:

1. The same corrections apply to the preflight phase of this vault as apply to the other half twist on vaults. Look for errors in:
   a. The dynamics of the run.
   b. The scoot step.
   c. The angle of the body on the board.
   d. Body tightness off the board.
   e. Angle of the body on the horse.
   f. Shoulder repulsion.

2. Specific corrections for this vault include insuring:
   a. Lower onflight.
   b. Early repulsion of the horse and early rotation (just prior to the moment the body reaches the perpendicular on the horse).
   c. More height in the off-flight and a tighter tuck or pike if rotation is incomplete (to increase rotation, shorten the radius of rotation).
   d. The opening and stretch of the body at the completion of one and a half revolutions so that a vertical descent occurs.
   e. A stick landing.

Spotting:

The spotting described for this vault can be used during the mimetic progression with the trampoline or the actual horse vault.

1. The spotter (# 1) on the preflight side of the horse assures that the gymnast accomplishes the half twist and reaches the horse by lifting and twisting the gymnast onto the horse without increasing her preflight angle.

2. One of the spotters (# 2) to the rear of the horse stands sideways close to the horse and gymnast. She quickly reaches in as the gymnast's hands touch the horse and lifts up under the shoulder of the gymnast in order to give her as much height and lift in the off-flight as possible (thereby providing more time in flight to accomplish the rotation necessary for the vault).

3. Another spotter (# 3) stands sideways opposite spotter # 2 but farther behind the horse and helps the gymnast complete the rotation by keeping her in the air and spinning her by quickly placing one arm in front of her waist and moving her other hand from the gymnast's hip to her back. The arm closer to the horse is in front of the waist; when the rotation is almost complete, the other arm should be in back of the waist finishing the rotation so that the gymnast's feet will be under her.

4. An optional, fourth spotter stands on the same side as spotter # 2 but further away from the horse to assist with the landing.

5. An experienced handler of the ropes and rig should be present during practice on the trampoline with an overhead spotting rig.

Hecht

An old and rarely performed vault is the hecht. This vault is not an inverted vault: the front of the body passes over the horse. With a good run, the gymnast scoots onto the board without a back lean. The body lean on the board should be just about perpendicular. The gymnast's body begins to rotate and achieves a greater than horizontal angle with the floor (her hips are slightly higher than her head). She affects a slight pike in the hips. The hands touch the horse simultaneously and the upper arms are at a right angle to the body. The gymnast forcefully lifts her chest and head and eliminates the pike in her hips as she blocks or repulses the horse with the same technique used in the handspring vault. The body then rises during the afterflight as the front of it passes over the horse. The gymnast lands the vault in a stick (Fig. 4.35).

Teaching techniques and progressions:

1. The prerequisite for this vault is the performance of the layout squat vault with much height in the off-flight.

2. It might help the gymnast to perform a hecht on the unevens first so that she may be aware of the action of dynamically piking (flexing) and extending in the hips.

3. The horse should be at regulation height for this vault. The gymnast lands in a crash pad.

Corrections:

1. A good run is essential.

2. If the preflight angle is not greater than the horizontal, perhaps the board

Figure 4.35 • Hecht

should be moved back or the gymnast is reaching for the horse with her hands before her feet have left the board (Fig. 4.36).

3. Lack of body rise in the off-flight could be due to:
   a. Elbow bending during the support phase.
   b. Poor timing of the pike and extension in the hips.
   c. The pike and extension not being explosive and quick enough.
   d. Failure to block the shoulders and repulse the horse.
   e. Failure to raise or lift the chest and head during the extension of the body.

Spotting:
1. Two spotters stand sideways facing each other on the back side of the horse. They spot the afterflight. The hands closer to the horse grasp the back of the gymnast's waist. The other arms reach in front of the gymnast's waist and help to raise her upward so that her landing will be vertical.

Figure 4.36 • Hecht arm delivery

This vault is extremely interesting and effective. Very few American women gymnasts use it as a part of their vaulting repertoire. Performed correctly, it is a difficult vault, although most gymnasts should be able to accomplish it in a moderate way. To add variety, the gymnast may include a combination classic and modern twist (see Chapter 2) at the completion of the hecht in the after-flight. Girls who have real problems inverting during vaulting may have success with this vault.

PSYCHOLOGY OF COACHING AND PERFORMING SIDE HORSE VAULTING

In Chapter 1 it was stated that the vaulter must attempt to assume the state of mind of the Japanese kamikaze pilots in World War II. These flyers knew only how to takeoff and not how to land. The vaulter must approach the horse with the same dedication; her one mission is all-out 100 percent effort on the run. Once the vaulter has begun to run, there is no turning back. It is important in all gymnastics skills that once a gymnast has initiated a skill she must finish it, both for her own safety and her spotter's. After she has started a skill, the gymnast cannot validly or accurately evaluate, make changes, and so on, without endangering herself or her spotter, who is anticipating certain movements. The gymnast must completely understand and attempt to be faithful to this idea. The coach can help the gymnast understand these concepts by rigidly enforcing, demanding, and expecting their demonstration:

1. After the vault run has begun, the gymnast vaults without equivocation. Some coaches permit their gymnasts to "balk." A vaulting balk occurs when the vaulter starts her run and then swerves off the runway or board and doesn't vault. This is a bad habit to develop, for if the gymnast balks in practice, she will do it in a meet. Balking can shake her confidence and destroy her concentration as well as the coach's patience. In a meet, only one aborted vaulting attempt is allowed per vault. If the gymnast touches the horse and then balks, she will receive a zero score for the vault. This is an extremely high price to pay purely for a lack of total commitment. The vaulter must run as hard and as fast as she can, in control, if she is to fly over the horse: the side horse will not part and divide for the gymnast as the Red Sea did for Moses. Moreover, if the vaulter is able to swerve off the runway, she is not running with the desire and commitment (mental discipline) that good vaulting requires.

2. When the vaulter leaves the board, her body should be as tight as possible. She must not "choke" or "chicken out." Her performance should be good if she understands that she must follow through in order to prevent injury to herself and, more importantly, to her spotter. The spotter has a preconceived idea of the vault's direction and a plan for spotting it. If the vaulter alters what the spotter expects, the spotter might not be able to get out of the way of swinging arms, legs, or body changes and might get hurt herself so that she will be unable to spot the gymnast properly. Spotting vaulting is a relatively

easy skill if the vaulter's body is kept *tight*. A tight body is much easier to turn because it does not require as much strength on the part of the spotter. Thus, a tight body likewise is in the gymnast's best interest. If the gymnast has confidence in her spotter, she will more likely follow through with the skill as planned rather than spot herself by attempting to change the original plan of movement when she feels she is going to have or is having difficulty. Confidence in the spotter develops over a period of time and only after the spotter has demonstrated her concentration, her desire to be in the proper position, and her determination to place some part of her body between the gymnast and a fall or the mat.

Vaulting must be practiced regularly, on a minimum of three out of five days, although it is more beneficial to practice this event daily. It is best for the coach/spotter to work with six to eight girls at a time. The vaulter should take a few warm-up vaults (squats, etc.) with sticks, then a few tilts followed by inverted vaults. An average of ten vaults daily should be sufficient. The time spent practicing the vault is probably the briefest practice time of the four events, yet the gymnast must concentrate and take each vault as though she were vaulting in a meet. There are always many distractions in a practice, so it is difficult for a gymnast to concentrate as much as she should on performing each vault perfectly.

Commonly, there is less emphasis on vaulting than on the other three events, yet the vault counts as much scorewise as the other three. The coach's attitude toward vaulting and the degree to which she emphasizes the event can alleviate this problem. The vaulter should be encouraged not to begin her run until she is in total control both mentally and physically.

The evaluation of the vault by the coach and/or spotter should be brief and concise; she should describe one or two corrections that will improve the vault. These corrections should be constructive. The coach/spotter should point out not just what was wrong but also what can be done to correct the errors. Videotaping a vaulting practice every two weeks is also extremely helpful. Sometimes it is necessary to take the gymnast right back to the beginning to improve her technique. If a gymnast is having a particularly frustrating experience during vaulting practice on a given day, she should go to another event. Sometimes we practice incorrect technique very hard so that it becomes habitual and difficult to change. Moving to another event allows the gymnast time before the next workout to pull herself together mentally in preparation to correct the error. The more times we do a skill with poor results, the more we think we can't do it. This kind of thinking raises the frustration level for coach and gymnast extremely high. Why practice errors?

Since vaulting is a mechanical skill, the coaching approach that seems to be most effective is purely factual and mechanical. Therefore, if the coach and gymnast understand and appreciate the body and its possibilities and its limitations and if they have a basic knowledge of biomechanics, learning should be easier and the vaulter's efforts should meet with success.

Because it is worrisome, one of the most difficult assignments for the coach in any of the events is to accurately assess when the gymnast no longer needs spotting. The gymnast cannot be expected to vault well in a meet without a spotter if she has been spotted during every practice. The transition from spotting to nonspotting requires a thorough understanding of the gymnast including a knowledge of her fears, confidence levels, competitive "gutsiness," and skill level. The skill level is the easiest variable to assess, for the lighter the gymnast is in the spotter's hands, the less she needs a spot, and slowly the transition from lift, to touch, to no touch can take place. The spotter should assume the proper spotting position as a precaution even though the gymnast does not expect an actual spot. The spotter has to realize that eventually the umbilical cord must be cut. This process is often a difficult one, the gymnast must be weaned from spotting gradually. Nevertheless the vaulter should have performed sufficiently regularly in practice without a spot to be able to perform in a meet without "choking."

The psychological variables involved in the decision to discontinue spotting are determined by the coach's knowledge of the individual. The more self-confidence the gymnast has, the sooner she can perform alone. The coach's (sincere) confidence in the gymnast and positive reinforcement of the proper skill demonstration will enhance the gymnast's confidence in herself. The gymnast's confidence in the coach, too, is extremely important in allaying her fears, for if she believes the coach who tells her that she can do something alone she will do it. At this point, the coach must be honest and realistic and not a dreamer. Some girls possess a competitive "gutsiness" that most likely developed at a very young age. This quality can be developed further through competitive experiences, beginning at a low level and gradually adding more and more successful experiences. The reality of the situation is that some girls are competitors, but others are not; sometimes it is not evident to the coach who the competitors are until the meet. One poor meet performance is not an indication of a lack of competitiveness at all; just as we all have bad practice days, we all have bad meet days as individuals, coaches, and teams.

Some spotters and coaches like to demonstrate their skill continually by lifting girls through skills they couldn't do alone. This type of spotting is an ego booster for the spotter, who comes to feel indispensable and who also receives a vicarious feeling of achievement from putting the gymnast through the skill. This kind of spotter and/or coach should not participate in women's gymnastics, which is supposed to be a sport for the gymnasts. Generally, this problem primarily affects males in these roles in women's gymnastics. Presumably, this kind of behavior is due to their strength and possibly their cultural roles as protectors of the female and not to their need for ego fulfillment. The female coach seems to be able to handle this weaning process effectively: Is this facility attributable to her expected cultural role? The role of the coach should be that of a catalyst, or facilitator.

One of the functions of a vaulting coach is to devise meet strategies, because there are two vaults and there is a choice of performing the same or different vaults. The coach should encourage the gymnast to perform the first vault as well as possible so that they can choose a second vault. If the vaulter can do only one type of vault, then the choice is limited to either doing the same vault or not taking a second vault. The second vault should be eliminated only if the gymnast is nursing an injury that could be aggravated by vaulting again. Although it is inconvenient, the judges can give an average vault score. With this information the coach and the gymnast can decide if it is necessary to take the second vault. The coach should ask for this information only if necessary (to protect a slightly injured gymnast) for it is a time-consuming process. If the score of the first vault is as expected or desired, the gymnast may try a different vault, one that she has not practiced as much, is newer, not as consistently performed, or more difficult. If dual meet scores are used as a qualifying criterion for individual or team championships, then the conservative approach of insuring at least one good vault score should prevail. If the first score isn't adequate, the gymnast should repeat the same vault. Usually the most consistent vault should be the first vault. This tactic takes the pressure off the gymnast on the second vault and can also serve as incentive: "If the first vault is good, you can do the new vault." The final decision depends not only upon the gymnast's consistency and skill level but also upon the expected closeness of the meet, the order of events, and the gymnast's position in the vaulting lineup. If the meet is expected to be close, then conservatism is advisable; if it is going to be one-sided and not a qualifying event, the gymnast may try the new vault. If the order of events is Olympic order (vault, bars, beam, floor) then conservatism is again advisable; if the event order puts vaulting near the end of the meet, then the team score can be evaluated as the meet progresses and used as a criterion. If the gymnast is near the beginning of the vaulting lineup, then conservatism is advisable; if she is near the end of the vaulting lineup, then the previous team members' performances can serve as additional criteria. The coach and gymnast should discuss the possible vaulting strategy for the meet ahead of time (at least a day), so that the alternatives are completely understood. The coach should accept input from the gymnast, but it is the coach's decision as to which vaults are thrown and when, and she should explain her reasoning for the final decision to the gymnast.

TRAINING

The importance of training specificity for side horse vaulting must be emphasized. Therefore, vaulting itself is the key to training, although the number of vaults performed during a practice should be controlled to prevent injury. Injuries occur when individuals are tired. Limiting the number of vaults also makes each vault important, so the gymnast can't use the excuse that the next will be better or plead for "just one more, please." Probably, the most vaults are thrown when learning a new one or during mid-season, and even then the practice number should not exceed twelve daily, eight if the vault or vaults are consistent.

A common complaint among gymnasts is shinsplints, an aching pain that extends the length of the shin. This condition is thought to be a pulling apart of the longitudinal fibers of the long muscles in the front of the lower leg. The cure for this discomfort is complete rest for an extensive period of time, a treatment that is usually impossible during the gymnastics season. So the coach must encourage the gymnast to "tell it to go away and grin and bear it." There are many different wrappings and tapings that will eliminate some of the discomfort; the most effective depends upon the individual, and consultation with a certified trainer or a book on care and prevention of athletic injuries is recommended. How much activity to permit the gymnast depends upon common sense and her pain tolerance. The shinsplints syndrome can become psychologically contagious among a whole team. Consequently, the coach should avoid excessive attention and discussion of it. Some suggestions for prevention of shinsplints are:

1. Increase ankle flexibility in all directions.
2. Increase heel cord or Achilles tendon stretch.
3. Practice specific exercises:
    a. Back-lying—supine position, lift legs against resistance at ankles.
    b. Front-lying—prone position, lift legs against resistance at back of ankles.
4. Keep vaulting practices short and limit the number of vaults practiced.
5. Provide soft running and landing areas with mats that don't "bottom out."

To insure against injured knees and ankles, landing surfaces should be even, mats flush, and no space between mats.

Proper spotting can also help to prevent injuries that might occur during vaulting.

Tilts (10), bench jumping (10), and sticking landings (20) can be effective specific conditioning techniques. The major portion of the conditioning should occur at the end of the practice to accommodate the "overload principle" of exercise physiology.

General conditioning exercises that might help the vaulter are stair running, wind sprints (with knees high in the beginning), and exercises to increase quadricep and plantar flexion (ankle extension), strength, and explosive power such as half squat jumps and straight leg jumps. All exercises should be performed at the speed at which the movement will be performed in vaulting. Any running practice by the gymnast should be done in sneakers or training shoes to help prevent shinsplints. For more general conditioning procedures, see Chapter 2.

5

STICKING

balance beam

The team that sticks or stays on the balance beam is the team that wins the meet. This is an often heard axiom in women's gymnastics. And from the beginning to high intermediate levels of competition, it is very valid. While performing on the beam, the gymnast must give the illusion that she is on the floor (Fig. 5.1).* The difference, of course, is that one can't fall off the floor; the floor is not four inches wide, nor is it suspended approximately four feet in the air.

The skills for the balance beam are, for the most part, closely related to floor exercise skills. Therefore the movement categories for the balance beam are the same as those of floor exercise: tumbling, dance, and acrobatics. These categories should be artistically combined in a routine that changes levels, direction, and tempo. A routine should present a picture of elegance. If the skill can be performed on the floor (which is the progression for all beam skills), why can't it be done on the beam? The frustration of this event is related to its psychology. The balance beam is not that difficult an event physically, but psychologically it can be devastating for the gymnast, teacher/coach, and team, for the smallest most insignificant error in execution can result in a fall, dramatically effecting the individual's standing and team's score.

The balance beam itself is 12 m. (meters), or 16 ft. 5 in., long by 0.1 m., or 4 in., wide. The beam is 1.2 m., or 3 ft. 11¼ in., from the floor to its top. A timer begins timing the routine the moment the gymnast's feet leave the floor or board and

*Figure 5.1 is on preceding page.

158

stops the watch when her feet land on the mat at the end of the routine. A beginning timer must be alert because within one routine there may be many unplanned dismounts and mounts; the timer does not reset her watch to zero until the head judge for the event gives her permission to do so. The routine must be a minimum of 1 min. 15 sec. and a maximum of 1 min. 35 sec. The gymnast receives a warning at 1 min. 30 sec., and she then has 5 sec. in which to dismount. The judges are instructed at 1:35 to stop watching the routine. If a girl falls from the beam during the routine, she has 10 sec. to get back on the beam and resume her routine. The timer continues timing the routine from beginning to conclusion including falls. It is a good idea for the timer to use two stopwatches as a precaution against possible mechanical failure or an itchy trigger finger.

Focus and proper body alignment are the keys to successful balance beam work. Focus while working the beam involves the eyes looking down at the end of the beam; the head should not be down. When turning, the gymnast focuses her eyes on a spot on one wall at eye level, and at the completion of the turn, she again locks her eyes on a spot on the wall at eye level. Proper body alignment includes shoulders and hips parallel and in line over the base support. Even a seemingly insignificant error, such as dropping one shoulder slightly lower than the other, can cause a fall. Poor focus and improper body alignment are the most common causes of falls from the beam. When a gymnast is beginning to lose her balance, she should quickly bend her knees, STG, and move into the next skill.

The art of balancing is an important part of most athletic activities, even to the extent that a few years ago football coaches encouraged their players to take ballet lessons to improve their ability to balance. What could demonstrate balance in athletics better than a football running back changing directions and leaning his center of gravity totally outside of his base support as he cuts through the line or the body lean of a baseball player rounding third base? Balance beams have been used since the 1600s as a means of learning and demonstrating balance prowess (Fig. 5.2).

Even as a beginner, the gymnast should make every effort to perform beam

Figure 5.2 • The art of balancing

work on her toes and the balls of her feet with her body completely stretched. The basic concepts of gymnastics apply to all beam work. Successful balance beam performance requires much practice. Actually, of the four Olympic events, the balance beam requires the most persistent and consistent practice. Balance beam is mental discipline.

The necessary apparatus and equipment for learning balance beam are a regulation height beam, a low beam (the beam stabilized on the floor), mirrors, mats (regular, dismount, and crash pads), chalk (magnesium carbonate), batters' rock rosin (for wooden beams), and a container to protect the gymnasium floor from the rosin (a rubber tray designed as a foot bath for locker room showers is an effective repository).

SAFETY

The safety techniques specifically applicable to the balance beam event are:

1. Good mat coverage; no overlaps or spaces between mats. A few equipment companies are now manufacturing mats that are precut to surround the apparatus. These are a wise and worthwhile investment.
2. A stabilized beam.
3. Proper skill explanation for both the gymnast and spotter.
4. Generally, with a beginner who is falling, proper spotting includes getting the gymnast away from the beam.
5. Proper supervision.

The skills for the balance beam will be discussed according to mounts (techniques for getting onto the apparatus), work on the beam, and dismounts (planned and practiced techniques for getting off the apparatus). During the learning process, the teacher/coach should constantly emphasize proper form: balance, composure, toes pointed, knees straight, and amplitude. Throughout balance beam work, the gymnast should squeeze everything in her body to the midline and STG. When she temporarily loses balance, the gymnast should bend her knees and stick.

MOUNTS
Front
Support
Mount

The most basic beam mount is the front support. Facing the beam, the gymnast approaches it, places both hands on the beam, shoulder width apart, and jumps or lifts into a front support position in which the fronts of her thighs touch the beam. The gymnast then swings one leg over the beam so that she is sitting astride it. From this position, she can bring one foot onto the beam in front of her and step up or bring one leg behind her into a kneeling position (knee scale). This skill is basic enough that it needs only explanation and possibly demonstration. There are no suggested teaching techniques, progressions, or spotting instructions.

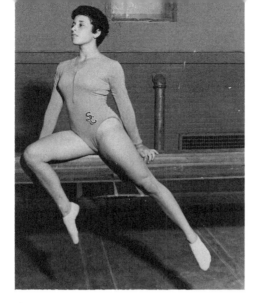

Figure 5.3 • Fence mount

Fence Mount

The gymnast approaches the beam obliquely, or diagonally, lifts the leg closer to the beam up and over it to the other side, and then lifts her other leg up and over. The hand closer to the beam clasps it for balance. The gymnast ends the mount sitting side forward on the beam (Fig. 5.3). This skill is a hitch kick to a sit on the beam.

Teaching techniques and progressions:

1. The fence mount is a relatively easy but pretty skill; therefore, there are no lead-up progressions to its performance other than performing a hitch kick on the floor.
2. A board may be used for this mount.
3. The mount should be attempted with a two-step approach.

Corrections:

1. The most common error a gymnast makes in attempting this skill is to vault over the beam rather than mount it. Therefore:
   a. The skill should be performed slowly and with control.
   b. The upper body should be kept in alignment (head and shoulders over the hips).

Spotting:

1. There is no recommended or necessary spot for this skill.

Forward Roll Mount

A very popular and often performed mount is the forward roll. This is an important part of a beginning gymnast's repertoire, for it is a basic skill to which variations may be added in order to increase its difficulty rating.

The gymnast approaches the end of the beam straight on or side of the beam

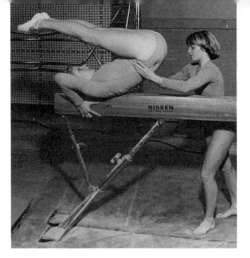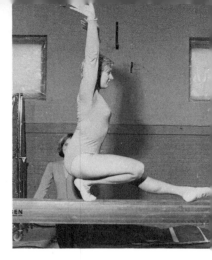

Figure 5.4 • Forward roll mount

from the diagonal, places her hands on the top of the beam while doing a two-foot takeoff, lifting her hips as high as possible, tucking her head, and placing the back of her neck on the beam. She then rolls (in tuck position) onto her feet (one slightly ahead of the other) to a stretched stand. There is no regrasp under the beam after the roll begins.

Teaching techniques and progressions:

1. The prerequisite for this skill is a forward roll on the floor mat.
2. The gymnast should take a preliminary run (two or three steps) and a two-foot takeoff from a board—not too close to the beam (see Fig. 5.4a). She places her hands on the beam and pikes her hips upward as high as possible. Her arms are straight. A spotter can aid with this progression by standing to the side between the board and the beam as the gymnast pikes her hips. The spotter extends her arm in the bend between the front of the hips and the thighs to help lift the hips.
3. When the gymnast can pike her hips high enough to accomplish the roll, she should perform the mount with spotting. A mat can be draped over the beam to prevent a hard landing.

Spotting:

1. One spotter may stand to the side between the board and the horse to help lift the hips as described previously.
2. The key spotter stands next to the beam facing the gymnast and just before the back of her neck comes in contact with the beam, the spotter grasps each side of the gymnast's waist and eases her onto the beam (Fig. 5.4b). She quickly releases this spot (Fig. 5.4c) as the roll continues and, with one arm, helps the gymnast to stand up while extending the other arm so that the gymnast can reach for it with her own hand.

Squat Mount This is a vaulting mount because the gymnast utilizes a two-foot takeoff from a board and places her hands on the beam in shoulder width position, lifting her

162

Figure 5.5 • Squat mount

hips and bringing her knees up to her chest in tuck position. The knees and feet go between the arms. The gymnast's thumbs are behind the beam to arrest forward motion. The feet are placed on the beam (Fig. 5.5).

Teaching techniques and progressions:

1. The prerequisite for this skill may be the performance of a squat vault.

Corrections:

1. The most common error in this mount is bringing the heels up to the glutes and landing in a kneeling position (on the shins), rather than bringing the knees up to the chest in tuck position and landing in a squat postion on the beam.

2. Vaulting over the beam can be corrected by:
   a. Proper body alignment; shoulders directly over the hips and head up.
   b. Keeping the thumbs on the back side of the beam.
   c. Not using a run to mount.

Spotting:

1. The spotter stands facing the gymnast on the opposite side of the beam. As the gymnast lifts off the floor or board, the spotter reaches up and clasps the gymnast's upper arms with her hands and helps her to stop in a squat position on the beam.

Combinations:

1. Mount, quarter turn, stand.

2. Mount, turn, tuck jump.

3. Mount, three-quarter turn in tuck, stand.

4. While performing this mount, the gymnast can squat through without allowing her feet to touch the beam. She can then bring her legs up into a V-seat position. The progressions and corrections are the same as for the squat mount. The spotter should change her position by moving slightly to the side of the gymnast so that the gymnast doesn't kick her as she brings her feet through.

5. By bringing both legs between the hands with the legs straight, the gymnast can perform the *stoop mount*. The gymnast must lift her hips high and overbalance her shoulders forward as her feet pass through her hands. The spot is the same as for the squat through described previously.

Straddle Mount

This mount is also a vaulting mount. The gymnast approaches the beam from the side and, after a two-foot takeoff, places her hands on the beam, thumbs back; straddles her legs as she lifts her hips up; and places her feet on the beam in a straddle position (Fig. 5.6).

Teaching techniques and progressions:

1. The prerequisite for this skill might be the performance of a straddle vault.

Corrections:

1. The gymnast should be encouraged to lift her hips high and not to straddle her legs too far apart so as to make a connector difficult.
2. The legs should not bend at the knees.
3. Vaulting over the beam can be corrected by:
   a. Effecting proper body alignment: shoulders directly over the hips and head up.
   b. Keeping the thumbs on the back side of the beam.
   c. Not using a run to mount.

Spotting:

1. The spotter stands facing the gymnast on the opposite side of the beam. As the gymnast lifts off the floor or board, the spotter reaches up and clasps the gymnast's upper arms with her hands and helps her to stop in a straddle stand on the beam.

Combinations:

1. Straddle mount, quarter turn lunge, stand.

Figure 5.6 • Straddle mount

2. On the mount, the gymnast doesn't place her feet on the beam but moves her feet over into a straddle position with support on the hands. The spot and corrections are the same as above. The progression for this mount is the straddle stand mount.

Wolf Mount
This mount is a combination of the squat and straddle mounts. Using a two-foot takeoff from the side of the beam, the gymnast lifts herself onto her hands on the beam (fingers pointing forward, thumbs behind the beam). The knee and foot of one leg go between the hands in a squat, while the other leg and foot extend to the side, as in a straddle (Fig. 5.7).

Teaching techniques and progressions:
1. The progressions for this mount are a squat mount and a straddle mount.

Corrections:
1. The gymnast should be encouraged to lift her hips high.
2. The straight leg should be just that: straight.
3. The bent leg should be in the tuck position, knee up to the chest.
4. Vaulting over the beam can be corrected by:
   a. Effecting proper body alignment: shoulders directly over the hips and head up.
   b. Keeping the thumbs on the back side of the beam.
   c. Not using a run to mount.

Combinations:
1. Wolf mount, quarter turn, stand.
2. Wolf mount, Japanese turn, stand. (A Japanese turn is performed by turning on the ball and toes of the tuck leg with the straight leg extended.)

Step-up Mount
The step-up mount is exactly what its name indicates. The gymnast can perform this mount facing the end, side, or diagonal of the beam. Using a board, the

Figure 5.7 • Wolf mount

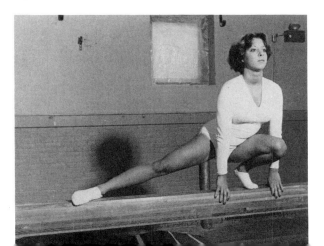

Figure 5.8 • Step-up mount with spot

gymnast steps onto the board with one foot; the other foot steps up onto the beam. Throughout this skill the gymnast should focus on the beam.

Teaching techniques and progressions:	1. The gymnast, if she is tall enough, can stand on the board on one foot and place the other foot on the beam so that, with the aid of two spotters who hold her hands, she stands up on the beam. This progression is helpful only if the gymnast's center of gravity is not excessive (fat).
	2. The gymnast can attempt the mount on a lower beam, with spotting.
Corrections:	1. A three- or four-step approach and push off the board will help insure a good lift.
	2. Proper body alignment includes hips and shoulders in line and head up. The gymnast should not reach for or lean forward in this mount. If she does, her center of gravity will be too far back or out of her base support.
	3. Focus on the beam.
Spotting:	1. One or two spotters stand, facing the gymnast, just next to the place where the gymnast's foot will land on the beam. Each extends an arm so that, if necessary, the gymnast can clasp a spotter's hand for help (Fig. 5.8).
Combinations:	1. Step-up mount, leap, step leap.
	2. Step-up mount, cartwheel.
	3. Step-up mount, the free leg held above the horizontal to the front or rear (increasing the mount's difficulty).
	4. Step-up, tour jêté (see Chapter 3), back walkover (this mount is difficult).

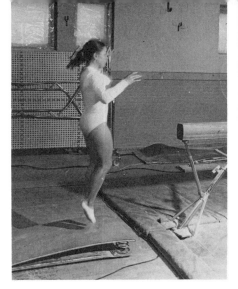

Figure 5.9   Squat jump

Squat Jump Mount	In this skill, the gymnast may again mount from the end, side, or on the diagonal of the beam. She approaches the board, performs a strong two-foot takeoff (the kind she would need for vaulting), bends her knees in front of her, and lands on the beam with one foot slightly in front of the other (Fig. 5.9).

Teaching techniques and progressions:

1.   The squat vault might be a proper prerequisite for this mount.
2.   The vaulting technique in which the vaulter runs, does a two-foot takeoff to a stretched body position, and lands on a Swedish box or horse also is an excellent progression for this mount.

Corrections:

1.   The most common error in this vault is the failure to get enough lift from the board, possibly because the gymnast "chickens out." She must "go for" the skill with 110 percent commitment. A lack of confidence should be dispelled by good spotting and the coach's understanding and encouragement.
2.   The gymnast must focus on the beam.
3.   She must also maintain good body alignment (shoulders over hips and feet).

Combinations:

1.   Squat jump, any dance or acrobatic skill.

Handstand Mount

As a skill on and for mounting the beam the handstand is valuable and necessary. The gymnast should begin working on it during her initial exposure to gymnastics.

Standing on a board next to the beam, the gymnast places both hands on the beam shoulder width apart. She jumps up and lifts her hips over her shoulders while straddling her legs (Fig. 5.10). When her hips are over her shoulders, she brings her legs together while completely stretching her body upward; she as-

Figure 5.10 • Handstand mount from the end of the beam

sumes a forward pelvic tilt, a neutral head position, and she STGs. If absolutely necessary, an approach of no more than two or three steps is permissible.

Teaching techniques and progressions:	1. The press handstand on the floor is a valuable progression for all handstands, whether on the bars, floor, or beam. The gymnast stands in a straddle position, places her hands on the floor in front of her, and leans forward in an attempt to bring her hips (center of gravity) over her shoulders and hands (base support). Her shoulders overbalance, or move forward over her hands. At this time, the legs release the floor and come together in the handstand. The gymnast slowly reverse-presses (elbows locked) out of the handstand. This skill should be done with a spotter; for more details, see Chapter 2.
	2. The gymnast should then attempt the press handstand while standing on the low beam, with spotting.
	3. The gymnast should then perform the press handstand while standing on the high beam, with spotting.
	4. A step two-foot takeoff press handstand on the trampoline will aid the gymnast with the kinesthesis of lifting the hips up and above the shoulders.
	5. Next the gymnast should try the handstand mount from a board, with spotting.
Corrections:	1. STG, and strive for forward pelvic tilt and stretched handstand (no banana back).
	2. The head should be in neutral position.
	3. Hands should be shoulder width apart.

168

4. Overbalance the shoulders as the hips are being brought over them and then stretch upward at the top.

5. Straddle the legs up and then together.

6. Do not take more than three steps during the approach; never approach this mount in a full run.

Spotting:

1. The spotter stands facing the gymnast, on the opposite side of the beam and slightly to the side. As the gymnast's feet leave the board, the spotter reaches over the beam with the arm closer to the beam and places her hand on the front of the gymnast's waist. With this hand she helps lift the hips. Once the hips have been helped up, the spotter places her hands on each side of the gymnast's waist and tries to aid her in stretching up and finding balance.

Combinations:

1. Handstand mount facing the end of the beam.

2. Handstand mount facing the beam diagonally.

3. Handstand mount from end or diagonal, forward roll. The shoulders must be overbalanced. (See Chapter 3 on the handstand forward roll and the early part of this chapter on the forward roll mount.)

4. Handstand mount at the end or diagonal on the beam, front walkout.

5. Handstand mount at side of the beam, cartwheel out of it.

6. Handstand mount, straddle back down to a straddle pike support on the hands.

7. Handstand mount, pirouette on the hands, step down out of it or forward roll or front walkout.

Figure 5.11 • Turning out of a handstand mount

8. Vary the position of the legs in the handstand, split, abstract (stag, one leg bent), or both legs bent in abstract.
9. Handstand mount from the side, split the legs, turn hips a quarter turn and either step back down out of it or front-tinsica out of it (Fig. 5.11).

This skill, the handstand mount, requires practice, practice, and more practice, for it demands perfect kinesthesis and control. The corrections for any of the above variations are correct handstand techniques. The spotting involves lifting the hips and stabilizing the handstand by spotting the waist.

Cartwheel Mount

This is a vaulting mount. It requires a three-step approach followed by a two-foot takeoff from a board. This mount is usually performed at the end of the beam, but it can be done by approaching the beam diagonally from the side adjacent to the first hand on the beam in the cartwheel. With a good lift from the board the hands are placed on the beam, one hand after the other, as in a cartwheel. After leaving the board, the legs straddle and the feet alternately contact the beam, also as in a cartwheel. The gymnast lands on the beam facing the direction from which she began the mount.

Teaching techniques and progressions:

1. A prerequisite for this mount might be a quarter on/quarter off vault, and/or cartwheel on the beam, and/or handspring vault.
2. This is one of those skills that the gymnast just has to pull up her "sockie straps" and "go for."

Corrections:

1. The most common error in this skill is the lack of commitment from the gymnast; she "chickens out."
2. The hips and feet must go over the shoulders and hands without "pancaking" the cartwheel. Pancaking the feet onto the beam is not a shortcut; it will result in a fall.

Spotting:

1. The spotter stands to the side between the board and the beam. The side on which the spotter stands is that of the gymnast's first hand in a cartwheel. As the gymnast leaves the board, the spotter uses the hand further from the beam to lift the side of the gymnast's waist closer to her (Fig. 5.12). The spotter moves and places the same hand on the upper part of the gymnast's other arm in the cartwheel. The spotter's free hand guides the first foot onto the beam by holding the front of the hip on that side.

Combinations:

1. Cartwheel mount, turn, and so on.
2. Cartwheel mount, back walkover.
3. Cartwheel mount, back handspring.

Figure 5.12 • Cartwheel mount with spot

Thief Mount

The thief mount is related to a very old vault called, surprisingly enough, the "thief vault." Facing the beam, the gymnast takes off from a board by lifting up one leg and then the other (Fig. 5.13). The outstretched legs (pike position) pass over the beam; then the hands catch the beam, with thumbs in the back of the beam stopping the forward momentum. The gymnast should pike prior to putting her glutes down on the beam.

Teaching techniques and progressions:

1. The gymnast may perform a thief vault over a side horse or beam once or twice with the apparatus lower than regulation height, but not too much lower.
2. Then she should try the skill on the high beam.

Corrections:

1. The head should be kept up.

Figure 5.13 • Thief mount

2. The board should not be too close to the beam.

3. The pike must be maintained so as to be able to stop the mount on the beam and not vault over it.

4. This skill should not be "thrown" with a great deal of force.

Spotting:

1. This skill does not require a spot.

2. If it would make the gymnast feel more comfortable, a spotter can stand on the other side of the beam but off to the side. Facing the gymnast, the spotter can spot her upper arm and the back of her thighs while she is on top of the beam.

Combinations:

1. Thief mount, V-seat, turn, stand.

2. Thief mount, one thigh roll squat the other leg to place the foot on the beam, stand.

3. Thief mount, V-seat, press through to a handstand (very difficult).

Aerial Mount

The front aerial mount is a gorgeous means of getting on the beam and it is not that difficult to learn. Standing in the classic lunge position on the board and facing the beam (Fig. 5.14), the gymnast *gently* lifts into a front aerial and completes the skill by sitting on the beam. The beam forms the horizontal axis of rotation for the aerial; thus this skill doesn't require the force from the legs of a front aerial on the floor. The hands don't touch the beam until the skill is almost completed.

Teaching techniques and progressions:

1. The gymnast should have tried a front aerial on the floor and should be able to do a front walkover.

2. Place a mat over the beam.

Figure 5.14 • Aerial mount

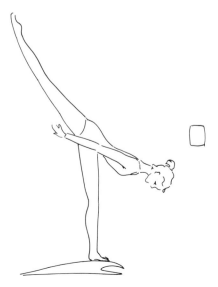

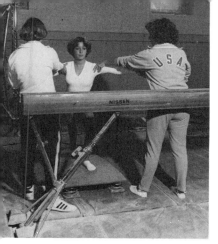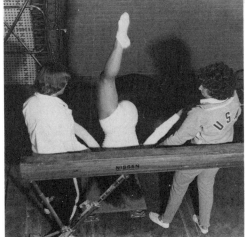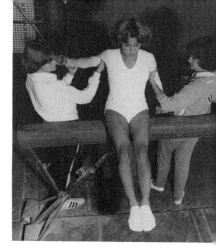

Figure 5.15 • Aerial mount with spot

3. The gymnast stands on a board in lunge position. Two spotters stand to the side and between the gymnast and the beam. Each spotter takes the gymnast's hand closer to her and the spotters' free hands are placed on top of the gymnast's shoulders (Fig. 5.15). As the gymnast finishes the skill, the spotters release her hands so that she can place them behind her on the beam.

4. Then the gymnast can perform the skill with only one spotter.

Corrections:

1. The skill should be performed very easily or gently.

2. The head and back should come as close as possible to the beam prior to lift-off.

3. At the end of the skill, the hands grasp the beam and the head stays back.

4. "Easy does it!"

Spotting:

1. The spotting for this skill is described in the section on teaching techniques and progressions.

Combinations:

1. Front aerial mount, thigh roll free leg over the beam to sitting position astride the beam.

2. Front aerial mount, thigh roll free leg squats onto beam, stand up.

SKILLS ON THE BALANCE BEAM

The gymnastic skills performed on the balance beam, in most cases, are those performed in floor exercise. These skills are tumbling, dance, and acrobatics. When the gymnast can perform the skills discussed in detail in Chapter 3, she may attempt those skills on the balance beam. The progression for all beam work is to perform the skill on the floor, then on the beam. In this section, only techniques that specifically apply to balance beam will be mentioned.

Tumbling Skills

Free Forward Roll (no hands)

This skill the gymnast performs in squat position on the beam. The roll itself should be long and low (for stability, keep the center of gravity as close to the base

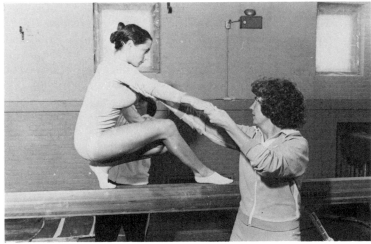

Figure 5.16 • Free forward roll with spot

support as possible). The gymnast tucks her head and begins the roll on the lower portion of her neck. With a tucked body, the gymnast rolls onto one foot and then the other and stands up. A key to this skill is tight body and STG. It is suggested that this be the first forward roll on the beam.

Teaching techniques and progressions:

1. A mat placed over the beam will help to make the practice of this skill more comfortable for the gymnast.
2. This skill is initially performed with two spotters (Fig. 5.16). The spotters, standing on opposite sides of the beam, each take the hand of the gymnast that is nearer to her. With the free hands (the ones that are further from the gymnast) they support the top of the gymnast's shoulder. The spotters move forward and stay ahead of the roll.

174

3. As the gymnast becomes more and more proficient, she needs less spotting.

Forward Roll

The gymnast begins the roll by placing the lower portion of the back of her neck on the beam in front of her hands. She is in tuck position as she rolls forward on her rounded back. She should not regrasp the beam or stop her momentum or wiggle her hips around as though she is trying to get into a tight pair of slacks. The roll should be continuous as the gymnast moves from a squat position on the beam to the roll and stands up. The key to success in this skill is an extremely tight body.

Teaching techniques and progressions:

1. The beam can be covered with a mat for the purpose of learning this skill.
2. The spotting is as prescribed for the forward roll #2; that is, the spotter holds both sides of the gymnast's waist until the hips approximate the beam and

Figure 5.17 • Forward roll with spot

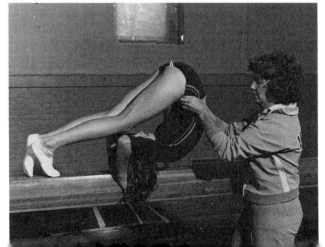

then the spotter releases the waist and helps the gymnast stand at the end of the roll by holding her hand or upper arm (Fig. 5.17).

*Handstand
Forward Roll*

Refer to the description of this skill in the mount section of this chapter or in Chapter 3. Key instructions are STG and pull everything in the body to the midline. The spotter holds the gymnast's waist on both sides.

Cartwheel

The cartwheel on the beam is slightly different from the cartwheel on the floor. The gymnast cartwheels into a straddle handstand; then in her hips she turns (90°) (Fig. 5.18) and places her first foot down on the beam pointing in the direction from which she began the skill. Standing on the side of the beam of the first hand down in the cartwheel, the spotter reaches up and holds the upper portion of the gymnast's second arm on the beam with her closer hand supinated and thumb down. The spotter's other arm grasps the side front of the hip of the first leg on the beam. This is a very safe and secure spot. The spotter concentrates on helping the gymnast place her first foot on the beam with pressure from the hand on the hip.

Back Roll

The back roll on the beam is the same as the back roll on the floor, except that the hands are placed on the top of the beam, elbows in, thumbs together. The gymnast should be tight and should pull everything to the midline of her body. This skill was once taught with the hands initially under the beam and then shifted to the top of the beam during the roll. The purpose of placing the hands under the beam was to help weak abdominals and quadriceps pull the legs up and over in the roll. Any female whose abdominals and quads are too weak to lift her legs up should not be doing back rolls on the beam.

This skill should be performed at first from a supine position on the beam (Fig. 5.19). The other teaching techniques and progressions, as well as the correc-

Figure 5.18 · Cartwheel

Figure 5.19 • Back roll with spot

tions, spotting, and combinations are the same as those previously discussed in Chapter 3.

Back Extension Roll
As a skill on the balance beam, the back extension roll has great possibilities for changing levels although it is difficult. It is performed on the beam as it is on the floor, except that the hand placement is thumbs together. The skill is begun from a supine position. The body must be tight—STG—for success. Because this skill is like its relative on the floor, a more complete description can be found in Chapter 3. The spotting is done by placing one hand on the front of the waist and the other on the back of the waist as the roll is completed to help lift the gymnast into a handstand.

Front Handspring
The differences between this skill in floor exercise and on the beam are very few. The skill itself is the same, but the emphasis is to make sure everything in the body is pulled to the midline, thus assuring that the first foot in the handspring will land on the beam. Since this maneuver involves a blind landing, the head should be kept back to maintain a stretched body and to insure a successful landing. The tendency is to pull the head down to look for the beam and this is a major error.

Figure 5.20 • Front handspring with spot

177

Figure 5.21 • Front aerial

The prerequisite for this skill on the beam is a front walkover. To spot this skill, the spotter reaches up as in a front aerial on the floor. She stands beside the beam next to the gymnast's bent knee in the lunge and grasps either the front of the gymnast's hip or the upper arm when her hands are placed on the beam (Fig. 5.20). The spotter's other hand is placed on the small of the gymnast's back when her hands touch the beam.

Front Aerial
From the lunge position, the gymnast executes an aerial as she would do it on the floor (see Chapter 3). When doing the skill on the beam, the gymnast must STG to insure a tight body and to guarantee that the foot of the first leg will land on the beam. The head must stay back (Fig. 5.21). This is a difficult skill because the landing is blind and it takes "guts" to go for it. The aerial cannot be the least bit dumped; therefore, good technique is extremely important. The progressions, corrections, spotting, and combinations are the same on the beam and on the floor (Fig. 5.22).

Side Aerial
The side aerial (Fig. 5.23) is a difficult skill to stick on the beam because of its landing position, but the techniques, progressions, corrections, spotting, and combinations are the same as they are on the floor.

Figure 5.22 • Front aerial with spot

Figure 5.23 • Side aerial with spot

*Back
Handspring*

The back handspring for the balance beam (Fig. 5.24) is a bit higher and lighter than its relative on the floor and it is performed with a walkout landing. The gymnast can think of this skill as a back jump to a handstand, which she follows by splitting the legs and walking out. The progressions again involve doing the skill on the floor, then on low beam, and finally on the high beam with good spotting. The corrections are the same as they would be for the handspring on floor. The spotter stands to the rear and side of the gymnast. The spotter places the hand closer to the gymnast between the gymnast's glutes and upper thigh to help lift and form the horizontal axis of rotation. When the gymnast jumps back into the handstand, this hand slips up to the back of the gymnast's waist. The free hand is then placed on the front of the hips just above the upper thigh to direct the first foot onto the beam. This skill, too, requires a tight body in complete control.

Figure 5.24 • Back handspring

Somersault   Somersaults, both back and front, are difficult skills on the beam. These skills are difficult on the floor, but they are usually preceded by other tumbling skills that set them up with power. On the beam, these skills are performed from a standing position. The prerequisites, of course, are their successful performance on the floor mat with very little or light spotting. The techniques, progressions, corrections, spotting, and combinations are the same whether the skill is in floor exercise or on the beam. On the beam though, these skills are usually performed in tuck position and the body must be tight—STG.

Again the reader is referred to Chapter 3 for detailed descriptions of the tumbling skills in floor exercise, which are and can be performed on the beam. The difficulty of any given tumbling skill performed on the beam is greater than on the floor.

Dance Skills   For dance skills that can be done in a routine, the reader is directed to the dance section of Chapter 3 for specific details. In brief, some of the dance skills on the beam are:

Leaps   1. Split leap (Fig. 5.25)
2. Switch leg, or scissors leap
3. Tour jêté
4. Cat leap (Fig. 5.26)
5. Hitch kick (Fig. 5.27)
6. Abstract leap (bending one or both legs)

Figure 5.25 · Split leap

Figure 5.26 • (left) Cat leap
Figure 5.27 • (middle) Hitch kick
Figure 5.28 • (right) Straddle pike jump

All leaps should be performed as high as possible. The landing leg should bend at the knee to absorb the force and to provide balance. Leaps must be practiced a great deal. The progression for leaps is from the floor to the low beam to the high beam. Occasionally, a female will fall while doing a high leap on the beam. The sound of the fall is appalling and tends to fill a gymnasium. Usually this type of fall does not injure the gymnast physically, although it will bruise the upper thighs, but the gymnast's pride is usually hurt. Application of cold will help the bruises and avoiding any further embarrassment will restore her pride.

Jumps

1. Hollow
2. Tuck
3. Pike
4. Straddle pike (Fig. 5.28)
5. Abstract (one leg bent, the other straight)
6. Arabesque
7. Turns

All jumps should be performed as high as possible. The knees bend upon landing for balance and lightness.

Turns

1. Pirouette at least 360° (Figs. 5.29 and 5.30)
2. Chêné (see p. 80).

Figure 5.29 • Full turn with free leg abstract

All turns should be performed on the toes and balls of the feet. Many beam falls are caused by improper turns. The most common errors that cause falls in turns are incorrect focus and improper body alignment. Turns must be practiced frequently on the high beam.

Contractions

Body waves or successions are also quite useful in beam routines for movement variety and torso movement.

Jazz and Folk Steps

These steps can serve as connectors in a beam routine. They, too, should be performed on the toes and balls of the feet.

Figure 5.30 • Full turn with free leg straight and extended

Arm and Head Positions Dance affectations of arm and head positions can lend character to a routine and should be considered in every position and skill.

Mirror Mirror work is also extremely important for the balance beam. Working in front of a mirror can help alleviate self-consciousness and eliminate errors caused by improper body alignment.

Acrobatic Skills Acrobatic skills for the balance beam are the same skills that are performed in floor exercise. For a complete description of these skills, see Chapter 3. The teaching progressions are to perform the skill on the floor, then on the low beam, and then on the high beam with the prescribed spotting.

Back Walkover and One-arm Back Walkover This skill is performed on the beam the same way it is on the floor mat (Fig. 5.31). The emphasis in the beam walkover is to cover distance and not just to go up and down. Two walkovers in a row is a beam difficulty and the key to receiving credit is to keep the hips moving so that there is no pause between the walkovers. The progressions, corrections, spotting, and combinations are given in Chapter 3.

 Many teachers and coaches prefer an alternate spotting technique for walkovers, one arms, or tinsicas. To do this spot, the spotter stands on one side of the beam with her back turned to the gymnast who is about to begin the walkover. As soon as the gymnast's hands touch on the beam, the spotter, looking up and over the shoulder that is next to the beam, places both her hands on the gymnast's waist to help her complete the skill.

Figure 5.31 • Back walkover with spot

Figure 5.32 • Back tinsica

<table>
<tr>
<td>*Back Tinsica*</td>
<td>This skill is as described in Chapter 3. The back tinsica is a particularly lovely skill on the balance beam, but it requires STG and pulling all body parts to the midline (Fig. 5.32).</td>
</tr>
<tr>
<td>*Front Walkover*</td>
<td>The front walkover (Fig. 5.33) is a skill that is more difficult to perform on the beam because it has a blind landing and not much of a margin for error (four inches). Thus the gymnast should again STG and pull to the midline as well as using her hands to push off from the beam as the first foot is touching the beam. To receive credit for two front walkovers in a row, the gymnast should keep her hips moving forward as she performs the two skills together. For more detail, see Chapter 3.</td>
</tr>
</table>

Figure 5.33 • Front walkover with alternate spot

Front Tinsica This skill is also described in detail in Chapter 3. The gymnast must remember to STG and pull to the midline. This skill also has a blind landing and the gymnast, although tempted to tuck her head to see the landing, should keep her head back. Tinsicas are beautiful beam skills because they travel, and the body should be stretched with amplitude throughout.

Handstands on the Beam Some form of a handstand, if at all possible, should be part of a beam routine. Handstands on the beam require a great deal of practice. The gymnast's body should be completely stretched upward. Also important are STG, pelvic tilt, and the major body parts in complete alignment (head, shoulders, and hips).

Teaching techniques and progressions:

1. The skill on the floor.
2. The skill on the low beam.
3. The skill on the high beam with spotting.

Corrections:

Falls from handstands are usually caused by the following errors:

1. A banana back.
2. A loose body.
3. Improper body alignment.
4. Poor speed control going into or out of the skill.
5. Lack of concentration.

Spotting:

1. In general, the spotting for handstands on the beam requires the spotter to place both hands on the gymnast's waist or upper arms or one hand on the waist and the other on the upper arm.

Combinations and Variations:

1. One direction of the handstand can be sideways or in line with the beam; this variation is an English handstand (Fig 5.34).

Figure 5.34 • English handstand, legs abstract

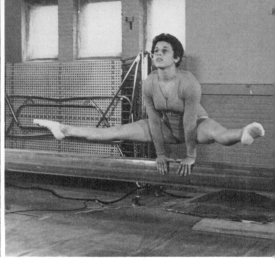

Figure 5.35 • (left) Handstand, legs abstract
Figure 5.36 • (middle) Coming down from a handstand one leg abstract, the other straddle
Figure 5.37 • (right) Coming down from a handstand straddle through

2. The leg positions in the handstand can be changed for variation:
   a. Split.
   b. Straddle.
   c. Abstract (one or both legs bent; Fig. 5.35).
   d. Circling.

3. The gymnast may go into the handstand in a variety of ways, including:
   a. Press (see Chapter 2).
   b. Cartwheel.
   c. Front walkover.
   d. Back walkover.
   e. Handstand pirouette (on the hands).
   f. Back extension roll.

4. The gymnast may come down from the handstand in a variety of ways, including:
   a. Back down as she kicked up.
   b. Front walkout.
   c. Cartwheel.
   d. Shoot through (English or regular).
   e. Stoop through (regular).
   f. Straddle down (regular, one leg abstract; Fig. 5.36).
   g. Straddle through (English or regular; Fig. 5.37).

For more specific information on shoot through and stoop through, refer to Chapter 3. It is important to emphasize overbalancing the shoulders in the performance of these skills.

Figure 5.38 • Roundoff dismount with spot

DISMOUNTS
Roundoff
Dismount

The roundoff dismount from the balance beam is a basic skill in which the gymnast gently places her hands on the beam as in a cartwheel with the second hand at the end. She kicks her legs up and over as her hands touch the beam. At the top of the inverted posture, her legs come together (Fig. 5.38) and she quarter-turns to a stick landing on the mat facing the beam.

Teaching
techniques and
progressions:

1. The prerequisite for this skill is a roundoff on the floor and then its performance on the end of a low beam.

Corrections:

1. The second hand should be placed at the end of the beam. The hands should be no more than shoulder width apart.

2. The gymnast must keep her head in neutral position and *lock* her elbows.

3. A pancaked roundoff can be corrected if the gymnast takes her legs up and over the beam. A stretched hand support, quarter turn.

Spotting:

1. The spotter stands at the end of the beam, beside the gymnast's first hand down on the roundoff. The spotter reaches up and clasps the gymnast's upper arms in her hands and can help her land the skill. This is an amazingly easy and successful spot. This spot is even good with Alice Adipose, for the spotter's hands can actually steer the gymnast just as one might drive or park a large truck.

The reader should review earlier discussions of the potential of danger to the knees from landing in the side plane. The cartwheel and side aerial dismounts from the beam should be avoided and not taught; therefore there is no explanation of these skills in this text.

Handstand Dismount

The handstand dismount is not a particularly spectacular skill, but it does increase the limited beginning repertoire. The skill is not enthusiastically recommended because its landing looks awkward. The gymnast kicks a handstand (English) at the end of the beam or cartwheels into a handstand (regular) anywhere on the beam's length. From a stretched, tight (no banana back) handstand, the gymnast blocks her shoulders and thus lifts up and away from the beam to a stick landing on a mat.

Teaching techniques and progressions:

1. The prerequisite for this skill is a controlled handstand on the floor.
2. The skill should then be done on a high beam with good spotting.

Corrections:

1. The most common error for the beginner performing this skill is to arch off the beam and thus land with her feet in past her hips. This is a very bad landing because it causes hyperextension of the low back (which smarts). To prevent this type of landing, the gymnast should shorten her abdominals with a forward pelvic tilt and STG. Good spotting to help prevent a banana back is very important.
2. The head should be kept in neutral position and not pulled down. The eyes can look down for help in anticipating the landing, but the head should not be tucked.
3. The elbows must be locked.

Spotting:

1. Initially the two spotters, one on each side at the point where the gymnast's feet will be landing, reach up and with their closer hands supinated, thumbs down, they hold the gymnast's upper arms in the handstand. The spotters place their other hands on the bottom of the gymnast's glutes to help prevent her from overarching in the low back. The spotters aid with the landing into mats.

Combinations:

1. Once she has accomplished the skill, the gymnast may want to add a half twist to it. The twist in this skill is a combination of the classic and modern twist (see Chapter 2). This is a fairly difficult skill to *do well*, although it is basic.

Front Handspring Dismount

The handspring dismount can be performed diagonally off the side or at the end of the beam. This skill is performed as it is described in Chapter 3, except that the thumbs of the hands are placed together on the beam. The gymnast does not throw this skill with the same force she must use in floor exercise.

Teaching techniques and progressions:

1. The prerequisite for this skill is a controlled handstand.
2. The gymnast should also have attempted with relative success a front handspring on the floor, although this skill is easier to perform as a beam dismount because the beam's height gives her more time to rotate her feet under herself.

Corrections:	1. The gymnast must block her shoulders in order for the skill to rise as it should.
	2. The elbows do not bend.
	3. There must be no banana back for this position will cause a bad landing in which hyperextension of the low back will occur.
	4. The head must be kept neutral rather than pulled down or tucked.
	5. The skill should be performed gently with very little effort, except for the shoulder block.
Spotting:	1. One or two spotters stand beside where the gymnast's feet will land. Each spotter places her closer hand supinated and thumb down on the gymnast's upper arm. The spotter's other hand supports the bottom of the glutes to prevent her from overarching the low back. The spotter aids with the landing into mats.
Combinations:	1. A half twist can be added to this skill. The twist is a combination of the classic and modern twists (see Chapter 2).
	2. A pike and layout can be added to this skill as the shoulders block and the hands leave the beam. Done this way the skill looks like the yamashita vault.
	3. Front walkover, front handspring dismount.

Back Handspring Dismount

As a dismount, it is best to do the back handspring with one arm from the side (diagonal). This is a difficult skill. It is performed in a dismount just as on the beam, except that the jump should take the gymnast up, back, and diagonally to the side. The hand that the gymnast places on the beam is the one that will be next to the beam upon landing.

Teaching techniques and progressions:	1. The prerequisite for this skill is a good back handspring in floor exercise and a back handspring on the beam.
	2. With spotting, the gymnast should try the one-arm back handspring on the floor, on the low beam, and then on the high beam.
	3. This is a "gutsy" skill.
Corrections:	1. The gymnast should be encouraged to achieve a high lift into the back handspring.
	2. The gymnast must have a straight arm and locked elbow and should block her shoulders (see Chapter 2).
	3. She should throw the snap-down phase of the back handspring very easily or she might undercut or overrotate. Because of the additional height that one doesn't have when performing this skill on the beam or in floor exercise, it is not necessary to have a forceful snap-down.

Spotting:
1. The spotter stands sideways and slightly back on the side of the beam opposite where the gymnast will land. The spotter places the hand that is closer to the gymnast upon her glutes to lift them up and over. The other hand goes on the front of the waist when the gymnast reaches the handstand position. With this same hand the spotter pushes or keeps the gymnast's body away from the beam for the landing.

Side Aerial Dismount

Aerials as dismounts are executed as are aerials in floor exercise, although these skills are easier to do as beam dismounts because the gymnast has height in which to rotate and get her feet under her. The keys to this skill are a good lunge position (Fig. 5.39), lifting from the legs, no banana back, STG, and anticipation of the landing by bending the knees when the feet touch the mat. All aerials should rise so as not to appear dumped.

The side aerial involves the risk of knee injury from landing sideways. Thus the barani, or roundoff without hands, is recommended instead. In this dismount, the gymnast begins to turn during the push-off stage of the roundoff.

Teaching techniques and progressions:
1. The gymnast should perform a slow roundoff on the floor from a lunge.
2. The gymnast should then perform a side aerial on the floor from a lunge with a spotter.
3. Then the gymnast should perform the skill on the beam with spotting (Fig. 5.40). She should have a good understanding of how and why completion of the half turn is important.

Corrections:
1. The corrections for the barani dismount are the same as they are for the side aerial (see Chapter 3).

Figure 5.39 • (left) Beginning aerial dismount (foot should be at the end of the beam)
Figure 5.40 • (right) Side aerial dismount

Spotting:

1. The spotter stands at the end and to the side of the forward leg in the lunge and where the gymnast will land. The spotter places the hand that is closer to the gymnast on the front of the hip to help with the lifting phase of the dismount. She can extend the other hand for the gymnast to grasp with the hand on the same side as her forward leg in the lunge. This position provides support during the rotation.

2. Eventually the spotter's second hand reaches behind the gymnast's waist to help her land. The first hand moves up to the front of the gymnast's waist.

Front Aerial Dismount

The front aerial dismount (Fig. 5.41) is like the front aerial in floor exercise and the front aerial on the beam. Consequently the teaching techniques and progressions, corrections, and spotting are the same (see Chapter 3). The only difference is that great force is not necessary for rotating this skill. The gymnast should get as much lift from her legs as possible and without reservation (i.e., no banana back).

Combinations:

1. Front aerial, half twist.
2. Front aerial, full twist.

(The twists are a combination of the classic and modern twist described in Chapter 2 and are predicated upon a high aerial.)

Back Somersault Dismount

Like many of the other tumbling skills for the beam, the back somersault dismount is performed as it is in floor exercise. The other progressions for this skill as a dismount include performing it on the floor or trampoline with good spotting and then from the high beam. The gymnast should reach and jump up and then rotate the skill to a stick landing in the crash pad.

Figure 5.41 • Front aerial dismount with spot

Spotting: 1. Two spotters, standing at the end and on opposite sides of the beam, place the hands closer to the beam on the gymnast's glutes to help with the lift and rotation. Their other hands can actually hold the gymnast in the air by holding the top of her shoulders when the gymnast inverts.

Combinations: 1. Back somersault in tuck (Fig. 5.42).
2. Back somersault in pike.
3. Back somersault in layout (Fig. 5.43).
4. Cartwheel, back somersault dismount.
5. Dismount from the side of the beam with a back somersault.
6. Dismount diagonally from the side of the beam with a back somersault.
7. Back handspring, back somersault dismount.
8. Back somersault, full twist (see Chapter 3).

Front Somersault Dismount

The front somersault dismount from the beam is related to the front somersault in floor exercise (see Chapter 3). The gymnast jumps up and then rotates the skill so as not to dump it. The other progressions for this skill are performance with spotting on the trampoline, then on the floor into a crash pad, and then on the high beam. A gymnast who cannot perform a good front somersault in floor exercise may be capable of doing this skill as a dismount because she will have enough height to complete the rotation. For other teaching techniques, progressions, and corrections refer to the description of this skill in Chapter 3.

Spotting: 1. Two spotters, standing at the end and to the side of the beam, reach up with the hands closer to the gymnast on the front of her hips and help her to lift off.

Figure 5.42 • Back somersault dismount in tuck with spot

Figure 5.43 • (left) Back somersault dismount in layout
Figure 5.44 • (right) Front somersault in tuck

With their other hands on the upper part of the gymnast's back, they help to finish the rotation. The two spotters continue to move forward with the gymnast, and when the rotation is almost completed, the spotters' second hand move to the front of the gymnast's waist and help her to stick-land the skill.

Combinations:
1. Front somersault dismount in tuck (Fig. 5.44).
2. Front somersault dismount in pike (Fig. 5.45).
3. Front somersault dismount in layout.

Figure 5.45 • (left) Front somersault dismount in pike
Figure 5.46 • (right) Front somersault dismount in tuck diagonally from side of beam

4. Front somersault dismount diagonally from side of the beam (Fig. 5.46).

5. Front walkover, front somersault dismount.

6. Front aerial, front somersault dismount.

7. Split leap, front somersault dismount.

8. Front somersault, full twist dismount. To perform this skill, the gymnast must have a relatively high front somersault. This skill utilizes a combination of the classic and modern twist. The spotting involves helping the gymnast to complete the twist with the spotter's hands on the side of the gymnast's waist and then in front and in back of her waist upon landing.

ROUTINE CONSTRUC-TION

A routine should contain one mount, work *on* the beam, and one dismount. Often balance beam routines sound like an artillery barrage because they are punctuated by more falls than sticks. Routine composition can help prevent falls. It is competitive suicide to have skills in a routine that a gymnast is unsure of or can't hit consistently.

The gymnast should compose her own routine with the coach's help. The routine should not be the coach's. The gymnast and her coach should try to develop a unique style using what the gymnast does well, and her routine should be an elegant presentation. Skills should follow each other logically and appear to belong together not thrown one after another without connection. The gymnast must use or work on the entire length of the beam but should not work only from one end to the other (i.e., pass, turn at end, pass, turn at end, etc.). Watching a routine that simply goes back and forth is like watching an exceedingly slow tennis match.

Poses, or balances (Figs. 5.47 and 5.48), have been purposely omitted from the skills discussion of balance beam since there are only three stops permitted in

Figure 5.47 • (left) Pose
Figure 5.48 • (middle) Needle scale
Figure 5.49 • (right) Split

a routine. A handstand and a split (Fig. 5.49) are stops and these are important to beam routines. Therefore, unless a pose demonstrates extreme flexibility, the gymnast should not choreograph any others into the routine.

The skills chosen for the beam should represent the movement categories of acrobatics, tumbling, and dance. It is suggested that in a routine there be:

1. Three acrobatic skills
2. A full turn (360°)
3. A jump
4. A leap
5. An inverted stretch support (handstand)
6. Hops
7. Running steps
8. A walkover
9. Torso movements with locomotor movements
10. Difficulties (listed in FIG *Code of Points*)

These skills should fit together harmoniously and should exhibit obvious changes in:

1. Level—high above the beam and on it (see Fig. 5.50, this should not predominate)
2. Tempo—most gymnasts work the beam too slowly; a routine should contain quick, light movements as well as slow movements
3. Direction—moving from one end to the middle and turning, working the entire length, and so on

Figure 5.50 • Pose on the beam

4. Force—each movement should convey a certain quality (smooth, angular, narrow, sharp, wide, percussive, etc.)

To prevent a malady that is common to poorly constructed routines, namely, boredom, the gymnast and coach should strive for an expressive routine (see Chapter 1). Expression requires:

1. Imagination
2. Use of the head (varying positions, although primarily it should be up)
3. Changes in facial expression
4. Changes in trunk position
5. Changes in limb position

The gymnast must perform all skills, whether from dance, acrobatics, or tumbling, with total stretch and extension or amplitude.

COACHING BALANCE BEAM

Balance beam is one of the difficult events to coach. The coach's frustration level often rises and falls according to her team's beam performance; in other words, she may lose her cool during this event. A gymnast may perform nearly perfectly on the beam in practice, but during a meet—BOOM!—who can predict what will happen? The composed, disciplined, determined, and usually experienced gymnast who performs consistently is the exception.

The physical or mechanical elements that the coach can provide to help the gymnast perform more consistently on the beam are insistence upon practicing routines, safety, a relaxed yet disciplined atmosphere, beam placement, good spotting, and an explanation of the proper body mechanics of the art of balancing.

The wise coach will establish and teach a compulsory beam routine to beginners. The coach can choreograph into the routine elements she thinks are important or adopt an NAGWS or USGF compulsory. After the gymnast has learned compulsories, the coach and the gymnast can compose an optional routine.

Routines are sacrosanct: there is no escaping the necessity for their practice. The coach should provide the gymnast with the opportunity to perform or practice a minimum of four full routines daily. If there is enough available apparatus and time, the gymnast should do up to eight full routines daily. It would be physically impossible for the coach of a team to fairly watch even all four routines of each team member and still help with the other three events. To compensate, team members might work in twos. While one gymnast does a routine, the other critiques and evaluates it; then they reverse roles. The personnel in the pairs should be changed weekly. It might help if the coach makes these assignments. Teaching emphasis should be placed on amplitude (Fig. 5.51). The routines

Figure 5.51 • (left) Amplitude
Figure 5.52 • (right)

should be timed at least twice a week, if not more regularly, to insure that the routine is within the time limit of 1 min. 15 sec. to 1 min. 35 sec.

The atmosphere of a beam workout should be relaxed yet disciplined. Jump-offs are intolerable. Landing in a balanced position off the beam is referred to as a "jump-off," which is not acceptable. Only if the gymnast's body is draped over the beam or lands extremely awkwardly or ends up hanging on the beam, like an opossum, has a genuine and valid fall occurred. To prevent jump-offs the gymnast must mentally discipline herself to stick. To prevent falls, the coach can encourage the gymnast to have proper body alignment, STG, pull everything to the midline of her body, and bend her knees for balance. Occasionally, a coach should evaluate the routine from a position facing the end of the beam. From this vantage point, she can see improper body alignment (i.e., one shoulder lower than the other, one hip or leg out to the side of the base support, or a banana back handstand). The whole team should develop a positive attitude toward sticking and should encourage each other to stick (Fig. 5.52).

The beam should be placed along the length of the gym, if at all possible. This placement makes it easier for the gymnast to focus. If longitudinal placement is not feasible, then the beam should be placed in line or parallel with the shorter walls. Beam placement should never be diagonal. As previously mentioned, the mat coverage should be adequate around the whole beam and there should be no overlaps or spaces between mats.

Effective spotting increases safety. A technique of piling crash pads and/or folding mats one upon the other in order to elevate the spotter is helpful. In addition, it provides added security for the gymnast. For skills such as aerials or somersaults on the beam, piling the mats on both sides of the high beam so that they are flush with it provides an extra measure of protection. As the gymnast feels more confident in the skill, the mats gradually can be removed.

The balance beam is psychologically the most difficult of all the events. Both the gymnast and her coach must develop a positive attitude about this event. The frame of reference should be sticking instead of falling. If a coach says to her gymnast just before she mounts beam "don't fall," the last thing in the gymnast's mind is "fall" and that's probably just what she will do to please her coach. Rather than discussing falls, talk about sticks. Reinforce the positive. The coach may want to develop a motivational chart on which the gymnasts record the number of beam routines they stick, instead of the number of falls.

The beam should be thought of as merely an extension of the floor (Fig. 5.53). To many, height means fear. This fear must be overcome for success on the beam. If the gymnast spends enough time (hours) on the high beam, her fear will diminish. If she can do a skill well on the floor and low beam and if she has confidence in her spotter as well as in her ability to do her routine, she will be less fearful. Once a gymnast has initiated a skill, it is obligatory that she complete it—"go for it." Completing the skill is essential for the gymnast's and spotter's safety. It is obvious from this discussion that mental discipline is the success variable of the balance beam. The "I can and I will and I did" attitude (of a humble nature) is necessary. In a quiet way, the gymnast must respect the psychological difficulty of the event by establishing a rapport with the beam. One approach to the beam is to think of it as a plant that needs to be talked to; it needs to be caressed. Composure and inner calm (if that's possible) should be the goal of the gymnast prior to and while performing on the beam. Concentration should be ultimate, and no distraction or interruption should break the balance beam performer's train of thought.

Falls from the balance beam occur because of poor concentration, improper body alignment, poor focus, and lack of confidence. Some of these variables are intangible and, as such, are very difficult to anticipate. The coach should make

Figure 5.53 • Elegance

every effort to know her gymnasts as individuals so that she can help them to strengthen their individual weaknesses. The "never give up" and "never jump off" attitude must be ingrained in the whole team. During a meet, it might be helpful for the girls who are to perform on the beam not to watch any other routines, for falls, unfortunately, are contagious. If the gymnast falls, it is absolutely necessary that she forget about the fall, continue as though nothing had happened, and finish strong. If she thinks about her fall, she will probably fall again.

To minimize nervousness prior to performing, the gymnast might slowly stretch, avoid watching other routines, and develop the confidence that she can perform the routine well. The coach has to be aware that if she herself is "hyper" during a meet, and all coaches are, she should not let her tension affect the beam performer. This is not the time for the "do this for the ole Gipper" pep talk. If the coach talks with the gymnast prior to her performance, she should use a very soft voice, in an unrushed way, and with limited verbiage. The coach's confidence and composure should positively affect the gymnast's beam performance.

CONDITION-ING

Conditioning for the balance beam should be primarily of a specific nature. Routines, routines, and more routines comprise the only path to success on the beam. The coach also may want her gymnasts to increase their flexibility by stretching their tighter muscle groups (see Chapter 2) because maximum flexibility is necessary for beam work.

Sticking is not easy, but a concerted and positive approach to the beam by the gymnast, team, and coach make it possible.

6

SWINGING
the uneven bars

The uneven-parallel-bar event in gymnastics is one of the most exciting and challenging sport activities for women today. The range and quality of movement is limited only by the imagination and thorough understanding of the apparatus itself. Successful performance in this event depends upon swing. There is a very rhythmical quality to an uneven bar routine. The gymnast smoothly and seemingly effortlessly swings from one bar to another (Fig. 6.1)*. In general, the routine should contain continuous, meaningful movements that are not punctuated with obvious stops or wasted movements. While working the unevens, the gymnast should strive to establish an even and steady sense of rhythm, so that the bars themselves help the performer in executing a routine, thus the title of this chapter: swinging.

Although the traditionally prescribed position for the thumbs on the unevens is pointing in the direction of the move and in opposition to the fingers, this writer strongly urges the gymnast to learn moves from the beginning with the thumb next to and pointing in the direction of the fingers so that the hand holds the bar. In the more advanced moves on the bars, the thumbs can prove to be a hindrance and actually prevent the completion of a move. The gymnast should also hold the bars tightly to insure an easier spot for the spotter.

In terms of spotting, the only way to become a proficient spotter on the unevens is to "get in there" and spot. Too many women shy away from spotting this

*Figure 6.1 is on the preceding page.

event because they feel it requires a lot of strength, but far more important than strength is the spotter's anticipatory powers and timing, which develop and improve through experience. In general, the best spotter always reaches under the low bar, never over it because reaching over the bar may result in injury to the spotter.

When a gymnast is learning a move for the first time, the teacher should enlist a helper to assist in carrying the gymnast through the move so that the gymnast will have a kinesthetic awareness of the body and its parts and what will be expected of her in this particular move.

The uneven-parallel-bar event is presently the most evolutionary event in women's gymnastics. Because this event is changing so very rapidly, many moves that were considered to be of superior difficulty a few years ago have now been classified as medium and, in some cases, beginning moves. Unfortunately for the beginner, there are very few "easy" moves on the unevens, but all participants should learn and always perform all the skills with straight legs and arms and a tight body.

SAFETY

To many observers, the unevens appear to be the event fraught with the most danger because the gymnast is moving so rapidly around, over, and under the bars while changing directions. However, adhering to the usual safety procedures insures that there is no more inherent danger in this event than in any of the others. For proper mat coverage, mats should be under and completely around the bars with no overlapping or spaces. The bar attachments and adjustments must be checked for tightness before each gymnast's performance. The top of the high bar is 2.3 m., or 7 ft. 9^{9}/$_{16}$ in., from the floor the top of the low bar is 1.5 m., or 4 ft. 11^{1}/$_{16}$ in. from the floor. If a board is used to mount the bars, it should quickly be removed. The gymnast should be instructed about the skill she is to perform and the spotter and gymnast should know what each intends to do. Spotting is necessary. Almost all skills can and should be learned on the low bar first. Chalk (magnesium carbonate) should be provided for the hands.

All work on the uneven bars requires a solid foundation of basics. For the purpose of this book, the skills on the uneven bars will be divided into these basic families of moves: hip circles, cast wraps, kips, seat circles, sole circles, pops, somersaults, and handstands.

HIP CIRCLES
Back Pullover
Mount

The approach for the back pullover can be made from either direction. The gymnast begins by facing the low bar with her hands in an overgrip position (both hands over the bar) shoulder width apart. The gymnast steps forward on one leg (so that it is directly under the bar) and then kicks her free leg up and backward around the bar (Fig. 6.2). As she brings her hips to the bar by pulling with her arms, she throws her head backward. Her body circles the bar in a backward direction and she completes the skill in a front support position on the low bar (body stretched, hands holding the bar in an overgrip, the upper front of the thighs resting upon the bar).

Figure 6.2 • Back pullover mount

Corrections:
1. The gymnast should not step too far under and past the front of the bar.
2. The gymnast should forcefully pull the bar into the "belly button" (as in a true naval salute).
3. The head must go back to move around the bar in a backward direction.

Spotting:
1. The spotter stands to the side of the performer in front of the bar. The spotter helps the gymnast rotate around the bar by lifting the glutes with the hand further from the bar. Her other hand should be on the gymnast's shoulders.

Figure 6.3 • Mill circle with spot

Combinations:	1. Back pullover mount, back hip circle.
	2. Back pullover mount, front hip circle.
	3. Back pullover mount, squat on or through.
	4. Back pullover from a piked hang between the bars to the high bar.

Mill Circle

This skill, which also has been called a "single leg circle" or "crotch circle," is not a pure hip circle. With one leg in front and the other leg behind the bar, the gymnast takes an undergrip. She lifts her *tightened* body up and out, away from the bar, and circles in a forward direction around the bar (Fig. 6.3).

Corrections:
1. The legs should not touch the bar.
2. The gymnast must keep her body tight as she lifts herself out and away from the bar. The initial impetus provides the force for the skill's completion. The skill should not be dumped.
3. The gymnast's hips and shoulders should stay in line and within the base support (hands) throughout the skill.

Spotting:
1. The spotter stands sideways between the bars. She reaches under the bar with the arm closer to it and tightly holds onto the gymnast's wrist because beginners may "peel off." She places the other hand on the small of the gymnast's back at the bottom of the circle to lift her up in the skill's completion.

Combinations:
1. Mill circle facing either direction.
2. Mill circle catch the high bar.

Back Hip Circle

From a front support position (Fig. 6.4a), the gymnast pikes her hips slightly, brings her legs in and under and bar, and then extends them (this preparatory effort is called a "beat") (Fig. 6.4b). She must keep her shoulders in front of the bar. As the front of the hips hits the bar at the completion of the beat, the force should cause the hips to pike. The gymnast then throws back her head and her body circles the bar backwards. The gymnast completes the skill in a front support. She keeps the bar against the hips by pulling with the arms.

Teaching techniques and progressions:
1. The progression for this skill is the back pullover.
2. The beat should be practiced separately before the hip circle is added.

Corrections:
1. The shoulders should be kept in front of the bar during the beat until the pike occurs.

Figure 6.4 • Back hip circle: (a) front support and (b) cast

2. The bar must pike the performer. The gymnast cannot anticipate this action.
3. The impetus from the beat should be the force for the skill.
4. The arms and legs must be straight and stretched—STG.

Spotting:

1. The spotter stands to the side of the performer. She keeps one of her hands on the back of the performer's thigh and as rotation begins, her hands switch. The spotter should always reach under the bar to prevent injury to herself. The spotter keeps the gymnast's hips into the bar and helps with rotation. At the end of the move, the spotter brings one of her hands up to the front of the gymnast's shoulders.

Combinations:

1. Back pullover, back hip circle.
2. Front hip circle, back hip circle.
3. Back hip circle (high bar), cast wrap.
4. Back hip circle, high bar or low bar, facing either direction.

Front Hip Circle The gymnast forcefully dives forward from a high front support position (bar lower on the thigh). At the bottom of the dive she pikes her hips and begins to circle the bar in a forward direction. The hands shift to the top of the bar as she extends her legs and completes the skill in a front support position.

Teaching techniques and progressions:

1. The progression for this skill is from a front support position. The gymnast performs a forward roll off the bar while holding on with the hands.
2. The gymnast can learn the front hip circle by assuming a front support position on the low bar facing the high bar (Fig. 6.5). The gymnast grasps the high bar (this insures her body being high enough on the low bar). She places

206

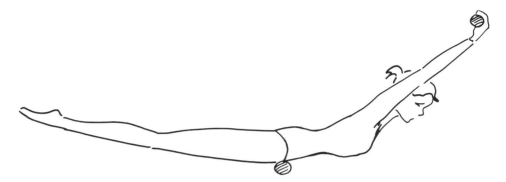

Figure 6.5 • Front hip circle (progression #2)

her hands on the low bar only as she is completing the skill. The spotter places one hand on the back of the gymnast's thighs and her other hand across the gymnast's upper back. The spotter must force the gymnast to pike.

3. The hands can be left loosely on the bar in the final progression, while the gymnast performs the hip circle in either direction.

Corrections:	1.	The body should be high on the bar.

Corrections:
1. The body should be high on the bar.
2. The skill should be initiated with great impetus.
3. A pike is essential.
4. The hands must shift to the top of the bar prior to the skill's conclusion.
5. The legs are extended to help lift the body to the top of the bar at the skill's conclusion.
6. Tight body, straight arms, and legs are important.

Spotting:
1. The spotter, who stands between the bars facing the gymnast, places one hand on the back of her thighs (Fig. 6.6). This hand insures that the body pikes by applying resistance to the legs. The spotter's other hand is between the gymnast's shoulder blades to insure a piking around the bar. The position of the spotter's hands reverses as the body completes its rotation.

Combinations:
1. Front hip circle on either bar, facing either direction.
2. Front hip circle, back hip circle.
3. Front hip circle, push away glide kip.
4. Front hip circle, handstand.
5. Front hip circle, somersault.
6. Front hip circle (back to high bar), catch high bar.

Figure 6.6 • Front hip circle with spot

Wrap (back hip circle from a long hang)

The width of the uneven bars should be adjusted for each gymnast. This adjustment can be determined by pushing the gymnast into the low bar while she is in a long hang (no shoulder sag) from the high bar (see Fig. 6.7). The low bar should contact the gymnast's body where her torso meets the upper part of her legs.

The wrap is a progression for a cast wrap but is never performed in a routine. The gymnast in a long hang position is either forcefully pushed into the low bar by the teacher/coach, or the gymnast pushes herself into the bar by using her foot to push away from the low bar. She then swings back into the low bar as hard as possible. The gymnast keeps her body tight, and there is no sag in the shoulders (this mistake is prevented by pulling the body up through the shoulders). As in the back hip circle, the gymnast must wait to react to the low bar before piking. When the gymnast's body is well into the low bar, she pikes and squeezes the bar between her legs and torso as hard as possible. When the gymnast can no longer hold onto the high bar with her hands—her knees are in close proximity to her cornea—she lets go and rotates around the low bar in a backward direction, ending in a front support on the low bar.

Figure 6.7 • Proper long-hang position

Teaching techniques and progressions:	1. The prerequisite for this skill is a back hip circle.
	2. The gymnast should swing and pike a few times prior to wrapping.

Corrections:	1. The shoulders should not sag.
	2. The pike should not be anticipated. The gymnast must *wait* for the bar, or she may taste her lunch for the second time.
	3. The gymnast should not let go of the high bar too soon.

Spotting:	1. Facing the gymnast, the spotter stands to the side between the bars. She places the hand that is closer to the high bar on the small of the gymnast's back and forces her into the bar. The other hand reaches under the low bar and holds the back of the gymnast's thighs to insure that the gymnast pikes in the skill.

Cast Wrap (cast from the high bar, back hip circle about the low bar) This is the first skill in which the body moves from one bar to and around the other bar. Initially, the body is in a front support position on the high bar. The gymnast beats slightly and lifts her tight body out and away from the bar with straight arms (Fig. 6.8). She keeps her head in neutral position and holds the bar very tightly with the hands. The gymnast does not sag her shoulders at the bottom of the cast. The ideal is to cast off the high bar with as much control and as slowly as possible. As the body approaches the low bar, the gymnast must not anticipate the wrap. She keeps her body tight and stretched and reacts to the low bar by piking and circling about the bar. Her body squeezes the bar to maintain the piked position. Her hands do not release the high bar until she can no longer hold on and she can see her knees in front of her eyes. The gymnast completes this maneuver by circling backward around the bar and finishing in a front support position on the low bar.

Figure 6.8 • Cast from high bar

Some gymnastics authorities relate the giant swing in men's gymnastics to the cast in women's gymnastics. The opinion of this writer is that these two skills are not synonymous in any way. At the bottom of the circling action in the giant swing, the male gymnast slides his hands more closely together and sags in the shoulders. This action gives more impetus for the last half of the giant or provides the force to complete the circle around the single bar. The purpose of the cast on the unevens is to provide as slow a means as possible for the gymnast to rotate around a bar that is at the bottom of her swing. Since the giant swing technique in men's gymnastics has a totally different purpose from the cast on the unevens, the two techniques of shoulder sag and sliding the hands together at the bottom of the cast should be avoided; they are counterproductive to the cast wrap.

Teaching techniques and progressions:

1. The cast should be learned from a front support on the low bar. The gymnast keeps her body excruciatingly tight while the teacher/coach/spotter lifts her backward off the bar.

2. The gymnast then goes to the high bar and is again lifted off in a cast.

3. When the gymnast is tight enough and is capable of doing the skill with her arms, she should cast from the high bar and the spotter should catch the front of her hips to prevent her from hitting the low bar.

4. As a prerequisite, the gymnast should have performed the wrap from a long hang, as previously described.

5. The cast and wrap are then combined (Fig. 6.9).

Corrections:

1. On the cast the gymnast should:
   a. Have a totally tight body—STG.
   b. Go out, not up and down.
   c. Hold tightly with the hands.
   d. Not sag or bottom out; no bent arms or banana back during the cast.

2. While wrapping, the gymnast should:
   a. Not anticipate the pike or wrap.
   b. Hold onto the high bar as long as possible to slow down the wrap.
   c. Tightly pike around the bar.
   d. Open her body at the wrap's completion to finish in a front support position with the hands in an overgrip on the low bar.

Spotting:

1. The spotter or spotters stand sideways between the bars and reach as high as possible with both hands. With the hand closer to the low bar, the spotter slows down the cast. She places her other hand on the gymnast's back to get her into the bar. The hand that has helped slow down the cast quickly shifts to the back of the thighs while reaching under the low bar to insure the pike on the wrap. This hand stays under and in front of the low bar and is in front of the gymnast's shoulder as she finishes the skill. The other hand helps

Figure 6.9 • Cast wrap with spot

to stop the gymnast's momentum, so that she can end in a front support, by applying upward pressure to the gluteal fold. The cast should always be spotted with beginners to intermediate gymnasts because, on occasion, the gymnast's hands may peel off the high bar, scaring her and her teacher/coach/spotter into a terrible state. This is especially true when, as the gymnast peels off the high bar, she approaches the low bar as if to perform a molar (like in teeth) circle.

Combinations:

1. Kip to the high bar, immediate cast wrap.
2. Cast wrap, eagle catch.
3. Cast wrap, hecht.
4. Cast wrap, push away glide kip.

Free Hip Circle

The free hip circle is a difficult skill that is performed in a backward direction. The term "free" refers to the fact that the hips do not touch the bar as they circle it. With an extremely tight body, the gymnast takes as great a beat as she can and then with only a very slight pike drives her feet in, under, and around the low bar. The initial impetus from the beat is the first determinant of the skill's completion. As her body begins to circle the bar, the gymnast drops her shoulders back. At the bottom of the circle, she quickly shifts her hands to the top of the bar and, with her body still tight, *attempts* to shoot for a handstand.

Teaching techniques and progressions:

1. The prerequisite for this skill are the performance of a back hip circle, uneven bar experience, and strong upper chest and arms.

Corrections:

The following are common errors:

1. A loose body.
2. Not enough force initially.
3. Too much of a pike.
4. Shifting the hands too late.

Spotting:

1. Standing sideways beside the bar the gymnast is on initially and will be on at the completion of the skill, the spotter helps the gymnast beat and drive into and under the low bar by keeping her hand and arm on the back of the gymnast's thighs. This hand follows the gymnast in and under the low bar. As the gymnast completes the circle the spotter reaches above the bar with both hands and helps keep the legs up so that the gymnast completes the cast or handstand.

Combinations:

1. Free hip circle low bar, push away glide.
2. Free hip circle high bar, cast wrap or cast belly bump.
3. Free hip circle either bar, either direction, cast handstand.

The free hip circle is currently a very popular skill for the unevens.

KIP

The single most important skill to learn on the uneven bars is the kip. The kip is critical to bar work. If one were to count kips in good to excellent uneven bar routines, there would probably be at least four or five variations of the kip in the eleven or twelve moves. The kip is an elusive skill to learn and the process is extremely frustrating, but the gymnast should persist in the quest for mastery of a kip. The kip is a basic concept in gymnastics, for by extending, bending, and extending in a kip in any event, the body goes from a low position to a high position.

Kip Between the Bars

This is the first kip to learn (Fig. 6.10). The gymnast performs it by sitting on the low bar while grasping the high bar in an overgrip. The body is extended (not arched) and piked at the waist so that the feet approximate the high bar. Then, while the legs are extended backward, the straight arms pull down as if the hands are pulling a pair of stockings or tights over the thighs and the gymnast completes the skill in a front support position on the high bar.

Teaching techniques and progressions:

1. A possible prerequisite for the kip between the bars might be a single- or double-leg stem rise.
2. The movement pattern of the skill can be performed mimetically from a supine position on the floor.
3. The rhythm of the kip is important: extend, bend, extend with an even quality.

Figure 6.10 • Kip between the bars

Corrections:

1. Not taking enough of an overgrip on the high bar results in the gymnast having to shift her hands to the top of the bar halfway through the kip and prevents her from completing the kip.

2. Bending the arms and pulling the bar in causes the kip to look like a "boob rise." When the arms are bent, the gymnast tries to wiggle her way up the bar.

3. Do not rush the kip. If the gymnast doesn't completely pike in the first phase of the kip, it will be most difficult to complete the skill.

4. Failure to extend the legs in the last phase of the kip results in a "muscle up" or poor technique.

5. Pulling more with one arm than the other results in a muscled kip or a very uneven or crooked-looking skill.

Spotting:

1. The spotter stands sideways between the bars. She places the hand closer to the low bar on the front of the gymnast's knee to help her with the initial and final extension. She places her other hand on the bottom of the glutes and helps the gymnast by lifting her upward.

Combinations:

1. Kip, cast wrap.
2. Kip, front hip circle.
3. Kip, back hip circle.
4. Kip, handstand.

Glide Kip

Standing behind the low bar, the gymnast pikes in the hips and lifts them back and upward while her hands reach forward and catch the low bar (Fig. 6.11). The glide forward then begins with the body in a piked position. The feet are kept as close to the floor as possible, until the end of the glide, when the body is extended. At the end of the glide, the gymnast forcefully pikes her body (the ankles are brought up to the low bar). As her hips start to drop back under the low bar, she extends her legs and simultaneously and forcefully pulls down her arms (straight).

Teaching techniques and progressions:

1. Standing behind the gymnast, the teacher/spotter grasps her waist and pulls her up and back. She instructs the gymnast to lift her feet from the floor while keeping them as close to the floor as possible without touching it.

2. The prerequisite for the glide kip is the kip between the bars.

3. If the gymnast's abdominals aren't strong enough to keep her feet up in the glide, it will be easier for her to straddle her legs after the jump and bring them quickly together at the end of the glide.

Corrections:

1. The head should remain in a neutral, unextended position.
2. The glide should not finish with an arch or banana back.

Figure 6.11 • Glide kip

3. Throughout the glide, the hands should remain over the bar in an overgrip so as to complete the kip.

4. The corrections for the kip part of the glide kip are the same as for the kip between the bars.

Spotting:

1. During the kip phases the spotter stands to the side of the gymnast and lifts her by placing her hand on the gymnast's glutes. If the legs are straddled in the glide, the spotter must step back and then move in to spot the kip after the feet pass by her during the glide.

Combinations:

1. Glide kip, squat through seat circle.
2. Glide kip, stoop up or straddle up sole circle (forward or backward).
3. Glide kip, front hip circle.

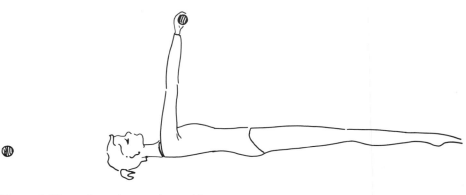

Figure 6.12 • Long hang prior to kip

4. Glide kip, back hip circle.
5. Kip from a long hang. This skill is very similar to the glide kip. The gymnast either squats on the low bar or sits on the low bar facing the high bar. She places her hands on the high bar in an overgrip and lifts her hips up and out. In the glide, the gymnast should attempt to reach a stretched body position parallel with the floor (Fig. 6.12), prior to performing the kip as described.
6. Glide kip, somersault.
7. Glide kip, handstand.

Glide Kip Catch   After performing the glide as instructed earlier, the gymnast initiates the first part of the kip. There is a pike at the end of the glide, followed by a forceful extension of the legs as the straight arms are pulled downward strongly. As the gymnast completes the last phase of the kip by extending her legs, she catches the high bar (Fig. 6.13).

Teaching techniques and progressions:

1. The prerequisites for this skill are a kip between the bars and a glide kip.

Corrections:

1. Often the performer will reach for the high bar before completing the kip. Thus, emphasize completing the downward thrust of the arms at the end of the kip, the move that will send the performer up! The move should not be rushed.

Spotting:

1. The spotter stands behind the low bar and to the side of the performer with her hands on the waist of the performer. At the end of the move, she gives the gymnast a lift to the high bar.

Combinations:

1. Glide kip catch, straddle over the low bar, kip to the high bar.
2. Glide kip half turn catch.
3. Glide kip full turn catch.
4. Glide kip catch, drop glide.

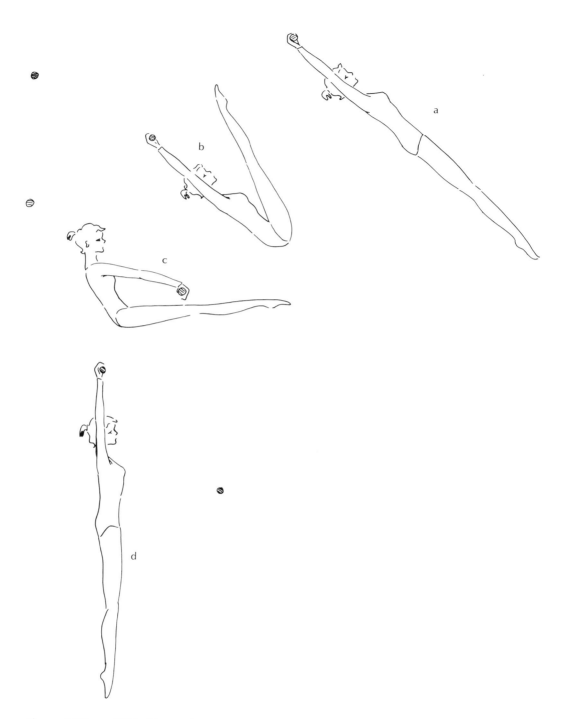

Figure 6.13 • Glide kip catch

**Glide
Overshoot**

At the end of the glide, the gymnast forcefully pikes her body and brings her feet between her hands. This backward momentum is allowed to continue as the performer pulls down with her arms (straight) and rides up around the back side of the low bar to a sitting position. She opens her body to stop forward momentum as she reaches the top of the bar.

Teaching
techniques and
progressions:

1. The prerequisite for this skill is an understanding of and the ability to do a kip.
2. The gymnast may have to increase her flexibility and abdominal strength to perform this skill.

Corrections:

1. Often the performer will become anxious about completing the move and place the back of her legs upon the bar before she has attained the proper sitting position *above* the bar. We often call this tendency "cheating the move." As its name implies, the move is an overshoot, which infers that the legs are brought over the bar and then pushed down.
2. The gymnast must quickly pike her legs in the initial stage of the kip.

Spotting:

1. The spotter stands behind the low bar with her hands on the gymnast's waist to help with the overshoot phase of the move.

Combinations:

1. Glide overshoot, front seat circle.
2. Glide overshoot, back beat underswing catch high bar.
3. Glide overshoot from a long hang on high bar.
4. Glide overshoot, straddle cut catch.
5. Glide overshoot on high bar.
6. Glide overshoot, reverse kip (Fig. 6.14).

Figure 6.14 • Glide double-leg overshoot with amplitude prior to reverse kip

Glide Overshoot Catch High Bar

This move begins in the same manner as a glide overshoot, but at the end of the move, the gymnast thrusts the backs of the thighs downward onto the low bar and reaches for the high bar with her hands.

The teaching techniques, progressions, corrections, and spotting are the same as for the glide overshoot.

Combinations:

1. Glide overshoot catch the high bar, kip to the high bar.
2. Glide overshoot catch the high bar, back somersault between the bars.

Glide Overshoot Straddle Cut Catch Low Bar

Upon completion of the overshoot, the gymnast pulls downward strongly with her arms. Then, as she straddles her legs, her hands release and regrip the low bar (see Fig. 6.15). The legs are straddled by circling them. This is an excellent skill with difficulty rating.

Teaching techniques and progressions:

1. The prerequisite for this skill is a glide overshoot.

Corrections:

1. The performer should pull down and be above the bar before straddling her legs. The legs should be straddled in a circular pattern to provide for the hips to be back and piked so that a glide can ensue.
2. This skill should not be rushed.

Spotting:

1. Standing to the side, the spotter moves in behind the gymnast and places her hands on both sides of the gymnast's waist after the glide to help the gymnast lift for the overshoot. Then she pulls the gymnast back for the straddle cut catch.

Figure 6.15 • Glide double-leg overshoot straddle cut catch

Combinations: 1.   Glide straddle cut catch the low bar, glide kip.

                         2.   Glide straddle cut catch the high bar.

Glide Mill-up   At the completion of a glide, the gymnast brings a single leg between the hands (as backward momentum picks up) and pulls her arms down strongly. She keeps her legs split and her rear leg "kips" up as she completes the move, ending in a split position above the low bar (one leg in front and one leg behind the bar).

Corrections: 1.   The legs should not touch the low bar until the move has been completed.

                         2.   The front leg must be piked very quickly on the jam.

                         3.   The arms pull forcefully downward on the bar to help lift the body up in the last position of the skill.

Spotting: 1.   The spotter stands between or in front of the bars. She places her hands on the gymnast's waist or glutes and assists her in completing the move (Fig. 6.16).

Combinations: 1.   Glide mill-up, mill circle.

                         2.   Glide mill-up, catch the high bar. The gymnast should not reach for the high bar until she has completed the kip phase of the mill-up.

Reverse Kip   The reverse kip is the most difficult kip, but it is an excellent skill on the bars because there is a dramatic change of direction within the skill. The gymnast performs a glide double-leg overshoot (Fig. 6.17), and just before her legs go over the bar to a sitting position, she reverses her direction and does $^{13}/_{15}$ of a rear or

Figure 6.16 • Glide single leg shoot through with spot

Figure 6.17 • Reverse kip, initial pump

back seat circle (Figs. 6.17, 6.18, and 6.19). She completes the skill in a sitting position on the bar.

Teaching techniques and progressions:

1. The prerequisite for this skill is the ability to perform a double-leg overshoot and a back seat circle (Fig. 6.17b).
2. These two skills should be reviewed separately and then performed together (Fig. 6.18).

Figure 6.18 • Reverse kip

Corrections:

1. Often a gymnast performs the pike-through (jam) too slowly in the initial stages of the overshoot.
2. The hips should remain as close to the bar as possible throughout the skill.
3. The jam, or pump, of the overshoot should go up, and not out (Fig. 6.19).
4. The hands must shift early to the top of the bar, at the bottom of the back hip circle phase to help the gymnast complete the skill.
5. A tight pike should be maintained throughout the skill, until the end, when the body opens up at the top of the bar to complete the skill.

Spotting:

1. The spotter helps the gymnast on the pump, or jam, by pushing the gymnast's hips up, not out (Fig. 6.20). Then the spotter helps the gymnast change direction by applying force with one hand in the back seat circle phase. Then the spotter reaches up under the bar with the same hand and places it on the rear of the thighs to lift the gymnast up during the last phase of the skill. She places her other hand on the back of the gymnast's shoulders at the end of the kip.

Combinations:

1. Reverse kip in either direction on the low or high bar.
2. Reverse kip (low bar facing high bar), kip from a long hang on the high bar.
3. Reverse kip, back beat underswing or back seat circle.

The importance of kips cannot be overemphasized. Gymnasts must begin practicing the kip between the bars as a basic skill in gymnastics. The kip accomplishment is elusive and the gymnast must pursue it as no other skill in gymnastics. It might take a week or two years to learn a kip, but neither the gymnast nor the teacher/coach should become discouraged—rather, more determined. Once the gymnast has mastered the kip, she can learn almost any other

Figure 6.19 · Reverse kip

skill. Kips are the invaluable connectors in uneven bar routines and they dominate the event. So "hang in there," or kip in there, anyway.

SOLE CIRCLES   The name "sole circle" derives from the fact that in this move the soles of the feet are placed on the bar. This family of moves can be performed on either bar facing either direction. These skills are hard on the hands and cannot be practiced for too long at one time.

Straddle Sole Circle Turn Cast Wrap   Standing on the low bar and facing the high bar, the gymnast takes an overgrip on the high bar. She then jumps so that her feet are straddled outside of her hands with the soles against the bar. She begins to gain backward momentum (see Fig. 6.21). As her hips begin to ride up the back side of the high bar, she forcefully extends her legs and brings them together. Then she initiates a 180° turn. The hands may be changed one at a time or both at the same time (more difficult but can be quite a classy move if the arms are flared) as the turn starts. If the turn is to be to the performer's left, she may place her left hand in an overgrip position on the high bar before beginning the move. Her right hand crosses behind the left and assumes an undergrip. After the turn, the body approaches the low bar in a long hang. The bar pikes the body and a "wrap" follows.

Teaching techniques and progressions: 1. Standing in a straddle position on the low bar and facing the high bar, the gymnast holds the high bar with her hands for balance (Fig. 6.22). A spotter stands behind the gymnast and places her hands on the gymnast's glutes. The

Figure 6.20 • (left) Reverse kip spot
Figure 6.21 • (middle) Beginning a straddle back sole circle
Figure 6.22 • (right) Straddle back sole circle

gymnast then places her hands on the low bar, and with the spotter's help, lowers herself slowly and with control under the low bar.

2. Then the gymnast should perform the sole circle on the high bar.

3. After the sole circle concept is a reality, the gymnast can add the wrap.

Corrections: 1. The gymnast should be as compact and tight as possible. To achieve this goal, she pushes down on the bar as hard as she can with her feet and pulls her hands on the bar against her feet.

2. The sole circle should be ridden as high as possible before the feet disengage for the turn.

3. The body should be extended and tight, then turned.

4. The corrections outlined for the wrap from the cast wrap apply to this skill also.

5. Often, poor leg form is common in straddle sole circles and it should be corrected.

Spotting: 1. The spotter stands between the bars on the opposite side from the direction the gymnast is turning toward. She places her hands under the gymnast's hips and the small of her back to help complete the turn and carry the body into the low bar.

Combinations: 1. Straddle sole circle, half turn, cast wrap, eagle.

2. Straddle sole circle, one and a half turns, cast wrap (difficult but beautiful).

3. Straddle sole circle, half turn, cast wrap, squat.

Figure 6.23 • Front straddle sole circle with spot (combination #6)

4. Straddle sole circle, half turn, cast wrap, push away glide kip.

5. Facing the other direction, straddle sole circle, belly bump, and so on.

6. Front straddle sole circle (Fig. 6.23).

Front Stoop Sole Circle

The name of this skill is not indicative of the gymnast's mentality. The gymnast places her feet between her hands on the bar. With her hands, she pulls the bar in an undergrip against the feet (see Fig. 6.24). The hips begin to move forward. The knees stay as close to the eyes as possible (a tight pike).

At the completion of the forward momentum (which is great), after the body has made a 270° rotation around the bar, the gymnast can change her hand position to an overgrip as she drops her feet from the bar and lifts her head. Then she executes a glide, which results in a change in the direction of movement.

Teaching techniques and progressions:

1. This skill can be performed first with a spotter standing on the side of the bar toward which the gymnast will initially circle. The spotter places her hands upon the top of the gymnast's shoulders while she faces her. The spotter then eases the gymnast forward (see Fig. 6.25).

2. This skill must be spotted, for considerable centrifugal force develops within it and the gymnast could quickly peel off the bar.

Corrections:

1. A tight pike must be maintained, so the hips must stay in line with the shoulders and hands throughout. A tight pike is accomplished by a hard and sustained effort of the arms throughout to pull the body, legs, and feet into the bar.

Figure 6.24 • Front stoop circle with spot

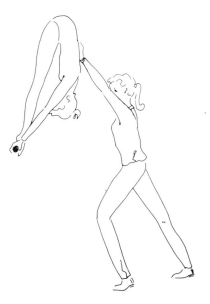

Figure 6.25 • Front stoop circle with alternate spot for learning skill

2. The skill should be initiated from the perpendicular above the bar.
3. The feet should not disengage until the circle is as high as possible.

Spotting:

1. The spotter stands behind the low bar, reaches under the low bar, and grips the wrist of the performer. As the gymnast initiates the regrip, the spotter moves to the back of the performer and grasps her waist with both hands. This positioning for the spotter occurs when the gymnast is facing away from the high bar.

Figure 6.26 • Front stoop circle on high bar, back somersault dismount (combination #3)

Combinations:	1.	Front stoop circle, reverse grip glide.
	2.	Front stoop circle, catch high bar.
	3.	Front stoop circle on high bar, back somersault dismount (Korbut) either over low bar or back off high bar (ride the sole circle high); Fig. 6.26.

Back Stoop Circle Catch High Bar in a Pike Hang

The gymnast places her feet between her hands on the low bar in an overgrip. Her body is in a tight pike. Backward momentum is begun. When facing the high bar, the performer can take the move in a tight pike rotating around the low bar to the high bar and catch. This is an older skill that is not in common use.

Teaching techniques and progressions:

1. The gymnast should perform the back stoop circle with good spotting as described in the progressions section of the straddle back sole circle.
2. She then should do the back stoop circle without a regrasp to the high bar.
3. Then the gymnast can attempt the whole skill.

Corrections:

1. The move begins high above the low bar when the performer's body is perpendicular to the floor.
2. The gymnast should not "sit out" the move.
3. A great deal of momentum is necessary and the gymnast can increase momentum with a tight pike.
4. The gymnast should not open up the body when releasing the low bar.
5. The head remains tucked throughout this move.

Spotting:

1. The spotting for this move is critical because the gymnast's body assumes a most vulnerable position for injury. The spotter stands between the bars and reaches under the low bar to grasp the gymnast's wrist with her hand. As the performer's body passes under the low bar, the spotter places both hands underneath the gymnast's back and keeps them there until the gymnast has securely caught the high bar.

Combinations:

1. Back stoop circle catch high bar, split legs to mill position on low bar.
2. Back stoop circle catch the high bar, dislocate pop to a handstand on low bar.
3. Back stoop circle (complete on the bar), back seat circle.
4. Back stoop circle catch high bar, half turn wrap low bar or drop glide.
5. Back stoop circle in either direction on low or high bar.
6. Back stoop circle on high bar, front somersault dismount (sole circle must be ridden as high as possible). Can be performed off high bar or off high bar over low bar (very difficult).
7. Back stoop circle low bar, handstand (toe on handstand)—a good stoop circle and push through the shoulders is essential.

**Back Stoop
Circle Cast
Catch High
Bar, Turn**

This move begins as does the sole circle with the exception that as the gymnast begins to ride up the back side of the low bar, she forces her legs out and her hands release the low bar and catch the high bar. When her body is extended, she initiates a turn so that her body faces the low bar (a change of grip occurs in the turn).

The teaching techniques, progressions, and corrections are the same as for the sole circle.

Spotting:

1. The spotter stands between the bars and reaches under the bar for the gymnast's wrist. As the gymnast's body passes under the low bar, the spotter places her hands on the small of the back and on the back of the thighs on the side away from the direction of the turn.

SEAT CIRCLES

Seat circles as a family of moves are distinguished by the fact the gymnast circles the bar with her body in a sitting position while supporting her weight on her hands.

**Back Seat Circle
Facing Out**

The gymnast sits on the low bar with her body in a piked position. Her hands are in an overgrip on the low bar. She raises her body off the bar so that only her hands support the weight of her body. The body should be very tight when the gymnast initiates the move. Her head is kept up and momentum is begun in a backward direction (Fig. 6.27). The body makes an arc around the bar. As the hips come up the front side of the bar, the gymnast quickly shifts her hands to the top of the bar and uses a straight arm pull to sit again on the low bar as she then extends her body.

Figure 6.27 • Back seat circle with amplitude

Figure 6.28 • Back seat circle or back beat (progression #1)

Teaching techniques and progressions:	1. The progression for the back seat circle is the back seat circle underswing on the low bar. The gymnast, in a sitting position, falls backward while maintaining a pike with her head tucked (Fig. 6.28). When beneath the bar, the gymnast changes direction and begins to ride back up the bar. She extends her legs and pushes down on the low bar then releases the low bar and grasps the high bar. The gymnast should remember to keep her head in and her knees extended. The spotter stands between the bars and places both hands on the small of the gymnast's back in the second phase of the move.
	2. After the back beat underswing, the gymnast should perform the back seat circle.
Corrections:	1. Amplitude should be the aim of the gymnast before she initiates this move.
	2. The hips, shoulders, and hands of the gymnast should all be in line throughout the move.
	3. The gymnast keeps her hips as close to the bar as possible through the move.
	4. The hands must shift quickly at the end of the move to insure its completion. Then the performer opens her body.
Spotting:	1. The spotter stands in front of the low bar and to the side of the gymnast (Fig. 6.29). The spotter then reaches under the low bar and places her hand on the gymnast's wrist. As the move nears completion, the spotter places her free hand on the front of the performer's shoulders or on the back of her thighs to keep her from falling forward.
Combinations:	1. Back seat circle, underswing catch high bar.
	2. Back seat circle, then catch high bar.

Figure 6.29 • Back seat circle with spot

3. High bar back seat circle (half), dislocate.
4. Back seat circle on either low bar or high bar (Fig. 6.30) facing either direction.

Front Seat Circle

Facing away from the high bar, the gymnast assumes a sitting position on the low bar. Her hands are in an undergrip position. Her body pikes tightly before she begins the move (see Fig. 6.31). The momentum is then started out and forward. As the body completes its rotation of the low bar, the performer extends her legs and completes the move by lifting the torso (Newton's law of action and reaction).

Figure 6.30 • Back seat circle on high bar

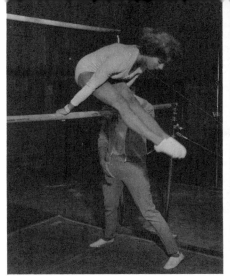

Figure 6.31 • Front seat circle with spot

Corrections: 1. The gymnast should assume a high and tight pike at the beginning and take the move out, not just down.
2. The hips, shoulders, and hands should be in line with each other.
3. The move should begin with a very strong impetus.

Spotting: 1. The spotter stands between the bars and to the side of the performer. The spotter's hand reaches under the low bar and grasps the performer's wrist. She places her free hand on the small of the gymnast's back and assists her in completing the move.

Combinations: 1. Front seat circle on either bar facing either direction.
2. Front seat circle on low bar, catch high bar.
3. Front seat circle, straddle cut catch low bar or high bar.
4. Front seat circle on high bar, straddle cut catch.

POPS The popping skills on the unevens are similar conceptually to kips. The body opens to layout from a piked position and this action should lift or cause the body to rise.

Eagle Catch This move is thrown from a back hip circle or wrap on the low bar. The cast and wrap are as essential to a good eagle catch as the roundoff is to good back handsprings.
 As the gymnast casts her body from the high bar, it must be tight and straight (no banana back). The body should pike only after hitting the low bar, as a reaction

231

Figure 6.32 • Eagle catch

to contact with it. The gymnast may slow down the speed of the wrap by holding on to the high bar as long as possible. The gymnast's body should be tightly piked; her torso and head, as well as her legs, should be "in." From this position, draped across the low bar, the gymnast "pops," or opens up, her body. Her hands are pronated to catch the high bar as shown in Fig. 6.32.

Teaching techniques and progressions:

1. The gymnast should kneel in front of the low bar, her back to it and piked forward. From this position she extends and catches the low bar in an eagle grip (Fig. 6.33).

Figure 6.33 • Eagle catch (progression #1)

Figure 6.34 • Eagle catch with spot

2. The gymnast should be in a piked position or draped over the low bar. She places her feet on the thigh of the spotter, who is standing directly behind her underneath the high bar. One of the spotter's arms reaches around the front of the gymnast's thighs. The spotter places her free hand on the gymnast's back, just above her waist. The gymnast then pops, or opens, her body and, with a lot of help from her friend, catches the high bar.

3. The gymnast then performs the skill from a swinging wrap and then a cast.

Corrections:
1. A good cast (no sag) and a tightly piked wrap are essential.
2. When the body opens up, the "belly button" is pushed against the low bar.
3. The gymnast should not throw with her arms but with the torso and legs.
4. This is a "soft" move.
5. Both legs and chest open simultaneously, not just one body section.
6. The eagle should rise . . . !

Spotting:
1. The spotter stands between the unevens and either places one hand on the small of the back of the gymnast and the other hand on the front of her thigh or places both hands around the back of the waist of the gymnast as she pops for the eagle catch (Fig. 6.34).

Combinations:
1. Eagle catch, drop glide to low bar.
2. Eagle catch, straddle over low bar, seat circle or leg over mill circle.
3. From a belly bump, wrap inside or reverse eagle, straddle low bar, turn drop glide to low bar (Fig. 6.35).
4. From a belly bump, wrap pop half turn catch high bar. This is one of the best

Figure 6.35 • Reverse or inside eagle catch, half turn drop glide (combination #3)

Figure 6.36 • (left) Eagle pop full twist (combination #5)
Figure 6.37 • (right) Eagle pop full twist (combination #5)

connectors for the bars and is not that difficult. The spotter places both hands on the gymnast's waist.

5. Eagle pop full twist (Figs. 6.36 and 6.37). The gymnast must pop the eagle and then twist. This is a combination of the classic and modern twist (see Chapter 2). If the gymnast is twisting toward her left, her right hand crosses under her left for the catch at the completion of three-fourths of the twist and vice versa for twisting in the other direction. The skill should rise, and the rhythm is: pop, twist. The spotter's hands are on both sides of the waist.

Hecht Dismount   This skill is executed exactly as an eagle catch with one large exception: the hecht is thrown earlier than the eagle catch. From a cast, the gymnast tightly pikes her body while wrapping. As she begins to approach the top of the low bar, she forcefully pops, or opens the pike, to a layout (Fig. 6.38) and consequently she sails up and away from the low bar to stick a landing.

Teaching techniques and progressions:

1. The gymnast drapes her body over the low bar, and two spotters in front of the low bar and slightly to the side lift her up from her piked position and off the low bar as she extends her body. Another spotter should stand between the bars to help lift the gymnast's legs out and over the low bar.

2. Then the gymnast should do the skill from a swinging cast.

3. Finally the gymnast should perform the skill with a slow, controlled, no-sag cast wrap.

Corrections:

1. Often the gymnast "rolls" her body off the low bar. There is no popping action, so the body does not rise above the low bar but, instead, rolls off in front of it. Rolling off causes the tops of the thighs to appear to be slightly abraded. To prevent this effect, the gymnast can achieve a tight pike and a more explosive pop by lifting both the chest and legs simultaneously.

Figure 6.38   •   Hecht dismount

2. At times, a gymnast will execute either too late or too early.

3. A poor cast is often the causative factor in a poor hecht.

Spotting:

1. The spotter or spotters stand in front of the low bar and to the side of the gymnast. As the gymnast completes her wrap, the spotter reaches in front of the gymnast so that one hand is on the gymnast's "belly." With her other hand on the small of the gymnast's back, the spotter helps to lift her up and away from the low bar.

Combinations:

1. Hecht dismount.

2. Hecht with a full twist (Fig. 6.39). The prerequisite for this skill is a good, tight, and high hecht. The spotter reaches under the gymnast's belly with one arm so that her hand is on the waist. She places her other hand on the near side of the gymnast's waist, and by pushing and pulling, she helps the gymnast execute the twist (Fig. 6.40).

3. Hecht, back somersault dismount. The prerequisite for this skill is an explosive and high hecht. The spotter helps lift the gymnast in the hecht and then spots as if spotting a back somersault on the floor.

4. Hecht from the high bar (Fig. 6.41). This skill is also known as a "single bar hecht." The progression for this skill is to attempt it on the low bar first. The gymnast must do a good back hip circle, which includes keeping her shoulders in front of the bar on the beat and then *piking tightly* during the back hip circle. The opening, or popping, is the same as for the hecht. Spotting is also the same. Once the gymnast can perform this skill on the low bar, she goes up to the bar and throws the move away from the low bar. Once she can perform the skill as such, then she can do it on the high bar over the low bar.

Figure 6.39 • Hecht with full twist (combination #2)

Figure 6.40 • Hecht with full twist with spot (combination #2)

5. Hecht from the high bar, full twist.
6. Hecht dismount with straddled legs (Fig. 6.42). This skill should not be taught initially, for poor technique can cause the gymnast to roll the skill. This mistake would preclude learning any of the other hecht variations.

The popping skills are exciting moves on the uneven bars for both the spectator and the gymnast when performed with proper technique, which, to summarize, includes tight body, tight pike, and forceful opening of the legs and chest simultaneously.

Figure 6.41 • (left) Hecht from high bar (combination #4)
Figure 6.42 • (right) Hecht with straddled legs (combination #6)

BELLY BUMPS   The moves in this family have also been called "suicides" (how's that for a confidence builder?) and "stomach whips." A belly bump is identifiable as such when the gymnast, facing the high bar with her back to the low bar and her hands on the high bar, drops to the front of her hips on the low bar. From this position she can bounce up and perform another skill or wrap around the low bar.

Belly Bump   In a layout position over the low bar with her hands on the high bar, the gymnast
Bounce   falls onto the low bar without a shoulder sag. When the bar touches the front of her hips, the gymnast pikes tightly and then pulls down on her shoulders lifting her body up and extends her legs up behind herself again.

Teaching
techniques and
progressions:

1. Initially the gymnast may perform this skill from a front support on the low bar as in Fig. 6.43.
2. This skill can be learned by standing on the low bar and facing the high bar, hands in an overgrip on the high bar. The gymnast jumps up slightly from the low bar, extends her tight body into a layout position, and bounces on the low bar with the front of her hips.
3. The gymnast can then perform the skill from a front support on the high bar, back to the low bar. The gymnast casts from the high bar, as in a cast wrap, and belly-bump bounces on the low bar.

Corrections:

1. The gymnast's shoulders should not sag.
2. The gymnast should not pike until the bar pikes her and then she should pike tightly.
3. The body must be very tight throughout the whole skill.
4. After piking, the gymnast should use her upper chest and shoulder muscles to pull her body up and as high away from the low bar as possible so that she attains a layout position (no banana back).

Figure 6.43 · Belly bump progression

Figure 6.44 • Belly bump with spot

Spotting: 1. Standing sideways in front of the low bar, the spotter eases the gymnast's body onto the low bar and helps her pike and extend by placing her hands on the front and back of the gymnast's thighs (Fig. 6.44).

Combinations: 1. Belly bump bounce, straddle legs over low bar, kip from a long hang.

2. Belly bump bounce, full twist, belly bump. The gymnast must not sag and should have a tight body in this skill to pull herself up as high off the bar as she can. At the top of the bounce she completes a full twist. The wrists of the hands naturally turn along the top of the high bar as the gymnast accomplishes the twist. Too often in this skill the gymnast becomes confused by too many grip changes and by anticipating them mentally. The complexity of the changes should be minimized. The spotter for this skill can either walk under the gymnast after the bump and turn the gymnast or place one hand on each side of the gymnast's waist and turn her by pushing with the closer hand and pulling with the far hand.

3. Belly bump bounce, hop to a handstand on the low bar. This skill should be spotted from a platform or mats piled to the side and at the height of the low bar or with the spotter standing on one leg on the low bar while her other leg is over the high bar. The spotter catches the gymnast's legs and helps with the handstand. Another spotter stands between the bars and spots the gymnast's shoulders, if necessary.

4. Belly bump bounce, front somersault catch the high bar (refer to the discussion of somersaults later in this chapter).

Belly Bump Wrap

In a layout position above and over the low bar with her hands on the high bar, the gymnast falls onto the low bar without a shoulder sag. When the bar touches the front of her hips, the gymnast pikes tightly holding onto the high bar as long as she can to slow down the wrap. Then she wraps around the low bar. The same principles of the cast wrap apply to this skill.

Teaching techniques and progressions:

1. The gymnast can learn this skill by standing on the low bar and facing the high bar with her hands in an overgrip on the high bar. The gymnast jumps up slightly from the low bar and extends her tight body into a layout position and wraps on the low bar with the front of her hips.
2. The gymnast then can perform the skill from a front support on the high bar with her back to the low bar. The gymnast casts from the high bar as in a cast wrap and belly-bump wraps on the low bar.

Corrections:

1. The gymnast's shoulders should not sag.
2. The gymnast should not pike until the bar pikes her and then she should pike tightly.
3. The body must be very tight throughout this skill.
4. The gymnast should hold onto the high bar as long as possible prior to wrapping to slow down the wrap and make the following skills easier to accomplish.

Spotting:

1. Standing between the bars, the spotter reaches up and over the low bar and momentarily touches the front of the gymnast's hips to help slow down the cast. When the gymnast pikes, the spotter reaches under the low bar and helps her by placing her hands on the back of the gymnast's thighs. The spotter must then prepare to spot the next skill out of the wrap.

Combinations:

1. Belly bump wrap, push-away glide.
2. Belly bump wrap, inside or reverse eagle (see the section on pops earlier in this chapter).
3. Belly bump wrap, pop half turn catch the high bar (this skill is also described in the pops section of this chapter).

SOMERSAULTS Front Somersault Between the Bars

It is with great fear and trepidation that the author includes a description of this skill in this text. The reason for this hesitation is that too often serious falls occur when a gymnast attempts this skill in a meet where her coach cannot stand between the bars to spot her. With spotting, this skill is relatively easy to learn. Thus, teaching it can propel a teacher/coach on a relatively high ego trip. When a gymnast falls while doing this skill, she lands on her upper back and lower neck and could injure her spinal cord or suffer a compression fracture of one of her vertebrae. At the very least, after falling during an attempt to perform this skill, the gymnast will suffer from both fright and a very stiff and sore back. The spill should also give the coach a hundred new grey hairs. Because this skill is performed and

Figure 6.45 • Front somersault between the bars with spot

taught, however, possibly a full explanation of the skill's dangers and the proper technique for its execution—although there are other somersaults that are safer and better advised—will help to prevent some unfortunate accidents.

The front somersault between the bars begins from a front support position on the low bar, back to the high bar (Fig. 6.45). The gymnast beats and casts her hips up as if casting to a handstand. From here the gymnast straddles her legs and reaches between them to grasp the higher bar. The body rotates about its horizontal axis between the bars, thereby somersaulting.

Teaching techniques and progressions:

1. The prerequisite for this skill is the ability to press a straddle handstand on the floor (see Chapter 2). The gymnast should be strong.
2. The gymnast should perform timers. The timer is the first portion of this skill. From a front support position, the gymnast casts up, straddles her legs, and catches her gluteal fold (where her glutes and upper thigh meet) on the high bar. The timer should be used as a review or refresher prior to the somersault performance even by gymnasts who can easily do the skill.
3. Then the gymnast tries the skill with two good spotters and a crash pad under the bars.

Corrections:

1. The gymnast must have a strong and powerful cast to the almost-handstand position.
2. The gymnast should not rush the skill. It has two distinct parts: the handstand and the rotation. If she turns the skill too soon (before reaching the almost-handstand), the catch will be impossible. Further, the hips should also be lifted backward as well as up.
3. The gymnast should not straddle her legs too soon.
4. This is a very strong and explosive skill.

Spotting:

1. The spotters, standing sideways between the bars, place their hands closer to the low bar on the gymnast's back just between the shoulder blades to help rotate and suspend the gymnast. They place their other hands on the front of the gymnast's thighs to help lift in the timer phase of the skill (see Fig. 6.45). This spot is relatively easy when the spotter can stand between the bars and start with her hands in the proper place on the gymnast. In competition, though, the spotter may not stand between the bars. At this time, this spot becomes next to impossible. The spotter gets as close as possible to being to the side and under the gymnast in as low a position (slight squat). She reaches out and if the gymnast does not catch attempts to break her fall.

   This skill is an excellent and nonworrisome skill when performed by a fine, experienced, and strong gymnast.

Combinations:

1. Front hip circle, front somersault between the bars, drop glide.
2. Mount by a jump front support, front somersault between the bars.
3. Glide kip, front somersault between the bars.

Front Somersault Facing the High Bar, from Low Bar to High Bar

From a front support position on the low bar facing the high bar, the gymnast casts to a handstand, leans her shoulders slightly forward, straddles her legs, rotates about her horizontal axis, and catches the high bar.

Teaching techniques and progressions:

1. The gymnast must be able to press a straddle handstand on the floor (see Chapter 2) and must be able to cast fairly well to a handstand on the bars.
2. The gymnast can be lifted through the skill by two spotters using the spot that will be described shortly.
3. The gymnast then goes for the move 110 percent.

Corrections:

1. The gymnast must strongly cast the handstand.
2. She should not drop her shoulders too far over the low bar.
3. This skill should be thought of and performed in two parts: the handstand and then somersault.
4. This is an explosive skill, not a lazy one.

Spotting:

1. The spotters stand between the bars on each side of the gymnast (Fig. 6.46). They place their hands closer to the low bar on the gymnast's upper arm, thumbs down and supinated. With their other hands on the gymnast's back, just above her waist, as the cast to the handstand finishes, they suspend the gymnast until she catches. The hands on the gymnast's arms must move to help her catch the high bar after she has begun the handstand and the rotation.

Figure 6.46 • Front somersault facing high bar with spot

The best part about this skill is that if the gymnast does not catch the bar she will land on her feet or, at the worst, her glutes.

Combinations:
1. Front somersault from low bar to high bar (facing the high bar), half turn drop glide.
2. Front hip circle, front somersault.
3. Glide kip, front somersault.
4. As a mount, front support to front somersault.
5. Belly bump bounce, front somersault. This is the same skill except that the hands start on the high bar, release, somersault, and regrasp the high bar (Fig.

Figure 6.47 • Belly bump front somersault (combination #5)

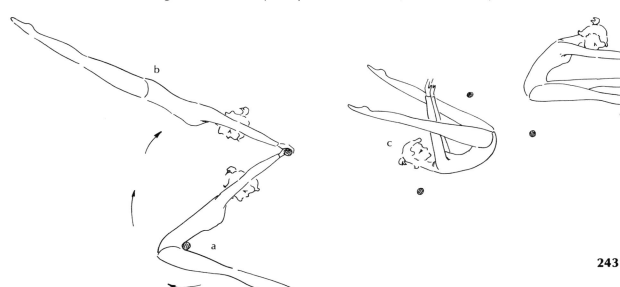

6.47). The gymnast must pull up as hard as she can before turning the somersault out of the belly bump. The spotters spot the gymnast's back while standing between the bars.

Back Somersault The back somersault between the bars is the easiest of the somersaults because rather than working against gravity, as in the previously described somersaults, in this skill the gymnast and gravity work together (finally). From a pike long hang position with the legs between the hands and the high bar (basket) the gymnast rotates backward then releases the high bar as she somersaults to a regrasp on the low bar and glide (Fig. 6.48).

Teaching techniques and progressions:

1. The gymnast assumes a basket position with her feet on the spotter's shoulder and the spotter's arms around her legs and simply reaches for the low bar. The spotter supports her until the catch then releases her legs for the glide (Fig. 6.49).
2. The gymnast then tries the skill again from the basket position and then adds the previous skill.
3. The gymnast should learn this skill in stoop position, for it is easier to spot than the straddle.

Corrections:

1. The gymnast must maintain a relatively tight pike.
2. The gymnast should let go of the high bar just before she sees the low bar so as to get a good push away from the low bar to a glide. Many gymnastics authorities advocate a late release, after the gymnast has glimpsed the low bar. Experience indicates that a late release can result in a molar (like in teeth)

Figure 6.48 • Back somersault

Figure 6.49 • Back somersault drop glide (progression #1) with spot

        circle and a poor glide or no glide at all. Whatever works for the gymnast she should use.

3. When the gymnast catches the low bar, her shoulders cannot sag nor can the pike open or her feet will touch the ground. This is the most difficult part of the skill.

Spotting: 1. Standing sideways between the bars, the spotter catches the back of the gymnast's thighs as she rotates down and tries to suspend her and prevent her feet from touching the ground.

Combinations: 1. Back somersault in straddle or stoop, glide.

            2. Sitting on the low bar hands on the high bar, jam or three-quarter overshoot (see kips), back somersault, glide.

3. Sitting on the high bar, back beat underswing or half a back seat circle (slow), back somersault, glide.

4. From a long hang on the high bar beat or pike into the low bar forcefully, extend legs and straddle them up and over the low bar to the basket position, back somersault (in straddle), glide.

The somersaults are very popular skills on the uneven bars. These are not skills for beginners or low intermediates.

HANDSTANDS

The premier family of skills on the unevens is the handstand. Just as gymnasts should train hard to accomplish a kip, they should also dedicate themselves to learning a handstand on the bars. The training commences with pressing straddle handstands (Chapter 2) and continues through attempts to cast handstands on a single bar (see Fig. 6.50). These efforts must be diligent and constant if success is to be the reward. All of the principles regarding the handstand, notably a tight body, forward pelvis (no banana back), STG, and no sagging in the shoulders, are very important on the unevens. In the Middle Ages of women's gymnastics (early 1970s), the trend was to jump into handstands on the unevens. This approach is no longer recommended, for jumping into a skill is typical of vaulting or floor exercise and not bars. It also adds an intermediate break in a routine.

Straddle Down Handstand

From a front support position on the high bar, facing the low bar, the gymnast pikes around the high bar and places her hands shoulder width apart on the low bar. The gymnast then casts her legs up into a handstand while pulling with her arms so that

Figure 6.50 • Cast handstand on high bar

Figure 6.51 • Straddle down handstand with spot

her shoulders and hips are directly in line with her base support (the hands). Once in the handstand (perpendicular with the floor), the gymnast straddles her legs and pikes (slightly) down with her shoulders overbalancing in front of the low bar (Fig. 6.51). She brings her legs together and, as the hips touch the low bar, pikes and performs a back hip circle.

Teaching techniques and progressions:	1. The prerequisite for this skill is the press handstand on the floor from the straddle stand and then the reverse press back down.
	2. The gymnast can then try this skill on the bars with good spotting.
Corrections:	1. The gymnast should have a tight body.
	2. The cast to the handstand should be done primarily with the arms and not the legs.
	3. To perform the back hip circle properly, the gymnast waits until the bar pikes her and then rotates backwards around it, rather than just collapsing on it.
Spotting:	1. The spotter can stand either between the bars (beware of the legs of the gymnast) or in front of the low bar facing sideways. She spots the upper arm of the gymnast as she casts to the handstand and as she overbalances the handstand. When the hips approach the bar, the spotter spots as if the gymnast were doing a back hip circle: hands on the back of the gymnast's thighs to help her pike around the low bar and open up to a front support at the skill's completion.
Combinations:	1. Kip between the bars, handstand straddle down, back hip circle.
	2. Handstand straddle down, back hip circle, push away glide.
	3. Handstand straddle down, back hip circle, eagle or eagle pop, full twist.

4. Handstand straddle down, back hip circle, press handstand (to high bar or pirouette low bar).

Handstand on Low Bar Cast and Press to Front Support on High Bar

This skill is the exact opposite or reverse of the previous skill. From a front support position with her back to the high bar, the gymnast casts to a handstand by pulling her hips over her shoulders (press). As she goes up, she straddles her legs and brings them together at the top of the handstand; then she pushes her stretched body back to rest the front of her hips on the high bar.

Teaching techniques and progressions:

1. The prerequisite for this skill is the straddle press handstand on the floor.
2. The gymnast might learn this skill by casting up into a handstand, doing a pirouette and half turn and then casting or jumping down on a single bar—with control.

Corrections:

1. A tight body is imperative.
2. Good control through the shoulders and low back is the aim—no banana back.
3. A good beat will help with the cast, but the shoulders should not be dumped in front of the low bar.

Spotting:

1. While standing between the bars and facing the gymnast, the spotter places the hand closer to the low bar under it and grasps the upper arm of the gymnast. The spotter places her other hand on the front of the gymnast's thigh and helps to lift her during the cast into the handstand.

Figure 6.52 • Handstand on low bar over high bar pop cast (combination #4)

Combinations:

1. Glide kip, handstand to high bar.
2. Front hip circle, handstand to high bar.
3. Handstand to high bar, cast wrap.
4. Handstand to the high bar, pop cast (pike and extend through hips to lift body away from the high bar, as shown in Fig. 6.52), flair arms (lift arms out to the side), and catch the high bar after the body is away from the bar and the cast has been started.

Figure 6.53 • Handstand from the high bar to low bar pirouette back hip circle with spot

Handstand from High Bar to Low Bar Pirouette Back Hip Circle

In a front support position on the high bar, the gymnast pikes and places her hands on the low bar shoulder width apart, casts to a stretched handstand over the low bar, pirouettes on her hands, performs a half turn, and begins to bring her hips down to the low bar while overbalancing her shoulders. When the front of the hips touch the low bar, the gymnast pikes and performs a back hip circle (Fig. 6.53).

Teaching techniques and progressions:

1. The prerequisite for this skill is a tight stretched handstand on the floor, pirouette turn.
2. The gymnast then can perform the skill with good spotting on the bars.

Corrections:

1. The gymnast must have a tight body in the stretched handstand.
2. The hands on the low bar should be close enough for an easy pirouette turn (taking the weight from both hands to one hand and then to both hands again).
3. The shoulders have to be overbalanced to perform a controlled back hip circle.
4. When the body is reverse-pressed down, it must be tight so as not to collapse on the low bar.

Spotting:

1. The spotter in the initial learning stages can stand with one leg on the low bar and the other leg hooked over the high bar. From this position, the spotter clasps the gymnast's legs and helps her into the handstand. Then the spotter helps support the gymnast while she pirouettes. The spotter further holds the legs up while the gymnast overbalances her shoulders for the back hip circle (see Fig. 6.53). This skill can also be spotted from a platform or a pile of mats.
2. Once the gymnast has learned the skill, the spotter stands between the bars and from here spots the handstand pirouette and then the back hip circle.

Combinations:

1. Kip between the bars, handstand.
2. Handstand pirouette back hip circle, push away glide.
3. Handstand back hip circle, inside or reverse eagle.
4. Handstand back hip circle, pop half turn catch high bar.

Cast to a Handstand

This is the handstand all gymnasts should aspire to do because its variations are innumerable. From a front support position on a bar, the gymnast beats and casts her legs up behind her. Simultaneously she pulls, through her shoulders and back muscles, her hips over her shoulders. Her legs straddle while her hips go up (Fig. 6.54), and at the top of the stretched handstand her legs come together.

Teaching techniques and progressions:

1. The prerequisite for this skill is the straddle press handstand on the floor (Chapter 2).
2. This skill should first be attempted on a low bar (adjustable men's high bar,

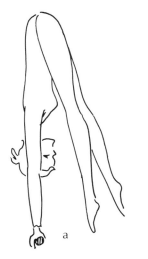
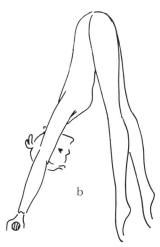

Figure 6.54 • (left) Cast handstand
Figure 6.55 • (right) Correction #1 for cast handstand: (a) correct and (b) incorrect

single bar of men's parallel bars, or the low bar of the unevens). From a front support position, the gymnast should cast up to the handstand half turn pirouette on the hands and land standing in a crash pad with both hands on the bar in the proper regrasp position.

Corrections:

1. The most common error in this skill occurs when the gymnast does not get her hips up and over her shoulders and hands. To correct it the gymnast must pull with her back muscles as well as her arms to get her hips over her shoulders: pull toward the low bar; don't push away from it (see Fig. 6.55).

2. The skill requires a tight back, pelvic tilt, STG, and no banana back.

3. The head should be neither tucked nor extended but, rather, in a neutral position.

Spotting:

1. In the initial stages on the low bar, the spotter stands next to and facing the gymnast while she is in the front support position and on the side of the gymnast that the gymnast's body will *not* pass over in the pirouette. The spotter reaches under the bar with the arm closer to it and grasps the gymnast's upper arm for support throughout the skill. The spotter places her free hand on the front of the gymnast's thigh to help lift her in the cast to the handstand.

2. When the gymnast can readily perform the cast to the handstand, the spotter then spots the cast after the pirouette into the move that the gymnast will perform next.

Combinations:

1. Cast handstand in either direction on either bar. A few suggestions are:
   a. Back to the low bar, cast handstand pirouette on the high bar cast wrap.

251

Figure 6.56 • Cast handstand pirouette belly bump

      b. Facing the low bar, cast handstand pirouette on the high bar, belly bump (see Fig. 6.56).
      c. Facing the high bar, cast handstand on the low bar pirouette, reverse press back hip circle or drape body back onto the high bar.
      d. Back to the high bar, cast handstand on the low bar pirouette turn glide (requires strong abdominals and controlled cast to keep the feet from touching the floor).

CONNECTORS

A few basic skills are invaluable as connectors. Routines are not built around these skills, but these skills can often provide the means of changing direction or body position so that the skills of the routine can be put together without stops.

Squat Through

From a front support position, the gymnast beats and casts her hips up high behind her, then squats or tucks and brings her feet between her hands on the bar. She must keep her shoulders in front of the bar until her feet and knees have passed over the bar. The spot for this skill is on the gymnast's upper arm (Fig. 6.57). This connector takes the gymnast from a front support to a sitting position or a squat position on the bar.

Thigh Roll

From a front support position, the gymnast lifts and rolls or turns on one thigh to a sitting position. This skill can be reversed so that from a sitting position on the bar, the gymnast lifts and rolls or turns over one thigh to a front support position. The whole body turns at once or together.

Figure 6.57 • (left) Squat through
Figure 6.58 • (right) Drop glide

Back Seat Circle Disengage Kip From a sitting position, the gymnast performs the first portion of a back seat circle. As her hips begin to go under the bar, her feet disengage or come from between her hands and she performs a kip. Thus she has gone from a sitting position to a front support position. This is not an easy skill and requires strong abdominals and good timing.

Drop Glide From a long hang position on the high bar, facing the low bar, the gymnast drops to a glide on the low bar (Fig. 6.58). Helpful hints for the proper performance of this skill include: let go of the high bar early, or when the hips are still in back of the high bar, to insure a glide rather than a drop or a molar catch; when catching the low bar push away or back for a good glide; as the hands release the high bar, straddle the legs in a circular fashion (out, back, around, and forward, together). This skill takes the gymnast from a hang on the high bar to a hang or glide on the low bar.

Push Away Glide From a back hip circle, wrap, or front hip circle (front support on either bar, facing either direction), the gymnast lifts her hips up and back by pushing the body up and away from the bar with her hands while piking in the hips. The legs are again straddled in a circular fashion (out, back, around, and forward, together) to a glide. This skill takes the gymnast from a front support to a glide, a long hang, or a cast.

253

ROUTINE CONSTRUC- TION

There are other variations of skills within the families of moves presented in this chapter, just as there are separate skills that have not been presented here. The teacher/coach and gymnast should let their imaginations run wild with variations of these skills. They also should watch for unique skills on the men's high bar that can be successfully and realistically adapted to the unevens within the limitations of the event—two bars instead of one and the female's limited (by comparison) strength. As a reminder, though, most uneven bar skills can be performed on either bar and moving in either direction.

An uneven bar routine should present one complete or total picture. The routine should appear to be one flowing sentence, from beginning to ending, without punctuation. There should be no stops in an uneven bar routine. The elimination of stops is largely up to the coach to enforce. The teacher/coach should encourage gymnasts to go through whole routines, rather than just isolated skills, even as beginners. Intermediate swings occur when a gymnast stops after a move and, prior to executing the next move, takes another beat or swing to get going again. An example of an intermediate swing is a move in which the gymnast kips to the high bar and then takes a beat and cast for a hecht dismount. To eliminate the intermediate swing she should use the end of the kip as the beat for the cast. Judges severely penalize intermediate swings and stops in uneven bar routines.

The basic skills are very important to further advancement on the unevens. The teacher/coach should systematically expose the gymnast to the cast wraps, hip circles, seat circles, sole circles, pops, and, most important, kips prior to teaching somersaults or handstands. While learning all of these skills, the gymnast must remember to keep her arms and legs straight. Continuous swing in a routine results not from bending the arms but from bending (piking) and extending (layout) the body. Bending and extending the body not only makes the routine swing but also makes it appear to be effortless. There should be no obvious demonstrations of strength ("strong like bull"), a stipulation that is almost contradictory since good bar work requires strength.

The current trends in uneven bar routines include:

1. Changing directions
2. Turning and twisting between the bars
3. Spectacular hand releases and regrasps
4. Skills performed around both bars

A general indication of the gymnast's skill level is the number of skills she performs over the high bar. Obviously, the more skills about the high bar, the more advanced the gymnast.

When composing a routine, even for this event, the gymnast should write down her uneven-bar movement vocabulary, and the coach and gymnast should choose the skills from this list. Since a bar routine is relatively short, the gymnast will not have time to perform all of the skills she can perform. The routine should contain an average of ten to thirteen moves. Long routines usually receive lower scores. Often, one or two of the more exciting or more difficult or more original skills the gymnast can perform form the basis for her routine. She then completes her routine by adding skills that fulfill the necessary difficulty requirements and provide for a total and continuous routine. As many teachers and coaches realize, connecting moves are critically important because they quite often create the problems in routine construction.

The teacher/coach should be able with ease, if thwarted in composition, to design a routine with a skill from each or a few of the families of moves presented here and bind them together with kips. The result should be at least a low-intermediate-level routine. Eventually, though, she should add a handstand, a somersault, and a twist. The teacher/coach may want to start her own file of skills and the different methods or skills that lead into it and out of it. Then, in the future, the gymnast or teacher/coach who is "stumped" for a connector can refer to the file.

COACHING

That routines are the key to uneven bar success cannot be overemphasized. Compulsory routines are quite helpful, for they usually contain important basic skills and help the gymnast learn to swing. The USGF and NAGWS have good compulsory exercises for beginning, intermediate, and advanced gymnasts. If the teacher/coach doesn't like the skills in these exercises she can compose her own compulsory for the whole team or class to work on. Some experienced coaches will not permit their gymnasts to perform optional exercises until they can perform a given compulsory.

Once a gymnast has put together her optional exercise, she should practice a minimum of two full routines daily before working on parts or new moves to substitute in or add to the routine. The coach should insist that there be no intermediate swings or lazy, unnecessary stops in the routine during practice. Regardless of the excuse, if the gymnast can't do a routine correctly in practice, she won't be able to do it in a meet—without divine intervention.

The gymnast's hands are extremely important and require proper care. Because of the friction generated between the hands and the bars, blisters (beginning stages) and calluses can form. The callus becomes thicker and thicker, and eventually most of the pressure and friction will be upon the callus (since it is elevated). Calluses should be taken down after practice, not before because the hands will be too tender to work bars. A pumice stone or a scraper designed for the feet is effective for this purpose. Taking down the callus makes it flush with the rest of the hand so that it won't rip or tear off. If a rip occurs, remove the dead skin closely and carefully with a small, sharp scissors. Then administer some form of antiseptic cream or salve to the area. A cold wet tea bag (tannic acid) will also help the wound. The teacher/coach and gymnast should be ever watchful for infection. In the event of infection, the gymnast should see a doctor immediately. As the rip is healing, keep soft and pliable as well as clean. If possible, the gymnast should wear palm guards. The palm guards selected for female gymnasts should be very soft and malleable. Some gymnasts prefer to use roller gauze as palm guards. Regardless of what material is used, palm guards will help to protect the hands. If the gymnast's hands, whether nude or palm-guarded, become hot during bar work, she should stop and let them cool down. The alert coach will admonish the gymnast who has badly ripped hands—hamburger—to discontinue her workout but will not baby the gymnast who ripped her hands a week ago and tries to use it as an excuse for inadequate performance. A gymnast should be able to work bars comfortably after giving her hands a day of rest, if the rip is not extensive or deep.

The gymnast's hips should be protected from constant bruising on the unevens. A bruise should result from piking too soon or being crooked when wrapping or bumping the bar. But the gymnast can wear "belly bumpers," squares of foam an inch thick that slip into each leotard leg to be worn over each side of the front of the hips whenever she is working the bars. The belly bumpers need to be removed only for the performance during a meet. Many gymnasts even wear them during their uneven bar warm-up in a meet.

The woman coach must spot unevens. The only way to learn to spot unevens is to get in there and do it. Even though the bar event goes quickly, the spotter can develop the quick reactions required to spot this event. As mentioned earlier, spotting the unevens does not require as much strength as it does timing. Women are and can be good spotters. To make it easier to reach the gymnast while she is learning a new skill, the spotter can stand to the side on a padded platform or mats piled up to the necessary height. In a meet, according to FIG rules, the spotter may not stand between the bars. This rule is quite valid for Olympic and elite level gymnasts. Unfortunately for the beginner and intermediate gymnast, the best position for spotting is between the bars. This rule is one that coaches in a league might suspend for the safety of the gymnast. Also, the coach may not walk under the bars when spotting in a meet.

In evaluating routines, the coach should constantly correct bent knees, bent elbows, intermediate swings, and a loose body—STG. In jest and facetiously, she might ask girls to bring a dollar bill to practice. When on the bars, each gymnast places a bill between her ankles; if the body is loose, the bill will fall to the floor and, of course, it then belongs to the coach. The coach should also help the gymnast establish the rhythm for the swing of the routine by talking her through the routine, by saying the names of the skills in tempo as the gymnast performs them. Some gymnasts need to be told when to take a breath in a routine. These suggestions as well as proper completion of each move (extending and not muscling) prior to going on to the next move should prevent rushing and make possible the performance of a total routine with swing.

PSYCHOLOGY OF THE UNEVENS

The gymnast must completely dominate the uneven bar event with her determination and aggression. This is not the event for a timid, shy, and gentle approach. The gymnast should begin this event by attacking it. She should almost feel that, if necessary, she could bite an uneven bar rail in half. There should be a total 110 percent commitment to beginning and finishing the routine. Just as she does when learning a skill on this apparatus, for her safety and her coach's, the gymnast must follow through once she has begun a move. She also must hold on to the bars with her hands no matter what trouble she gets into, for if she holds on, she can be spotted. The teacher/coach helps to develop this attitude or approach to the event by showing her confidence in and giving positive reinforcement to the gymnast who demonstrates this attitude.

Fear is a psychological variable that is often associated with the bars. If, however, the gymnast learns all skills on the low bar first and knows that a qualified spotter will be helping her, fear will not be a major factor in her performance. The coach must decide how much obvious fear she will condone in the gymnast. If a gymnast's fear takes time away from the other individuals on the team, it is excessive and should be brought under better control.

TRAINING   Specific conditioning or training for the unevens obviously includes full routines (minimum of two per practice). Even outright beginners should practice routines such as this sequence: back pullover, front hip circle, back hip circle. If the hands can stand it, another good conditioner is:

1. Front support on the high bar
2. Cast wrap
3. Squat through
4. Back beat underswing catch the high bar
5. Kip between the bars

This routine can be repeated several times, although two or three repetitions should help develop endurance and swing.

Based on the overload principle, ten kips between the bars at the end of practice one day and, on alternate days, glide kip catch drop glide kip catch repeated as many times as the gymnast and her hands can stand will provide good conditioning. Other conditioning exercises include:

1. Cast to a handstand pirouette on a single bar and land; repeat at least five times.
2. Front support position. On the low bar back to the high bar, cast straddle up to a handstand and then a front support on the high bar. Then handstand straddle back down to back hip circle on the low bar (see handstands).

These skills can also be done one right after another without stopping.

General conditioning to strengthen the abdominals and upper arms for the uneven bar event can be achieved with the following exercises:

1. Press straddle handstand up and down on the floor (see Chapter 2)
2. Bent knee sit-ups
3. Push-ups
4. Handstand push-ups (Chapter 2)
5. From a long hang on the high bar of the unevens, lift the feet up to touch the high bar without swinging; ten repetitions

The uneven bar event is the most exciting of the Olympic gymnastics events for women. This event continues to change because of its relative youth, and the teacher/coach must make every attempt to keep her knowledge and understanding current while helping her gymnast to swing in this "swinging" event.

7

DIRECTING
coaching

COACHING PHILOSOPHY

The philosophy of coaching adopted by a particular coach should constantly be reevaluated during the coaching experience. The measures of good coaching are that the coach is being true to herself, her philosophy of life, and her goals and aspirations for the team and that she is meeting the needs and goals of her team and its members as individuals (Fig. 7.1).* The coach should attempt to understand her own motivations for coaching, possibly including money, prestige, ego fulfillment, power, pleasure, and/or service. These are just a few of the common reasons one coaches. The coach should be honest with herself about what needs she is attempting to fulfill through coaching.

The coach should examine her own philosophy in relation to winning and losing. How important is winning? Is it everything, à la Lombardi? Is it possible for the final score to indicate a win and yet the team's performance spells "loss"? Is the coach more interested in building a strong foundation of basics or in having her gymnast fulfill the difficulty requirements for each event? Is competition for very young girls helpful or wholesome? Why do so many female swimmers and gymnasts "burn out"? Optionals or compulsories—which will help the gymnast more in the future?

After a loss, the team needs the coach to fairly evaluate the performance, to take some of the responsibility for the loss, and to establish a route to future success. At this time, however, the coach may feel less like being with the team

*Figure 7.1 is on preceding page.

260

than at any other time because she needs to reevaluate her role and input. Ironically, after the team wins, the team could care less about being with the coach, and yet this is the time when the coach would probably enjoy being with the team.

The coach should examine her expectations for the team. The coach cannot expect the team to give or to sacrifice more than she will. If the team rules include promptness to practice, then the coach can't be tardy. If there is a "no smoking" rule, then the coach can't smoke on the bus to the meet. If the coach expects the team to work hard, then she, too, must work hard. There are too many "crash pad coaches" in women's gymnastics. Crash pad coaches move from the supine or prone position on one crash pad to another during practices and give verbal commands. If the coach expects enthusiasm and support from her team, then she must be enthusiastic about and supportive of them. Often, though, we don't push our athletes as hard as they want to be pushed. Physically the female athlete can do and take more than she has been exposed to.

Within the coach's philosophy there should be some cognizance of how she wants to motivate her team. Is she going to use the positive or negative approach to reinforce behavior? Or will she use a combination of both? If she selects the positive approach, it should be truly positive. It is not enough to say "good routine, but your legs are bent on your aerial, you are ahead of the music in the slow part, your head is down throughout, your back tumbling was heavy," and so on. This kind of shallow praise does not constitute a positive approach. To be truly positive, we must clearly enumerate the successes and then select one or two things in the routine that need correction. The next step is critical, for in noting what needs correction the coach should also indicate how to make the correction. Occasionally the negative approach can be effective, especially when tempered with consistency and understanding. There are times when all of us feel better after we have been "reamed out." A dressing down can almost act as a catharsis for us when prudently used. Maybe a combination of motivational approaches would be helpful. Possibly, the old adage "you get more flies with honey" is not so far removed from recent findings about what motivates a team.

What efforts will the coach employ to communicate with a team? Communication is more effective if the coach knows the team members as individuals and as a group. The team should also have the chance to know who their coach is. Of course, it is not necessary for the coach or team to know all of each other's personal intimacies. The team does need to know that the coach is human, and, yes, there may be times when the coach is having difficulty dealing with a problem, not feeling well, is angry, and has fears. Understanding is a two-way street.

Communication further involves listening with genuine sincerity and really hearing another person. The coach may want to limit what her gymnasts tell her, but she should still hear what is offered within those limitations. In communicating with individuals and with the whole team, the most successful approach is frankness. The individuals on a team deserve to know if they are going to compete and why or why not. One of the more difficult things a coach has to do is to cut a team. Certainly, the easiest practice is for the coach to post a cut list at midnight and sneak out a side door. However, a better practice is to tell the individuals why they have been cut or why they haven't. Communication could be abetted if the coach knew what each individual's goals are for herself and the team. The team should also know the coach's goals and aspirations for herself and the team.

One researcher, Joseph Massimo,[1] determined what gymnasts want most from or in a coach. According to Massimo, gymnasts desire a coach who:

1. Uses minimal verbiage. Too many of us overcoach, perhaps because we are insecure and are trying too hard: "When you're number 2, you try harder." Many female coaches have this attitude about themselves. Yet we should select only one or two key corrections for the gymnast to work on in each skill.

2. Has a sense of humor. A coach must careful not to overuse humor, especially if it takes the form of sarcasm. Humor involves laughing at one's self and not *at* another.

3. Uses individual psychology. This practice implies dealing with each team member as an individual. Some gymnasts need lots of coaching and attention, and others can just about coach themselves. The concept of fairness is something that female gymnasts seem to get hung up on. There is no way a coach can be completely fair. There will always be some girls who will get more of the coach's attention on a given day than others. But, maybe, if the team understands why the coach is giving more time to a certain gymnast, there will be a better understanding: this is communication. All of us have different needs and the coach should attempt to determine what they are and provide for them in her own philosophy.

4. Has technical competency. Anyone who cares enough to take the time and is willing to learn and can analyze human movement can coach women's gymnastics. Knowledge of the sport can be acquired.

5. Appreciates the sociology of the team. The coach not only must deal with the individuals on the team but also must be aware of how these individuals interact. The coach should know what the team personality is.

What does a coach want from the team? Coaches probably all want to be liked. This desire is a dream. There will be individuals on a team with whom the coach will be unable to communicate or whom she will not even like. Personality clashes must be dealt with by the coach. Without acceptance or reduction of the tension and anxiety such clashes cause the interaction of these personalities to become counterproductive to the team's growth, so the coach must eliminate the clash one way or another. It might mean asking the individual to resign for the sake

[1] Joseph Massimo, Presentation to New England Gymnastic Clinic, Newton, Massachusetts, November 1975.

of the team. Respect might be a more realistic goal for a coach to want from a team than being liked. Respect is always mutual, for to gain a person's respect you must respect the person. Respect is built upon time and genuine caring for others.

The philosophic concerns of a coach are many. They should be determined, examined, and continually reexamined. A coach cannot effectively deal with and lead a team if she doesn't know herself.

THE COACH'S ROLE

The role of coach is elusive. What is a coach? Is a coach a maid, a mother, a friend, an omnipotent autocrat, or facilitator? This author perceives the role of a coach as a catalyst, or facilitator. The implication of this role is not that it is a super ego trip, which coaching can be, nor is it a vicarious athletic experience. Being a facilitator involves providing the best gymnastic experience possible for the gymnast. The best gymnastic experience comes from a good gymnastics facility, competent coaching personnel, an organized schedule, and safety consciousness.

The facility for gymnastics should be a gymnasium with adequate floor space and ceiling height to accommodate the four gymnastics events and apparatus. The apparatus should meet the current FIG specifications. The apparatus should be distributed about the gymnasium so that a gymnast will not injure herself because she has to cross one event to reach another.

The head coach must make every effort to keep her knowledge of gymnastics current. As the administrator, the coach must determine duties and responsibilities of the rest of the coaching personnel, if there is more than one person on staff. Additional personnel might include an assistant coach, a manager, and a spotter and/or trainer. All members of the coaching staff should have up-to-date information about the team's activities and direction as the head coach perceives it. It is essential that there be good communication among the coaching staff.

An organized schedule is the duty of a facilitator. The schedule involves preseason and season expectations for the team. If the team is to condition during preseason, the conditioning program should be written and disseminated to the individuals on the team. The season's expectations for the team should include a written proposal of practices, including time, location, and length, as well as the dates and locations of meets. The first team meeting is an ideal time to discuss:

1. Practices
2. Meets
3. Team rules and the consequences of breaking them, if there are any
4. The team's aspirations
5. The coach's aspirations for the team
6. Conditioning and weight expectations

Experience has shown that the coach and the gymnast must have scheduled workouts or practices. Since gymnastics is such an individual sport, conceivably we could borrow the idea of individual written daily practice schedules employed by track and field coaches. Regardless, the gymnast should know her practice schedule a day, a week, or even a season ahead of time. She should know what she will be working on and for approximately how long, as well as when the coach will be working with her. The all-around philosophy requires consideration at this stage. Does the coach believe in the all-around concept (i.e., each gymnast working all four events)? This is the ideal of gymnastics and should be the ultimate goal of coach and gymnast alike. Practicality and flexibility will determine, in part, whether the coach will insist on all girls working the all-around category. Experience shows that idleness in a gym breeds discontent and "bitchiness."

Coaching efficiency demands strict adherence to the practice schedule, but the coach and the gymnast should be flexible enough to recognize the need for and value of an occasional day off. It is also advisable to discourage routine composition during practice time. The coach and gymnast should work closely on a one-to-one basis to put together a routine. The coach might, if it is feasible, schedule individual practice sessions in addition to the regular team practices.

Regular videotaping (once every two weeks) can prove very helpful for the team. After the taping, the coach might audio-over the tape so that the gymnast can watch the tape without the coach having to be there. Videotape viewing is more educational outside of practice and if only a few individuals view themselves at one time.

Special days can help alleviate the inevitable boredom and frustration of the necessary repetitions in practice. Special days might include a day of contests of gymnastics-related activities. Dress-up days prior to a meet are also helpful. On dress-up day, the gymnast should wear the underwear, leotard, sockies (no pom-pom balls on the back of socks), and hairstyle that she will wear in a meet (Fig. 7.2). So attired, the team should go through the practice as if it were a meet. Proper presentation for the occasion would require no jewelry, no gum, addressing the

Figure 7.2

judges prior to and at the conclusion of the routine, no pulling the leotard down, no pushing hair out of the face, proper body carriage, and composure. Of course, these qualities should characterize every practice as well as meets and dress-up days. The coach should enforce proper presentation daily but look for the fine points of presentation on dress-up day, such as proper leotard fit, no holes in arm pits, no long bangs to cause a shadow over the eyes, and so on. Another special day would be an intrasquad meet.

The day before a meet, realistically, is no time to learn a new skill or a routine. If the gymnastics season is a long one, the day prior to a meet might best be utilized as a day off. If the season is a short one, the practice prior to a meet should consist of a light and easy workout. This is the day of all days to build confidence.

On meet day the coach should strive for an evenness of disposition and be as positive as possible. This is not the time for the coach to share her anxieties and fears with the team. If the coach isn't confident, how can she expect the gymnasts to be? The meet should be an occasion for the gymnasts. The coach should not be burdened with administrative meet responsibilities the day of the meet. These responsibilities should have been performed earlier. The coach should adopt a check list for each meet. An example follows:

1. Date _____ Time _____ Place _____

2. _____ vs. _____

3. Judges: names, addresses, and social security numbers

     _____   _____   _____

     _____   _____   _____

     _____   _____   _____

     _____   _____   _____

4. Flags for opening ceremonies

5. March music for opening ceremonies

6. Lineup for each team in order of performance/event

7. Visitors wish to go up on _____ and _____ events last

8. Judges' score sheets listing:
   a. Name of gymnast, team and skeleton of point breakdown to be filled in by judge
   b. Place for final score
   c. Place for judges' signatures

9. Master score sheet to be duplicated at the end of the meet and given to both teams
10. Floor exercise tapes
11. Tape recorder
12. First-aid supplies
13. Rosin
14. Chalk
15. Apparatus
16. Sufficient mat coverage
17. A description of opening ceremonies for visiting team
18. Tape measure
19. Rule book
20. Two stopwatches
21. Calculator
22. Timer
23. Two scorers (to average scores)
24. Three runners (to run judges' scores to head judge and score table)
25. Meet director
26. Flasher (not what you're thinking! This individual flashes each gymnast's average score)
27. Head scorekeeper
28. Announcer
29. Score board (meet running score)
30. Supplies:
    a. Stapler
    b. Staples
    c. Cellophane tape
    d. Ditto
    e. Ditto paper
    f. Scrap paper
    g. Razor blade (for corrections not wrists)
    h. Pencils
    i. Pens
    j. Paper clips
31. Team members assigned to help move apparatus and pull boards and mats
32. Videotaping

During the warm-up for the meet (Fig. 7.3), the coach should be ever-watchful for the gymnast who does too much warming up and doesn't have anything left for the meet. This tendency is typical of beginning gymnasts and gymnasts who lack confidence in themselves and their routines. Warm-up serves as a brief refresher and the gymnast should not throw whole routines.

When the meet is over, scores can't be changed unless there is a mathematical error; falls from the beam can't be erased and poor performances can't be changed. The coach must go on and not harp on the past but rather build positively upon the errors toward a better future.

The practice on the day after the meet should be designed to correct and work on the shortcomings that showed up in the meet. The coach should prepare a sound and objective evaluation for the team. The team should also be able to view the videotapes. Videotape viewing should be positive in nature.

Generally, motor learning theory cautions that practices should be short and intense so as to maximize learning. We also are aware that a fatigued gymnast does not learn well and runs a greater risk of injury. Occasionally, the coach must encourage the gymnast to work on another skill if she continues to practice one skill incorrectly. There is no *reason* to develop and overlearn incorrect movement patterns and to incur the frustration that accompanies repeated failure.

SAFETY

Safety considerations are quite important to the continuing operation of a vital gymnastics program. Our society seems to be law-suit conscious and the gymnastics teacher/coach should be aware of the potential for accidents that is inherent in the gymnastics environment. Accidents can be kept to the minimum if, during program preparation, care is taken to avoid negligence. Preparation and care involve:

Figure 7.3

1. The clear, concise explanation of the skills that the student will be expected to perform

2. Constant supervision of the students in a gymnastics situation (supervision implies the teacher's ability to observe the whole gymnasium and control the class or group at each moment)

3. Skills selected for importance and in accordance with the student's skill level and ability

4. The use of progressions

5. A teacher/coach who is knowledgeable in gymnastics

6. Safe equipment that is properly assembled, maintained, and checked daily

7. Mat coverage of high quality that is flat, complete, flush, and nonoverlapping

8. Spotting by individuals who have been taught how to spot

9. No jewelry worn by the teacher/coach or gymnast since it can injure the gymnast or her spotter

10. A proper uniform (i.e., a leotard); well-fitted shorts and shirt is a second-rate substitute

11. Keeping hair from falling in the gymnast's eyes. Elastic bands are an invaluable expendable supply of teachers and coaches

12. No gum chewing (gum can be aspirated by a gymnast when she inverts)

Proper strengthening and flexibility will prevent injuries. The gymnast should have equal amounts of these variables. The gymnast and her coach must be aware that aches and pains are an inescapable part of gymnastics. The gymnast will just have to learn to deal with discomfort and accept it stoically. A discussion of common gymnastic-related injuries and suggested preventatives and treatment follows.

To avoid shinsplints, heel cord stretching, increased ankle flexibility, and strengthening of the lower leg are valuable. Conditioning on the hard floor is inadvisable. There is no cure for shinsplints other than complete rest. For some relief from the pain of shinsplints, try an arch support or analgesic applied to the shin with a stockinette pulled over it, or taping to pull up the arch. Forearm splints are due to lack of wrist flexibility. If severe pain is present, the gymnast should see a doctor, for it might signify a compression fracture or damage to the muscle capsule.

To guard against ankle sprains the gymnast must strive for maximum ankle flexibility and strength and learn to land with bent knees, the feet slightly apart and forward on even surfaces. Ice is the immediate treatment for a sprained ankle. The gymnast should see a doctor and have X rays taken. When she is able to practice again, her ankle should be taped. There is a real art to taping: basically a pretape substance, an undertape, and then adhesive tape should be applied. Lots of tape does not mean a good taping. There should be no openings or windows in the taping. The side of the ankle that was sprained should be pulled up in the taping. The most common sprain, the inversion sprain, involves the outside of the foot. The eversion sprain occurs on the inside of the foot. During meets, flesh-colored material (tape or elastic tape) should be used or wrapped over the white tape; otherwise, the gymnast appears to have on high socks and the long line of the leg is broken.

Prevention of knee injuries depends on developing and increasing the strength of the quadriceps (Fig. 7.4), the muscles of the front of the thighs (see Chapter 2). The gymnast should learn to bend her knees upon landing with her feet slightly apart and pointing forward. All sideward landings, such as aerial or cartwheel dismounts from the beam and the cartwheel vault, are prohibitive because of their potential for knee injury. The landing surface for dismounts should be even. The immediate treatment of a knee injury is the application of ice and the gymnast should quickly get to a doctor.

Ripped hands from the uneven bars were discussed in the coaching section of Chapter 6. Dislocated elbows in gymnastics usually occur when, as the gymnast is falling backward, she reaches back with her hand to break the fall. To prevent this injury, she should just land on her glutes, where there is usually enough padding to absorb the fall. The application of ice and a doctor's care are the treatment for an elbow injury.

To decrease the risk of a back injury, proper warm-up, stretching, strong abdominals, learning to bend the knees upon landing, proper body alignment, and using both sides on walkovers and splits are in order. If the gymnast takes a bad fall onto her back, neck, or head, she may receive a spinal cord injury and she *should not be moved.* Call a doctor immediately!

Bruises are fairly common in gymnastics. At times it may seem that the team colors should be black and blue. To prevent bruises to the hips from working

Figure 7.4

the uneven bars, a pad should cover the bar or the gymnast should use belly bumpers (refer to the coaching section of Chapter 6). Cold is the proper treatment for a bruise.

A well-qualified trainer is one of the finest assets a team can have. The trainer and team doctor can give advice on preventing, treating, and rushing injuries (aiding the healing process, i.e., whirlpool, heat, massage, and so on) and establishing a good conditioning program. These are a few concerns of the coach who perceives herself as a facilitator.

THE ASPIRING GYMNAST

It is advisable for very young children (four, five, or six years old) to spend their first year in gymnastics developing a movement vocabulary and tumbling. The movement vocabulary should include:

1. Locomotor movements
    a. Walk
    b. Run
    c. Leap
    d. Skip
    e. Slide
    f. Gallop
    g. Hop
    h. Jump
    i. Combinations of the above
2. Axial movements
    a. Fall and recovery or fold and unfold or bend and extend (using the whole body, especially the torso)
    b. Swing
    c. Sway
    d. Twist
    e. Turn
    f. Strike
    g. Dodge
    h. Combinations of the above, together with locomotor movements

The children should be encouraged to move efficiently and, eventually, with amplitude to their own rhythm and then to an imposed rhythm.

Tumbling can be encouraged and taught as suggested in the following order:

1. Forward rolls
2. Cartwheels
3. Walkovers (front and back)
4. Back somersaults (with spotting)

5. Back handsprings (with spotting)
6. Roundoff
7. Front handsprings (with spotting)
8. Butterflies
9. Aerials (side and front)
10. Combinations of all of the above (for a complete description of these skills, see Chapter 3)

By the age of eight, the gymnast can be vaulting (squat, handspring, and hecht, described in Chapter 4) and working the balance beam. At nine years old, the gymnast is ready for the uneven bars. These are suggestions and are certainly not inflexible.

Fortunately the negative social sanctions that have plagued female athletes for many years are slowly changing. Those who have been coaching for a few years can see conspicuous changes—changes in both the girls on their team and the attitudes of many who initially doubted the need for a highly competitive gymnastics program. Now people are beginning to appreciate what females can accomplish and are trying to achieve in sports. Women are proving to be fine athletes—it is a popular activity. Gymnasts today are more skilled, more aggressive within their sport, more self-directed, and more dedicated to excellence, thanks to the growing programs and dedicated teaching and coaching in the elementary, junior, and senior high schools and in private clubs.

Some people labor under the illusion that women aren't competitive by nature. Maybe not all women are, but neither are all men competitive. The desire to excel develops while a child is very young primarily as a result of child-rearing practices. In our society in the past, girls were not taught to excel; that drive was reserved for boys. These practices are changing for the good of women's athletics.

Figure 7.5

Yes, gymnastics is a beautiful sport to watch (Fig. 7.5). It is fun for the performer for about ten seconds after completing a good routine. Yes, the joy of effort is truly an intrinsic response, to be able to express self through movement, but most of the time it is hard, boring, tedious, exhausting, and frustrating. And it is certainly challenging and elusive.

Earlier it was mentioned that today's female athletes are more self-directed and dedicated to excellence, which is an indication of their desire and need for a fine sports program. We all know that to become good at anything requires practice and effort. An example is how much the woman athlete is willing to do to be a better gymnast:

1. She sacrifices time for year-round practice.
2. She works all-around, preferably (all four events—gymnastics has no specialists).
3. She conditions—overload principle.
4. She must give up some social activities to get proper rest.
5. Diet is a great problem for women. It is desirable for team members to carry between 10 and 13 percent fat, by volume on their bodies. The average college female, in contrast, has 22 percent fat; the male distance runner in good condition has about 6 to 8 percent.
6. Another sacrifice is money, if private lessons are necessary.

So women have demonstrated a determination to work hard to become better athletes and to prove that they deserve the opportunity to compete.

Female gymnasts try to discipline themselves mentally, too. The way some females achieve mental discipline is through:

Figure 7.6

1. A positive attitude on the part of both the coach and the gymnast (Fig. 7.6)
2. Enough confidence in self and coach so that the word "no" isn't heard
3. Following through a skill once she has begun
4. No tears—well, almost none because they take time from the rest of the team and workout, and that's selfish
5. Accepting the premise that open and constructive criticism is the only way the whole team can improve
6. Honest, frank, straight, and sincere communication—for all (coach and gymnast)
7. Emphasis on the individual's performance as well as a team responsibility: *Wants* us to be good!
8. The knowledge that proper conditioning or physical shape is the first step toward good mental discipline: "sound mind in sound body"
9. Hoping that each gymnast will be capable of fulfilling her potential by showing buoyancy, enthusiasm, sincerity and honesty, perseverance, and, yes, guts

If those of us who coach female athletes desire a better understanding, our role or goal should be to provide the best possible program and to be willing to sacrifice as much as we expect our athletes to sacrifice. In order to provide the best program we must have the best leadership and the best facilities we can provide and we must provide competitive experiences of good caliber for our teams. Then our efforts and the results of these efforts will be seen as necessary, vital, and unique.

MECHANICAL ANALYSIS

Earlier in this chapter it was mentioned that anyone with interest, concern, and the ability to analyze movement can coach gymnastics. An in-depth study of biomechanics is invaluable for everyone genuinely interested in improving their gymnastics coaching. A few of the basic principles that apply to the skills presented in this text will be mentioned here.

Newton's laws of motion relate directly to women's gymnastics. The first law, the law of inertia, holds that a body in motion will tend to stay in motion and a body at rest will tend to stay at rest unless acted upon by some external force, such as friction, gravity, wind, and so on. This law applies to vaulting and all tumbling skills. The second law, the law of momentum or acceleration stipulates that the acceleration (change in speed) of a body is proportional to the force causing the acceleration and inversely proportional to the body (mass). This law applies to tumbling, lightness, and speed. The third law is familiar to readers as the action-reaction law (also law of reaction or law of rebound): for every action there is an equal and opposite reaction. This law applies to many varied skills in gymnastics. An example is pushing down on the mat to leap up.

The parallelogram of forces represents a resolution of forces that occurs in blocking (Chapters 2, 3, and 4) and can be demonstrated graphically by the necessary angle of takeoff of the body on the board for inverted vaults. The parallelogram of forces derives from the law of conservation of energy, which states that energy can only be transferred or directed in its flow and cannot be created or destroyed.

The principle involved in the cast wrap on the unevens is that the angular momentum of a body will continue despite a change in the axis of rotation. Initially, the axis of rotation in this skill is the hands and the change is to the hips.

To complete gymnastics skills, the gymnast learns to land with her feet slightly apart (increasing the base support for more equilibrium) and to bend her knees upon contact with the mat. This method spreads the resistance over as long a period of time as possible and thus prevents the force from becoming too large. Landing the feet slightly in front of the center of gravity of the body allows for arresting the horizontal force upon landing.

Chapter 2 explains twisting techniques that are based upon the previously described principles.

The radius of rotation or the momentum and the principles that apply to gymnastics are:

1. Shortening the radius of rotation will increase speed.

2. Lengthening the radius of rotation will decrease speed.

These principles are applicable to the decision to perform the skill in tuck, pike, or layout position, especially with respect to tumbling and tumbling dismounts from apparatus.

An understanding of the principles of equilibrium is critical in balance beam work and in dismounting. The center of gravity is the exact center of the body's matter. Although there are techniques for determining the center of gravity for males, there is (to this writer's knowledge) no such technique to apply to females. For females, the center of gravity is located approximately in the hips. Variations in the location of the center of gravity are due to differences in somatotype, height (length of lever arms), weight, and weight distribution. Equilibrium, or balance, is related to the distance of the center of gravity from its base support as well as to the size of the base support. For balance, the center of gravity must fall within the base support, whether it be the feet, as in most locomotor skills, or the hands, as in tumbling, inverted vaulting, and bar work. Often difficulty is determined by how high the center of gravity is within a skill.

These are just a few of the most basic principles of physics and mechanics that apply to gymnastic skills. Again, the earnest coach will study kinesiology, or biomechanics, in depth. The gymnast should analyze her own movements when viewing videotape records of her performance.

SPOTTING   Spotting is the aid given to a gymnast during her performance of a skill (Fig. 7.7). Spotting can be mechanical (a spotting belt or an overhead spotting rig) or by

Figure 7.7

hand. The mechanical means of spotting should by used only when the gymnast is learning a very difficult skill or one that the spotter has never spotted. This form of spotting, if it is overused, can become a crutch or security blanket for the gymnast, and even though the ropes are slack, the gymnast will not feel secure performing the skill without the belt. Hand spotting is a marvelous technique, for it helps the gymnast with the kinesthesis for a skill she could not perform alone and it can protect her from the possibility on an injury due to a fall.

Often in physical education and sport we allow ourselves the luxury of thinking we affect the attitudes and values of our students just by exposing them to sport. The structure and methodology currently in vogue in physical education do not support this notion. Yet, in the sport of gymnastics there is an ideal opportunity to teach responsibility for others, if this attitude is desirable, by having the students learn to spot each other.

Spotting is a learned skill, just as a back handspring or a vault is. Therefore it can be taught. Just as in the development of other motor skills, spotting requires practice; spotting is *moving*. The key to good spotting is *good footwork*. The spotter must be able to use her feet to move herself into the proper positions to break a fall most effectively or to help a gymnast through a skill. Spotting is dependent not solely upon strength but also on timing, and proper positioning, and the proper placement of the hands. Therefore women can spot. A women's gymnastics team does not require a male spotter. Many female coaches do and should take pride in their ability to spot.

To spot properly, the spotter must have a thorough knowledge of the skill to be performed and she should be able to analyze the skill for the time and place in which the gymnast will need a spot. Often the spotter simply helps lift the gymnast's center of gravity either over or through the skill. Generally, when spotting the bars, vaulting, or skills on the beam, the spotter should be reaching up prior to the skill's execution, for reaching up while the skill is in progress will take too much time for a good spot. For skills over the horse or on the high bar of the unevens or on the high beam, the spotter may want to stand on an elevated pile of mats or on a covered platform of sorts (Swedish box) to insure that she can comfortably reach the gymnast. Often the spotter must be prepared to move in to spot, so that she does not prevent the gymnast from initiating a skill (e.g., tumbling) or in which the gymnast may straddle her legs (e.g., skills on the uneven bars). The gymnast and the spotter should thoroughly understand what the spotter is going to do. If the spotter tells the gymnast she is going to spot her, she must make every effort to at least get a hand on her. There will be times when the spotter will be unable to catch the gymnast, but the fall should be broken somehow, even if the spotter has to put her own body between the gymnast and the mat. From the previous statement, it's obvious that the spotter places the gymnast's welfare above her own. She often is in more danger than the gymnast. Thus the spotter should protect herself, especially her hands and arms, when spotting bars. She should learn to bend her knees and use her legs instead of her back when spotting tumbling. If the spotter uses her feet properly, her body should be in the strongest and safest position for both the gymnast and herself.

Some women hesitate to touch a gymnast, but that's the sport of gymnastics: there are no other connotations or implications. For a good spot, the hands must be on the gymnast before she begins to fall or needs help. If the spotter waits to put her hands on the gymnast until she needs it, the spot is usually inadequate and ineffective. Initially the need to place her hands on a gymnast might prove to be uncomfortable for the spotter, but the gymnast is not aware of it and would be displeased if she were not spotted. Occasionally the spotter may want to use her whole forearm to lift if she anticipates a heavy spot.

When spotting a gymnast who is going to be moving backward, the spotter can lightly touch the gymnast's back to indicate that she is ready to spot. Otherwise, some gymnasts will keep looking over their shoulders to see if the spotter is prepared and concentrating. This action can result in poor body alignment in the skill.

The trampoline is quite a valuable teaching aid for more advanced tumbling and vaulting. Spotting the trampoline involves pushing the gymnast back onto the bed and/or seeing that she does not land on her neck or head. Regardless of the gymnast's experience, there should always be five spotters, one on each side of the trampoline and one on the bed or frame of the trampoline.

The difficulty in spotting is initially getting in there and spotting. Once that hurdle has been overcome, the spotter must learn when not to spot. As a gymnast becomes lighter and lighter in the spotter's hands, the spotter should spot less and less and move further and further away, yet be ever ready, just in case. Knowing when and when not to spot takes time, experience, and an understanding of the gymnast's security, confidence, and guts.

Spotting is a sport skill. As such, it requires practice. It is a challenge and the feeling of accomplishment after a "good spot" is immeasurable. Women are and can be good spotters.

DEMONSTRA-TIONS

Because gymnastics is such an aesthetic sport it is the ideal mode for demonstrations. Even the most inexperienced gymnasts can provide a form of visual entertainment that will be most pleasing to an audience and, in particular, to parents. What to include in an exhibition is solely dependent upon the skill level of the gymnasts as well as their audience's appreciation. The utmost principle to adhere to is: short is beautiful. A performance should be no longer than an hour and a half. The beginning and ending should be exciting. If the demonstration is primarily for parents, then every effort should be made to have all girls perform.

A successful number might be called a "pot pourri," in which all the girls demonstrate a skill on all four events at once. Dance numbers, vaulting, and tumbling also provide opportunities for many girls to perform (Fig. 7.8). In coed performances, pyramids on the symmetric arrangement of couples demonstrating dual stunts also appeal to audiences. Well-chosen music can greatly add to the quality of the exhibition. An effective announcer can further enhance a gymnastics exhibition. It is often helpful to select a theme to unify the show.

If the purpose of the exhibition is to demonstrate skills taught in physical education classes, then it should be light and involve as many people as possible. If the purpose is to demonstrate the sport of gymnastics, then the performances should be of high quality but with very little opportunity in the routines for injury, and so on. Injury can put a damper on any exhibition. Often exhibitions are a yearly event, in which case the directors of the program should continually search for different numbers, be creative, and dare to be different. Costuming and lighting can certainly add to the overall effect. Exhibitions are time consuming and require a great deal of effort and input.

Figure 7.8 • Dance routine

Figure 7.9 • Ribbon scarf routine

A suggested program follows:

1. Entrance (march in)
2. Opening ceremonies
3. Group tumbling, utilizing intricate floor patterns, tumbling, and graceful running
4. Pot pourri (see earlier description) or two balance beam performances or two floor exercises
5. Dance
6. Pot pourri or four uneven bar routines
7. Group vaulting, rapid fire (well spotted)

Figure 7.10 • Amplitude

8. Dance, group floor exercise, or rhythmic gymnastics (Fig. 7.9)

9. Contest (obstacle course, etc.)

10. Exit (march out)

The exhibition should move quickly without long delays between numbers. If the gymnasts don't enjoy themselves, the audience will not. Well-executed demonstrations can sell a gymnastics program.

AMEN, OR "THE LAST HURRAH"

This text has explained very specific techniques. This is just one approach to the teaching of gymnastics and the old cliché "if it works, use it" is applicable. In teaching there is no right or wrong; there are many approaches, each of which can be effective with a bit of insight and preparation. Therefore it would be presumptuous to say this is the only way. However, these techniques have been successful for many years of teaching gymnastics. As miners die of "black lung," this coach will undoubtedly die of "white lung" from the chalkdust, and were this coach paid a penny for each pound lifted she would be a millionaire.

To briefly reemphasize, all skills should be taught, learned, and performed with amplitude (stretch), proper technique, and form, not just during a meet but every minute of every practice as well. The sport of gymnastics epitomizes the elusive search for perfection (Fig. 7.10). Routine practice is the key to the success of the team and individuals alike. Genuine individual concern for each gymnast and her development can only breed success. Once the coach has discovered the formula for helping a gymnast to develop her self-confidence, she can become purely a technician, but until that time, she must be all things to all people. The meaningful rewards in coaching show up in the expression on a girl's face the first time she does a cartwheel or a hecht on the unevens. These rewards make the time, frustration, commitment, and aches (physical, mental, and emotional) well worthwhile (Fig. 7.11).

Figure 7.11 • The joy of gymnastics

GLOSSARY

Abstract Leap
A skill in which the gymnast transfers weight from one foot to the other and bends one leg or both while airborne.

Acrobatics
A school of movement that emphasizes skills demonstrating flexibility.

Aerial
A skill in which the gymnast lifts her body into space, utilizing an alternate foot push-off, and makes a complete (360°) rotation about the horizontal axis of her body to land one foot after the other. The aerial can be through the front plane (front aerial or aerial walkover) or through the side plane (side aerial or aerial cartwheel).

Afterflight
That part of the vault in which the body is in space, from the time the hands leave the horse until the feet touch the mat; the dismount in vaulting, postflight, or off-flight.

All-Around
A category of gymnastics that includes all four of the women's gymnastics events; the gymnast who performs all four events.

Amplitude
The completeness or magnitude of a skill; total stretch.

Artistic Gymnastics
The four Olympic events.

Axial
Movements about a fixed point.

Banana Back
Overarched back.

Beat
Preparatory swing on the unevens that involves a pike and extension in the hips.

Belly Bump
A skill performed on the unevens (also commonly referred to as a "suicide" or "stomach whip"): with the

hands on the high bar and the body over the low bar the gymnast bounces on top of the low bar on the front of her hips, pikes, and extends.

Belly Bumpers
Pieces of foam placed over the hips to prevent excessive bruising from the unevens.

Blind Landing
A landing in which the gymnast cannot see the mat; common in forward turning skills such as handspring vault, front somersault on the floor, front aerial, and front somersault on the beam.

Blocking
Changing vertical to horizontal movement by preventing the shoulders from moving forward when in a hand support position or preventing the hips from moving forward in the lunge position.

Body Slap
A loud sound that occurs when the body hits the floor mat; it indicates lack of control or poor technique.

Body Wave
A body technique involving successive movements within a limb or the whole body; succession or contraction.

Bottom-Out
Landing mats that are worn out or poorly designed so the gymnast's force continues through the mat to the floor.

Cast
A movement on the uneven bars in which the gymnast in a front support position, hands in an overgrip, pushes her body away from the bar.

Cat Leap
A transfer of weight from one foot to the other in which the knees are bent and kept in front of the body.

Center of Gravity
The exact midpoint of a mass or of the body.

Chalk
Magnesium carbonate usually applied to the hands of the gymnast.

Chené
A turn involving a half turn on each foot, translated to chain.

Choke
A poor performance not caused by a lack of ability.

Compulsory
A prescribed routine that must be performed as it is written.

Contraction
A technique involving successive body movements usually within the torso; succession.

Crash Pad
A landing mat, usually eight inches or more in thickness.

Dance Fall
A planned technique for changing levels through a graceful fall to the floor exercise mat.

Danish Lift
A Danish mother's technique for helping young children up the stairs.

Dismount
A means of leaving the apparatus upon completing a routine.

Dismount Mat
A landing surface that is legal in competition; a mat four inches thick.

Dumped
A skill without amplitude; a *low* skill.

Eagle
A means of catching the bar in an uneven bar routine: the hands are pronated with the arms raised diagonally sideways from the shoulders.

English
A handstand on the beam in which the gymnast faces the length of the beam.

FIG
International Gymnastics Federation, the governing body for world gymnastics.

Focus
The eye direction, extremely important for balance.

Fouetté
A pirouette turn; whip.

Free Hip
A circling action of the body on the unevens in which the hips do not touch the bar.

Front Support
A body position on the uneven bars in which the hands are in an overgrip shoulder width apart and the front of the hips rest on the bar.

Glutes
Slang for the gluteal muscle group, located between the back of the waist and the top of the thighs.

Gymnast
An individual who participates in gymnastics.

Gymnastics
A sport; artistic involves the four Olympic events.

Handspring
The body makes a 360° rotation about the horizontal axis from feet to hands to feet.

Hecht
A means of dismounting from the unevens in which the body, after circling around the bar, flies off the top of the bar in a forward direction; in vaulting the front of the body passes over the horse horizontally.

Hip Circle
A family of moves on the uneven bars initiated from a front support position on the low bar from which the body circles either forward or backward about the bar while the front of the hips maintains contact with the bar.

Hit
The consistent and successful performance of a routine.

Hitchkick
A transfer of weight from one foot to the other in which the legs are straight and brought up in front of the body, or to the rear in a rear hitchkick.

Hollow Jump
An arched, straight leg jump.

Imagery
A technique of suggesting a mental picture to help the gymnast move correctly.

Jam
A technique for bringing the feet and legs between the hands when in a hang position on the uneven bars (double-leg overshoot).

Kip
A means of moving the body from a lower to a higher position by forcefully bending and extending.

Layout
A completely stretched and extended body, which is one of three basic body positions in gymnastics.

Leg Skill
Movement that primarily requires the use of the legs, such as tumbling and vaulting.

Locomotor
A movement in space from one place to another.

Long Hang
A position on the uneven bars in which the hands are in an overgrip and the body is stretched under a bar.

Mat
A protective covering for the floor.

Meet
The competitive experience in gymnastics.

Mimetics
A method of pantomime or going through a skill, usually with spotting or in slow motion.

Mixed Grip
A hand position on the uneven bars in which one hand is in the overgrip and the other hand is in the undergrip.

Monkey Jump
A poorly done back handspring that moves in an up-and-down path rather than a long and low one.

Mount
A means of getting on the apparatus or beginning an exercise.

Muscle-Up
In women's gymnastics, not extending in the hips at the end of a skill on the unevens, particularly in kips.

NAGWS
National Association for Girls and Womens Sports, which publishes a rule book for gymnastics (AAHPER, Washington, D.C.).

Neutral
In this book, applies to a head position that is neither tucked nor extended.

Off-Flight
A phase of the vault during which the body is in the air, from the time the hands leave the horse until the feet land on the mat; postflight; afterflight.

Onflight
A phase of the vault during which the body is in the air, from the time the feet leave the board until the hands land on the horse.

Optional
An unprescribed routine of the gymnast's own composition.

Overgrip
A position of the hands on the uneven bars: palms down on top of the bar; regular grip.

Overhead Spotting
A means of spotting a gymnast in a spotting belt that is suspended from the ceiling by ropes or cables.

Pancake
The body piked while inverted.

Peel Off
When the gymnast falls from the bars because her hands can hold on no longer, she is said to "peel off."

Pike
One of three basic body positions in gymnastics: the body is bent at the waist and the arms and legs are straight in a "jackknife" position.

Piqué
A turn that is a form of pirouette.

Pirouette
A turn on one foot.

Pommels
Handles on the side horse.

Pops
A family of moves on the bars in which the body extends to layout from a pike position.

Postflight
A phase of the vault during which the body is in space, from the time the hands leave the horse until the feet land on the mat; off-flight, afterflight.

Preflight
A phase of the vault during which the body is in space, from the time the feet leave the board until the hands land on the horse; onflight.

Press
A technique of lifting the body away from the floor or the apparatus by using the arms and upper body.

Punch
The lift or power for a skill, usually initiated by the legs.

Repulsion
The push away from the horse that causes a rise in the afterflight of the vault.

Reverse Press
A technique for letting the body down onto the floor or apparatus by using the arms and upper body.

Rosin
Batter's rock rosin, used on the gymnast's sockies to prevent slipping.

Russian Lift
A technique of forcefully pulling the elbows of stretched arms down and into the body to cause the body to rise; most commonly seen in front somersaults.

Scissors Leap
Performed by reversing or changing the position of the front and rear legs while in the air; switch leg leap.

Scoot
Refers to the vaulter's last step onto the board; ideally it should be long and low.

Snap Down
The last half of a roundoff or a back handspring, wherein the legs are forcefully piked down to the floor from the hand support position.

Sole Circle
A skill on the uneven bars performed by placing the soles of the feet and hands on one bar. The body circles the bar either forward or backward in a piked position.

Somersault
A 360° rotation of the body about its horizontal axis. The gymnast leaves the floor by a push from the feet, makes a complete turn and lands on the feet. This skill can be performed in a forward or backward direction in tuck, pike, and/or layout position.

Split Leap
This dance skill entails a transfer of weight from one

foot to the other and should be performed with amplitude, height, and both legs parallel with the floor while airborne.

Spot
The assistance received while learning or performing a skill. This assistance is protection for the gymnast.

Spotter
The trained individual who provides assistance and protection to the gymnast who is learning or performing a gymnastic skill.

Spotting Belt
A belt with ropes attached to either side designed to protect the gymnast from falling. Two spotters are required.

Stalled
The effect that occurs when a skill's momentum fades; an incomplete skill, often caused by a loose body.

Static Stretch
A technique for increasing flexibility: the muscle group is stretched slowly and in a sustained way without bouncing. Currently, this is the advocated technique for increasing flexibility.

STG
The initials for "squeeze those glutes" (the gluteals are the large muscle group in the back between the waist and the top of the thighs). This technique is a basic concept for tightening the whole body so that skills can be accomplished.

Stick
A descriptive term for landing a skill in balance, without the necessity for taking steps.

Stomach Whip
An uneven bar skill also called a "belly bump": the hands are on the high bar of the unevens and the front of the hips bounces on the low bar.

Straddle
A body position in which the legs are apart.

Succession
A contraction of connected body parts; often occurs in the torso and moves outward to extremities.

Suicide
A skill on the uneven bars also called a "belly bump"

or "stomach whip": the hands are on the high bar of the unevens and the front of the hips bounces on the low bar.

Swedish Box
Apparatus made of wood with a padded top that can be utilized for certain vaulting skills or as a spotting platform.

Switch Leg Leap
A dance skill also called a "scissors leap": while airborne in a leap (transfer of weight), the gymnast switches the position of her front and back legs.

Technical Execution
The performance of a skill with ultimate amplitude and as correctly as possible.

Throwing
Giving impetus or initiating a skill.

Thrown
The skill has been initiated.

Tick-Tock
Initiating a skill, such as a walkover, in a forward direction and changing to a backward direction; the direction of the skill is reversed.

Tilt
The gymnast lifts her body (STG) into the air in layout position; she must be spotted. A tilt is a progression for the handspring vault or roundoff (see these skills for more details).

Tour Jêté
A dance turn in which there is a transfer of weight from one foot to the other while a half turn is executed in the air. The gymnast should face the direction she came from upon the skill's completion.

Trampoline Vaulting
A technique and/or progression for learning the on-flight (bouncing from the trampoline onto the horse) or the off-flight (leaving the horse in a hand support and landing on the trampoline).

Tuck
Basic body position in which the knees are brought up to the chest, the back is rounded, and the chin is in and down.

Turn
In dance, a rotation about the vertical plane of the

body; in tumbling, a rotation about the horizontal axis; a twist is a rotation about the vertical axis.

Twisting Belt
A spotting belt in which the gymnast can turn (about the horizontal axis) and twist (about the vertical axis).

Undergrip
A basic hand position on the uneven bars in which the hands are supinated and hold the bottom of the rail.

USGF
Initials for the United States Gymnastic Federation located in Tucson, Arizona, which is the governing body of gymnastics in the United States and the national association of the International Gymnastics Federation (FIG).

Vault
A jumping skill in gymnastics. Usually the gymnast jumps over the horse or as in a mount.

Walkout
A landing on one foot and then the other (alternately).

Wrap
A skill on the unevens in which the body pikes around the bar: the bar is held into the waist by flexing the legs and torso as the body turns about the low bar in a backward direction. The hands are initially in contact with the high bar and regrasp the low bar at the skill's completion.

Yamashita
A vault that is initiated as a handspring and completed by forcefully piking and extending the body.

INDEX

Note: Numbers in bold face indicate a reference to an illustration.